VORWORT

Das neu entwickelte **Business Matters** ist ein Lehrwerk für kaufmännische Berufe, das für die Ausbildung in Berufsschulen und die innerbetriebliche Aus- und Weiterbildung konzipiert wurde. Das Lehrwerk orientiert sich an den Lehrplänen der Bundesländer für Berufsschulen. Darüber hinaus werden alle in den KMK-Rahmenlehrplänen geforderten fremdsprachlichen Inhalte vermittelt.

Es ist auf Lernende zugeschnitten, deren Englischkenntnisse den Anforderungen eines mittleren Bildungsabschlusses (B1) entsprechen. In verschiedenen Situationen und auf einer Seite *Extra material* pro Unit wird für fortgeschrittene Lernende anspruchsvollerer Lernstoff für die Weiterarbeit auf der Stufe B2 angeboten, während Arbeitsblätter auf der Lehrer-CD als Trainingsmöglichkeiten überwiegend auf Stufen A2 und B1 zur Verfügung stehen.

Business Matters vermittelt in zehn voneinander unabhängigen Units anwendungsorientiert alle wichtigen Kompetenzen für die Berufspraxis auf Englisch. Es bereitet Lernende in kaufmännischen Berufen praxisnah und durchgängig auf die KMK-Zertifikatsprüfung in Englisch (Stufe II) vor. Dies geschieht anhand prüfungsbezogener und mit einem KMK-Symbol gekennzeichneten Aufgaben und wird verstärkt durch eine KMK-Seite am Ende jeder Unit sowie einer kompletten Musterprüfung *(KMK mock exam)* im Anhang.

Die Units sind in sich geschlossen und können in beliebiger Reihenfolge oder auch unter Auslassung einzelner Kapitel bearbeitet werden. Im Mittelpunkt steht die Vermittlung kommunikativer Kompetenzen mit abwechslungsreichen Übungen. Dazu werden in fallstudienartigen Units Gesprächssituationen mit englischsprachigen Geschäftspartnern geübt. Wichtige Ausdrücke und Redewendungen stehen in *Language boxes* und in ausführlicherer Form im Anhang mit deutschen Übersetzungen *(Useful phrases)* bereit und werden in Rollenspielen gefestigt.

Neben der rein fachlichen wird auch die soziale Komponente des Arbeitsalltags berücksichtigt. Außerdem werden das Lese- und Hörverständnis sowie das eigenständige Verfassen englischsprachiger Geschäftskorrespondenz (E-Mail, Brief) trainiert. In den Lernsituationen nach jeder geraden Unit, die das kompetenz- und anwendungsorientierte Lernen unterstützen, bekommen Lernende die Chance, realitätsnahe Situationen nachzuspielen. Webcodes fördern die Lernenden, eigenverantwortlich zu arbeiten.

Das praxisorientierte Lernen wird durch authentische Texte wie Internetseiten, Geschäftskorrespondenz und Hörtexte sichergestellt. Vielfältige Übungen vermitteln das notwendige sprachliche Hintergrundwissen. Die **Handreichungen** enthalten didaktische Hinweise, die **Audio-CD** sowie eine **CD-ROM** mit einem breiten Spektrum an Zusatzmaterialien zur Erweiterung der Arbeit mit dem Schulbuch, u.a. editierbare Kopiervorlagen.

Neben der Aufarbeitung des Fachvokabulars und der spezifischen Redemittel werden auch Grundlagen der Grammatik zur Wiederholung angeboten. Sie werden in deutscher Sprache mit Hilfe von Beispielen erklärt und im handlungsbezogenen Kontext geübt. Der Anhang enthält verschiedene Wortlisten: eine Grundwortschatzliste, eine nach Units chronologisch gegliederte sowie eine alphabetische Wortliste, die das schnelle Auffinden von Vokabeln ermöglichen.

Die wichtigsten Wortfelder stehen zum Nachschlagen und Lernen in einem kurzen deutsch-englischen Glossar *(Basic business word list)* zur Verfügung. Den Schluss bildet eine Liste der am häufigsten gebrauchten unregelmäßigen Verben.

Liste der Symbole: ⊚ Hörverständnistext auf der Audio-CD   **KMK** Übungen zur Vorbereitung auf die KMK-Zertifikatsprüfung

WEBCODE **BMU0601**

TABLE OF CONTENTS

UNIT	Title	Content
1	**Getting to know a company**	Introductions Company structure Departments and tasks
2	**In the office**	Office tasks Ordering stationery Asking for help
	Situation 1	
3	**Marketing and advertising**	Marketing strategies Effective advertisements Online advertising
4	**Making an order on the telephone**	Telephone enquiries Offers Confirmation of orders
	Situation 2	
5	**A trade fair and an order**	Meeting customers and making appointments Orders and shipment Payments and reminders
6	**Customer care**	Customer care guidelines Customer service mistakes Handling customer complaints
	Situation 3	
7	**Business travel**	A business trip Airport and hotel Small talk
8	**Presentations**	Audio-visual equipment Preparing presentations Presentation strategies
	Situation 4	
9	**Logistics**	The logistics process Safety rules and regulations Just-in-time production
10	**Applying for a job**	Career planning Applying for a job A job interview
	Situation 5	

Appendix

KMK mock exam	114
Incoterms	119
Useful phrases	122
Basic word list	133

TABLE OF CONTENTS

Language & skills	Grammar	KMK exam	Extra material	
Welcoming a trainee Describing a company's structure Asking and giving directions Describing daily work routines	Simple present and present continuous	Hörverstehen Interaktion	Different company types	6
Describing office tasks Ordering stationery Asking for and giving instructions	Comparatives and superlatives of adjectives	Leseverstehen	New office organisation: homeworking and hot desking	15
				25
Explaining the marketing process Assessing customer's attitudes to advertising Developing marketing strategies	Questions	Mediation	Viral and guerrilla marketing	27
Making a telephone enquiry Making a telephone order Writing a confirmation email	Modal verbs	Produktion	Email dos and don'ts	38
				47
Meeting customers Making appointments on the telephone Writing an invoice Writing a first reminder	Conditional I and II	Hörverstehen Interaktion	Incoterms 2011	49
Avoiding customer care mistakes Reacting to customer complaints	*-ing* form and/or infinitive	Produktion	Customer retention	59
				69
Arranging a business trip on the telephone Finding your way around an airport Booking and arriving at a hotel Small talk	Future with the simple present and present continuous	Leseverstehen	Cutting the costs of business travel	71
Booking audio-visual equipment by telephone Preparing for a presentation Making a presentation with visuals	The will future with *will* and *going to*	Mediation	Presentation body language	80
				89
Describing the logistics processs Warehouse logistics Getting familiar with delivery notes	The passive	Produktion	Quality assurance and quality control	91
Planning a career Writing a covering letter Writing a CV Preparing for a job interview	Simple past and present perfect	Hörverstehen Interaktion	Assessment centres	101
				112

Chronological word list	´38
Alphabetical word list	´58
Basic business vocabulary (German – English)	´69
Common irregular verbs	´72

UNIT 1 — Getting to know a company

- introductions
- company structure
- departments & tasks

1 Warm-up

A Which of these phrases would you use when meeting someone for the first time?

1. Pleased to meet you.
2. Good to see you again.
3. Great to meet you in person at last.
4. How do you do?

B Work with a partner and think of other phrases for greeting people. Write a list. Present this to the class.

GETTING TO KNOW A COMPANY

UNIT 1

2 | A visit to a company

A **Read the dialogue. Why is Amy visiting Peterson Sports Shoes Ltd?**

Receptionist Good morning. Can I help you?

Amy Good morning. Yes. My name's Amy Austin. It's the first day of my ==traineeship== I have an ==appointment== with Jack Ryder.

Receptionist Okay, Ms Austin. Welcome to Peterson Sports Shoes. I'll let Mr Ryder know that you're here … Hello, Mr Ryder. There's a Amy Austin in ==reception== for you. Okay. I'll ask her to wait … Ms Austin, Mr Ryder is in a meeting at the moment. He apologises for being late, but he'll come down in about fifteen minutes.

Amy Great. Thank you.

Jack Amy? Amy Austin?

Amy Hello, yes, I'm Amy.

Jack Hello, Amy. Pleased to meet you. I'm Jack Ryder. I'm the Assistant Human Resources Manager. I'm responsible for looking after our ==trainees==.

Amy Hello, Mr Ryder. Pleased to meet you too.

Jack Amy, let me introduce you to Ruby Whitlam.

Ruby Hello, Amy. Pleased to meet you. I'm the ==Human Resources Manager==. Please call me Ruby.

Amy Hello, Ruby. Nice to meet you too.

Jack So, welcome on the first day of your traineeship. We have three more trainees starting today. They aren't here yet but, when they arrive, we'll give you an ==introduction to the company== and a bit of background information about us.

Amy Great!

Jack Then I'm going to show you round the company and explain what the different departments do. After that you can go for lunch. In the afternoon, Ruby will introduce you to Allen Bennet who is our ==Sales Manager==. You'll be doing your traineeship in his department.

Ruby Yes, I'll be taking all the trainees into the ==departments== they'll be working in after lunch. You won't start to work properly until tomorrow. Today is really going to be about getting to know our company. How does that sound?

Amy Absolutely great, thanks.

Jack Okay. Well, let's get going then.

B **Look at the dialogue again and match the ==highlighted== words and phrases in the dialogue above to the German translations.**

1 Abteilungen
2 Ausbildung
3 Auszubildende
4 Empfang

5 Personalleiterin
6 Termin
7 Verkaufsleiter
8 Vorstellung der Firma

C **Read the dialogue again and find phrases which can be used to do the following things.**

1 Finding out what you can do for someone
2 Saying that someone is sorry for not being there
3 Saying that you're happy to meet someone
4 Saying what your job consists of
5 Introducing people who have never met

7

GETTING TO KNOW A COMPANY

3 Questions about the dialogue

Which answer is correct: a, b or c?

1 Amy is …
a visiting the company for a job interview.
b beginning her training with the company.
c visiting the company to sell it some shoes.

2 Jack will be late because he …
a missed the bus to work.
b is meeting with some colleagues.
c is taking a telephone call.

3 Jack is …
a Assistant Human Resources Manager.
b the Human Resources Manager's assistant.
c Resources Manager.

4 Ruby is responsible for the …
a people who work for the company.
b company's customers.
c company's resources.

5 The other three trainees …
a are being given some information about the company when Amy arrives.
b have already gone to their departments.
c haven't arrived yet.

4 Vocabulary

Use five of the words and phrases in the box to complete the sentences from the dialogue. Three words or phrases which do not fit will be left at the end.

1 Hello, Mr Ryder. Pleased … too.
2 I'm … looking after our trainees.
3 I have an … with Jack Ryder.
4 Amy, let me … Ruby Whitlam.
5 Please … Ruby.

> appointment • call me • introduce you to • introduction • responsible for • responsible to • say to me • to meet you

WEBCODE **BMU0101**

5 Role-play: welcoming a trainee

Üben Sie das Rollenspiel mit einem Partner / einer Partnerin.

Student A

Sie sind der/die Ausbildungsleiter/in in Ihrer Firma. Heißen Sie den neuen Auszubildenden / die neue Auszubildende am ersten Tag der Ausbildung willkommen. Stellen Sie sich dem/der Auszubildenden vor und sagen Sie, dass Sie mit dem Vornamen angesprochen werden möchten. Stellen Sie dann Ihren Kollegen Frank Stevens, den Personalleiter, vor.
Erläutern Sie dem/der Auszubildenden, dass Sie mit einem Rundgang durch die Firma beginnen werden, um ihm/ihr die Abteilungen vorzustellen. Nach dem Mittagessen wird er/sie dann Hintergrundinformationen zur Firma erhalten.

Student B

Sie sind ein neuer Auszubildender / eine neue Auszubildende. Es ist Ihr erster Tag in der Firma. Stellen Sie sich dem/der Ausbildungsleiter/in und dem/der Personalleiter/in vor, die Ihnen ebenfalls vorgestellt werden.
Sagen Sie, dass Sie sich auf die Ausbildung freuen und dass Sie sehr daran interessiert sind, verschiedene Abteilungen kennen zu lernen. Hören Sie sich das Programm des Ausbildungsleiters / der Ausbildungsleiterin an und bezeugen Sie Ihr Interesse.

GETTING TO KNOW A COMPANY

6 Company structure

A Match words and expressions from the text to their definitions (1–8).

1 founded
2 gives work to
3 employees
4 base
5 factories
6 situated
7 clients
8 hiring

Peterson Sport Shoes Ltd

Information for new trainees

In 1983, Peterson Sport Shoes was established near Nottingham with just five employees to produce shoes for runners. The company now employs over 250 staff and has an annual turnover of £7 million. With its headquarters still in Nottingham, the company has two production facilities in nearby towns. Our distribution centre is located further north in Manchester.

The company is organised around the following key departments:

Sales Department

This department's job is incredibly important, but it can be described in a few words. Basically, the department's job is to sell our shoes – and as many of them as possible. Members of the Sales team are also responsible for maintaining good relations with our customers.

Marketing Department

The Marketing Department has two main functions. Firstly, it looks at the market and decides which products people want to buy at the moment: trendy sports shoes or functional ones for running. This is very important because we don't want to make shoes that nobody wants to buy. The department also looks at the best way to sell our products. They decide what sort of advertising will work and which shops are best for our shoes.

Human Resources Department

The Human Resources Department looks after our staff and makes sure that they are doing their work properly. Human Resources also looks after things like how much holiday people take and how much they get paid. The department is also responsible for recruiting new staff when the company needs them.

B Work with a group and choose one of the departments from the list. Brainstorm everything you know about the function of the department. Present this to the class.

- Production Department
- Administration Department
- Accounting Department
- Distribution Department

C Discuss which department of the company you would most like to work in. Explain why.

GETTING TO KNOW A COMPANY

7 Mediation

KMK

Übertragen Sie den Text auf Seite 9 sinngemäß in die deutsche Sprache.

8 Vocabulary

Use the words in the box to complete the sentences about work relationships in Ruby Whitlam's department.

| alongside • charge • heads • report • responsible • responsibility |

1 Ruby Whitlam … the Human Resources Department.
2 She is … for looking after the company's employees.
3 Ruby's assistant manager, Jack Ryder, is in … of training the company's trainees.
4 Jack has a team of three training staff who … to him.
5 Today, Jack Ryder has the … of welcoming Amy Austin to the company.
6 He works … the other staff in the Human Resources Department.

9 Who does what?

Read the sentences below which describe work relationships at Peterson Sport Shoes and decide who does which job.

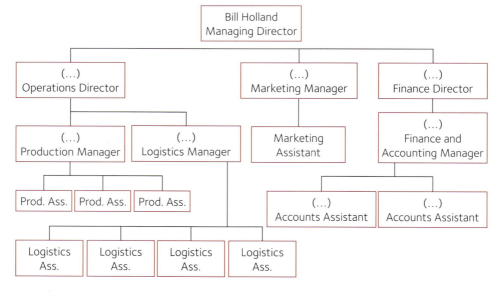

1 Alison Wakeman has responsibility for the work of four members of staff.
2 Jane Rogers reports directly to Bill Holland and is responsible for one staff member.
3 Thomas Kirk is in charge of two members of staff and reports to Irene Stewart.
4 Dave Scott reports to Thomas Kirk.
5 Tony Armstrong has responsibility for a team of three members of staff.
6 Steve Smith is in charge of two managers in the company.
7 Helen Street works alongside her colleague Dave Scott.
8 Irene Stewart reports to Bill Holland and has responsibility for one manager and his team.

GETTING TO KNOW A COMPANY

UNIT 1

10 A tour of the company

Draw the plan of the company in your notebook then listen as Amy is given a tour. Write the names of the departments in the right places.

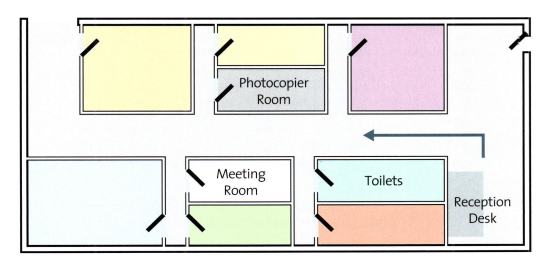

11 Asking for and giving directions

A Look at the plan of the company and match the questions (1–4) to the answers (a–d). Each set of directions starts at the corridor beside the reception desk.

1 Excuse me. Can you tell me how to get to the Sales Department, please?
2 Hi. How do you get to the Accounting Department, please?
3 Hello. Can you tell me how to find the staff café?
4 Morning. Can you please give me directions to the photocopier room?

a Go along the corridor. Take the second turning on the right. It's the first door on the right.
b Go along the corridor and take the second turn on the left. It's the first door on the right.
c Go up the corridor and take the first turn on the left. It's the second door on the left.
d Go up the corridor. Take the second turn on the right. It's the second door on the right.

B Now write down the phrases which you could use to ask for and give directions.

C Work with a partner. Take turns to say where you are on the plan and ask directions to different departments. Your partner should give you clear instructions.

11

GETTING TO KNOW A COMPANY

UNIT 1

12 Ross's job responsibilities

03

A Listen as Ross explains his job to Amy and decide whether he's talking about:

1 things he regularly does,
2 things he is only responsible for at the moment, or
3 both.

B Listen again and complete the sentences from the dialogue.

1 My main … is to give Jack the help he needs with his work.
2 I … of a few regular tasks.
3 For example, I … office supplies.
4 I … that everyone in the department has enough of these.
5 I also … the post for the department every morning from the reception desk.
6 What … Jack with just now?
7 At the moment he … a new training plan.
8 I … him to collect information for the plan.
9 I … a lot to our trainees at the moment.

GRAMMAR

Simple present and present continuous

1 I **look** after office supplies.
2 Jack Ryder **looks** after the trainees.
3 **Do** you **like** your job in the Human Resources Department?
4 Ross **is showing** Amy round the company.
5 **Is** Amy **doing** her training in the Sales or the Marketing Department?

- Das *simple present* wird verwendet, um Gewohnheiten und Tätigkeiten zu beschreiben, die man regelmäßig verrichtet. Es wird mit dem Infinitiv des Verbs gebildet. (1)
- In der 3. Person Singular *(he/she/it)* wird ein -s an das Verb gehängt. (2)
- Außer bei dem Verb *to be* und bei Modalverben (zum Beispiel *can*) werden Fragen und Verneinungen mit dem Hilfsverb *do* (Verneinung *don't*) gebildet. In der 3. Person Singular werden Fragen mit *does* (Verneinung *doesn't*) gebildet. (3)
- Das *present continuous* beschreibt Handlungen bzw. Zustände, die im Moment des Sprechens geschehen bzw. Gültigkeit haben oder zeitlich begrenzt sind. Es wird mit einer Form des Verbs *to be* und der *-ing*-Form des Hauptverbs gebildet. (4, 5)

13 Practice

A Use the simple present or the present continuous to make complete sentences.

1 Ross usually / work / in the office
2 Today, he / show / Amy around the company
3 At the moment, Jack / have / a meeting about the training plan
4 Amy normally / work / in the Sales Department
5 At the moment, Scott / help / in the Marketing Department
6 Tina / fetch / coffee for a visitor

B Now imagine that the sentences above (1–6) are answers to questions. What were the questions? Write them down.

12

KMK exam practice

14 Rezeption – Hörverstehen

04

Machen Sie sich Notizen und beantworten Sie die Fragen auf Deutsch.
Lesen Sie sich die Aufgaben vorher gut durch. Sie hören den Dialog zweimal.

1. Wie viele neue Stellen schafft das Unternehmen?
2. Warum stellt das Unternehmen neue Arbeitskräfte ein?
3. Wann wurde das Unternehmen gegründet?
4. Welche Gründe werden für den Erfolg des Unternehmens in den 1960er Jahren gegeben?
5. Was geschah 1975?
6. Was machten die neuen Eigentümer des Unternehmens?
7. Welche Märkte sind die Hauptabnehmer des Unternehmens?

15 Interaktion

Berichten Sie einem Partner / einer Partnerin über das auf Ihrer Karte beschriebene Unternehmen. Hören Sie, was ihr Partner / Ihre Partnerin Ihnen berichtet. Vergleichen Sie die beiden Unternehmen mit Ihrem Partner / Ihrer Partnerin.

Student A

Company name: Fizzi Ltd
Products: Soft drinks (like lemonade)
Established: 1991
Based: Swindon, England
Number of employees: 237
Export markets: Sweden, Holland, Belgium

Student B

Company name: Fruity Tradition plc
Products: Sweets made with real fruit juice
Established: 1972
Based: Dundee, Scotland
Number of employees: 312
Export markets: US, Australia

Extra material

A brief guide to the different company types

sole trader / sole proprietorship
In a way, this is the simplest company form. The company is owned by a single person who can keep all of its profits but, at the same time, must take responsibility for all debts the company might run up or for losses it might make.

limited partnership / general partnership
When two or more people want to start a business together, they could choose this form of company. In some way, it's similar to a sole trader; the partners can keep any profit made by the business, however, they are liable for all of its debts and losses. In the limited partnerhip there are general partners with unlimited liability and limited partners whose liability is restricted to their fixed contributions to the partnership.

private limited company (Ltd)
A limited company is more complicated than a partnership or a sole trader structure. It's what's called a joint stock company. That means that the company is funded by money from various sources. The company gives its shareholders shares in proportion to the amount they have backed the company by. A limited company is also private: that is, shares in the company are not traded on the stock exchange. In a limited company, the liability of the company's owners is restricted to the amount they have invested in the company. So, if the owner of a limited company originally invested £20,000 and the company runs into trouble, the owner will only have to pay £20,000 towards the company's debts.

public limited company (plc)
More complicated to set up than a limited company, this type of company offers the same limited liability to its owners as a limited company. The major difference, however, is that it can sell shares in the company to the public on the stock market. In contrast to a limited company then, this type of company is publicly owned.

---

1 Key vocabulary

Match the German expressions to the highlighted words in the text.

1	Aktien		**5**	Haftung
2	beschränkt		**6**	Verbindlichkeiten, Schulden
3	Eigentümer/in		**7**	Verluste
4	Gewinne			

---

2 German company forms

A Work with a partner and decide which German company forms can be matched to those described in the text.

B Explain the company form of the company you work for.

---

3 Advantages and disadvantages

Work in a group to carry out these tasks.

A Make a list of the advantages and disadvantages described in the text of each type of company to its owners.

B Which other advantages and disadvantages for each company type can you think of? Extend your lists. Present these to the class.

In the office

UNIT 2

- office tasks
- ordering stationery
- asking for help

1 Warm-up

A

B

C

D

    A   Work with a partner and look at the photographs. Take turns to describe what the people are doing.

    B   Now work with your partner and make a list of other things that people who work in offices do.

15

IN THE OFFICE

2 An email to David

Read the email and decide which statement is true.

1 David is Sarah's boss.
2 Sarah and David do not normally work together.
3 Sarah is David's boss.

From: Sarah Thurgood
To: David Walmsley
Subject: To-do list

Morning David

Sorry, I'm not in the office this morning. I have to go to London for an interview with a potential new team member. I'll be back in the middle of the afternoon. Here are a few things you can do while I'm away. If you need help, ask Lena Kuhn, our new trainee from Germany.

First of all, just as I left the office yesterday, I received an email from a chain of shops called Top Store which is based in Nottingham. (You'll find the email in my inbox.) They are interested in our clothing and want our current list of prices. Could you please email them back and attach our price list. Please don't forget to do this. It's your most important task this morning.

Also, The Trendsetter Clothing Company sent me an email yesterday which I didn't have time to reply to. They would like to order 450 of our new skater caps; they want to know how much this will cost them. Can you please find the file about this customer in my filing cabinet and find out what price they have paid before? Then write a letter including a quote based on this. Please print out the letter so that I can sign it when I get back to the office.

Next on the list, we need to arrange a meeting between the Sales and Marketing Departments for Friday 27 May. Could you please book a meeting room? Try to get the large meeting room on the first floor from 11 in the morning until 4 in the afternoon. Could you also make sure that there's refreshments in the morning and afternoon and sandwiches for lunch, please? You can order both of them from the staff café.

Another thing: our Sales peoples' cars all need to go into the garage for their annual check. Could you please contact the garage which we normally use and get a list of dates when they could do this. Then ask our Sales team which dates would suit them.

And please order some stationery from the Administration Department. I personally need new marker pens and paper for my printer. Please ask around the other team members and find out what they need.

And one last thing – could you explain the company structure to Lena, please? I promised that I would talk to her about it this morning.

Alright, that's all for now. Have a good morning. I'll see you back in the office later.

Best
Sarah

Sarah Thurgood
Sales Manager
Cool Street (UK) Ltd

IN THE OFFICE

UNIT 2

3 | What David should do

David asks Lena to read Sarah's email and to help him make a to-do list of the tasks described in it. Write the to-do list for Lena.

4 | Mediation

KMK

Damit Lena auch ganz sicher ist, dass sie alle Informationen der E-Mail verstanden hat, möchte sie sie auf Deutsch zusammenfassen. Übernehmen Sie diese Aufgabe für sie.

5 | David and Lena's to-do list

Read David and Lena's to-do list. Which tasks have they forgotten? Also, which mistake have they made?

> To-do – Wednesday morning
> 1 book large meeting room on the first floor – 27 May, 11 a.m. until 4 p.m.
> 2 order tea, coffee, fruit juice, water and sandwiches from staff café for meeting
> 3 write letter to Top Store giving price for 450 skater caps
> 4 call the garage for possible dates
> 5 order stationery

6 | Key vocabulary

Match the words from the text (1–6) to the definitions (a–f).

1 file
2 interview
3 quote
4 refreshments
5 stationery
6 task

a price offer
b items that are needed in an office
c job
d tea, coffee, fruit juice and water
e a document which provides information about something
f a meeting between a company and someone who would like to work for it

17

IN THE OFFICE

7 Key verbs

Find the right verbs in Sarah's email to complete the sentences. Make sure you use the correct tense. Who said the sentences: Sarah, David or Lena?

1 We should … a meeting between Marketing and Sales.
2 I'd like to … the meeting room on the first floor for 27th May, please.
3 Did you … the garage about the Sales peoples' cars, David?
4 Could you please … the company structure to me? I don't understand it yet.
5 I'd like to … tea, coffee and sandwiches for next Friday, please.
6 I … out the letter and it's ready for you to sign.

8 Stationery items

One of the last things David has to do is order some stationery. Match the photographs (A–J) with the items of office stationery (1–10) he has to order.

1 printer paper
2 calculator
3 staples
4 note pads
5 stapler
6 paper clips
7 printer cartridge
8 highlighters
9 hole punch
10 envelopes

18

IN THE OFFICE

UNIT 2

9 Making an order for stationery

05 David is explaining how to order stationery. What is the importance of the number 46793?

10 Key terms from the dialogue

05 Listen and match the German words and expressions on the left to the English words and expressions from the dialogue on the right.

1	Aktenschrank	a	account number
2	Artikel	b	desk
3	bestätigen	c	filing cabinet
4	Formular	d	form
5	Kostenstelle	e	items
6	Notiz	f	note
7	Schreibtisch	g	to confirm
8	unterschreiben	h	to sign

11 Making a stationery order

Put the stages of ordering stationery into the order Lena has to do them in.

a Find and fill out a form.
b Take the order to the Administration Department.
c Ask the Department Manager to sign the form.
d Find out what is needed.
e Give the stationery to the relevant people.
f Sign the order form.
g Wait for a phone call and then collect the order.

12 Changing a printer cartridge

A Work with a partner and read the phrases. Discuss what purposes they could be used for.

1 Could you tell me what to do though, please?
2 I'll explain what you have to do. Is that OK?
3 So, first of all you have to ...
4 Just ... and then ...
5 Okay. And what should I do next?
6 Then you have to ...
7 You need to ...
8 When you have ...
9 Okay. And then what do I do?

I don't think any of the phrases could be used to thank somebody for doing something.

Right, but perhaps a few of them could be used to ...

19

IN THE OFFICE

B Now work with a partner and take turns explaining the steps in changing a printer cartridge. Use phrases from part A.

Example: **Student A:** *I want to change my printer cartridge. What should I do first?*
Student B: *Well, the first step is to …. Could you please tell me what the next step is?*

Student A

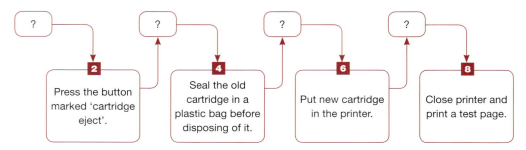

Student B

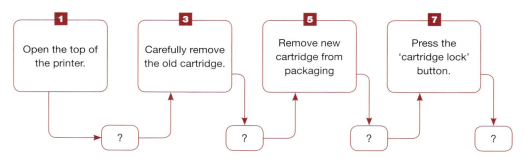

Comparatives and superlatives

1. Our office in Manchester is **smaller than** the one in Nottingham.
2. We want a new system on the intranet for ordering office supplies so that it's **simpler**.
3. The price of printer cartridges is **more important than** who they are made by.
4. We shouldn't just buy the **cheapest** ink cartridges we can find.
5. We should spend **as** much money **as** necessary on cartridges to get the right quality.

- Alle **einsilbigen Adjektive** werden mit -er und -est gesteigert. (1, 4)
- Einzelkonsonanten nach einem kurzen Vokal werden dabei verdoppelt: *big – bigger – the biggest*.
- **Zweisilbige Adjektive** mit den Endungen -y, -er und -le werden ebenfalls mit -er und -est gesteigert. (2) Dabei wird -y in -i umgewandelt: *thirsty – thirstier – the thirstiest*.
- Alle **anderen zwei- und mehrsilbigen Adjektive** werden mit *more* und *most* gesteigert. (3)
- Einige Adjektive haben unregelmäßige Steigerungsformen: *good – better – best*; *bad – worse – worst*; **little** (wenig) – *less – least*; *much/many – more – most*.
- Vergleiche bildet man mit *than* (als) (1, 3) oder *as … as* (so … wie). (5)

20

IN THE OFFICE

UNIT 2

13 Practice

Complete the sentences with the comparative or superlative of the adjectives in brackets.

1. I work for the … office supplies company in the Midwest. (large)
2. This year we have taken on … trainees than last year. (many)
3. Our department is the … growing part of the company right now. (fast)
4. Our office is in a small side street. It's not the … place to find. (easy)
5. I don't think we should buy this printer. It's much … than this one here. (expensive)
6. This is the … quality printer cartridge on the market at the moment. (good)

WEBCODE **BMU0201**

14 Features of printer cartridges

A Unscramble the words a–e and match them to their definitions 1–5.

1. What other people who have used the product thought of it
2. The time a product is guaranteed by the manufacturer
3. The time a product can be stored before it is used
4. The amount a product is sold for
5. A specific type of product

a. ciper
b. doelm
c. neghlt fo rawtnary
d. somtecru ganitr
e. fehsl fiel

B Decide whether the adjectives in the box are in the positive, comparative or superlative form. Then write down the three different forms for each adjective

bigger • difficult • easier • simplest • simple

C Sie arbeiten in der Abteilung Ihrer Firma, die für den Einkauf von Druckerpatronen zuständig ist. Verwenden Sie geeignete Adjektive, um Ihrem Kollegen / Ihrer Kollegin über die auf Ihrer Karte beschriebenen Druckerpatronen zu berichten. Besprechen Sie dann das Für und Wider der Modelle, bevor Sie sich entscheiden, welches Ihre Firma kaufen sollte.

Student A

Cartridge model	Price	Length of warranty	Shelf life	Customer rating (* –****)
Trix 234Q	£24.52	2 years	1 year	**
Ceuz K7654	£14.99	1 year	1.5 years	**
Inkloop 3	£17.90	1 year	2.5 years	***

Student B

Cartridge model	Price	Length of warranty	Shelf life	Customer rating (* –****)
Peaqy 88(a)	£11.50	6 months	2 years	*
Quyro 629	£22.90	2 years	2.5 years	****
Zintic 89	£21.50	6 months	2.5 years	****

21

KMK exam practice

15 | Rezeption – Leseverstehen

Sie sind Mitarbeiter/in einer Firma, die ein Büro in New York eröffnen will. Bevor langfristig Büroräume angemietet werden, bittet Ihr Chef Sie, nach Alternativen zu suchen. Sie finden in einer Fachzeitschrift folgenden Artikel.

Offices to rent! ... by the month, week, day or even hour

Businesses often don't own the premises they operate from and companies have probably rented their offices for as long as they have existed. Though they rent this commercial space, the companies themselves are generally
5 responsible for furnishing it with tables, chairs and other office equipment.

Now, however, a new trend in the office rental market is taking this all one step further. This is the trend for fully-furnished and equipped offices which businesses can rent
10 for short periods of time. In more traditional rental agreements, offices are rented for quite long periods of time, often several years. The new 'ready to go' offices can be rented for just a month, a couple of weeks, a few days or even just several hours if required.
15 Chris Hyslop is marketing director of Office Latte, a real estate company which specialises in providing this type of office accommodation for businesses and individual freelancers: "Whether you're a large company or a one-man business, we can provide you with fully-fitted office space
20 in most major cities in the US. What you get is not only an office of the size you need furnished with desks, chairs and tables, sofas and so on. You also get telephone lines, broadband internet connections, Wi-Fi, printers, photocopiers, pictures on the wall and potted plants. We even give you a kitchen with a refrigerator and microwave. The 25 only thing you have to pay for yourself is your coffee!"

Obviously, the facilities which Office Latte's accommodation provides is included in the rental price. None of this comes for free – you pay for it all down to the last potted plant with the rent – but it's certainly convenient. 30

"Convenience really is the key here. Our service gives you a professional, fully-equipped office. All you need to do is sign the rental agreement. This makes life easy, in particular for one-person operations. If you have a small business, you need to spend your time on your core activities, 35 like selling your product or services. What you don't need is to waste time fitting out your office space. We're happy to do that for you."

The appeal to small businesses is clear, but what about larger companies? What's in it for them? 40

Hyslop explains: "Let's say I run a company on the West coast – let's say in San Francisco, just for fun. I want to set up a sales team in the Midwest, but I don't have an office anywhere in the region where I can hold job interviews. That's where we come in. You can rent an absolutely pro- 45 fessional office suite from us, impress your potential new employees, carry out your interviews and set up your new team. All at minimum cost and with little effort."

A **Entscheiden Sie, welche der Aussagen über den vorstehenden Text richtig oder falsch sind. Begründen Sie Ihre Antworten auf Deutsch.**

1 It's normal for companies not to own the buildings they do business from.
2 Companies usually get the furniture and equipment in their offices as part of their rental deal.
3 The new type of offices is suitable only for companies.
4 The 'ready to go' offices offer more flexible rental periods than traditional office rental agreements.
5 Office Latte does not have offices in every large city in the US.
6 The new type of office makes life easy for very small companies as it allows them to get on with their business.
7 The service to the company from San Francisco described by Hyslop would cost a lot of money.

B **Ihr Chef bittet Sie herauszufinden, was Office Latte anbietet und welche Vorteile für kleine oder große Firmen genannt werden. Erläutern Sie dies auf Deutsch.**

Angebot	
Vorteile für kleine Firmen	Vorteile für große Firmen

Extra material

Cool Street (UK) Ltd

Report into new office organisation for the Sales team

The current situation: Sales team has its own office and each member of Sales staff has their own desk

The company's aim: to cut costs and create more interaction between Sales staff and other colleagues

5 **Our brief:** to investigate alternative ways of organising the Sales teams' office space

Summary of recommendations

Hot desking

Under this method of office organisation, staff members no longer have their own desks. Rather, they can use any one of several desks in a company's offices. The idea
10 behind this is that it leads to more flexible team working and interaction between staff. Staff members take their places at work depending on which projects they are currently working on and which other team members they need to work most closely with. Clearly, hot desking is made easier if members of staff have portable laptop or tablet computers and Wi-Fi access to a company's network, intranets and the internet.
15 As the Sales staff at Cool Street (UK) Ltd have both portable devices and Wi-Fi network access, we are in a position to start hot desking! We recommend that the Sales Department office is closed and that several desks are made available for Sales staff in the Marketing and Product Development Departments. Cool Street (UK) Ltd places a great deal of importance on the feedback which members of the Sales team receive
20 from customers. We believe that giving Sales staff hot desks in these departments would allow members of the Sales team to pass on important feedback to their colleagues in Marketing and Product Development on a day-to-day basis.

Homeworking

Our other recommendation is that members of the Sales team are allowed to work
25 from home when they are not meeting with customers and do not have to come to the office. This would allow Sales staff who live quite far from our headquarters to spend less time driving. Our Sales people already spend much of their time in their cars driving to meetings with customers or into the office. It would be a positive development to reduce the need for this.

30 Additionally, adopting homeworking in combination with the hot desking scheme described above would allow the company to cut the cost of the Sales team's current office. There may be some investment needed at first in setting up home offices for the Sales staff but the cost savings of no longer having a sales office would be bigger.

Extra material

1 Ideas behind the report

Read the report and decide which two statements best summarise the ideas of the people who wrote it.

1. We really should cut our Sales team's petrol costs by getting them to work from home.
2. The Sales staff need to spend more time in the office learning from their colleagues in Marketing and Product Development.
3. One of the best ways of finding out quickly what our customers are thinking is to listen to our Sales staff. That's why we want them moving around different offices when they're at headquarters.
4. We could take some of the pressure off our Sales staff by giving them the chance to work at home when they don't need to be in the office.

2 Advantages and disadvantages

A. Work with a partner and make a list of the advantages of hot desking and homeworking mentioned in the report. Which other advantages can you think of?

B. The report's authors don't mention any disadvantages. How many can you think of? Make a list with your partner.

C. Present the advantages and disadvantages which you have thought of to the class.

3 Role-play

Two colleagues discuss the advantages and disadvantages of the ideas described in the report in the staff canteen. Write out their conversation with a partner then role-play it for the class.

Situation 1

The Bunbury Chocolate Company in the UK is having money problems. Shashi, an Indian food company, is interested in expanding its business into Western Europe. It has sent Mr Lal to visit the Bunbury factory and to find out more.

1 Welcoming the visitors

Look at the cards and act out the role-play.

Student A

You are Ron Nodes, Bunbury's Head of Production: your job is to meet the visitor and to explain about the company and the area. Here are the topics you should discuss:
- Welcome Mr Lal
- Ask about flight and hotel
- Say Bunbury is a small, friendly town
- Company well known in UK, good reputation …
- Now looking to build international links
- Will show them factory
- Managing Director will see them at 11 a.m.; can answer questions
- Invite visitors for tea

Student B

You are Mr Lal. React to Ron's topics. The responses below may help you. (They are not in the right order.)
- Thank you very much.
- Oh, really? That's interesting.
- Maybe we can help you there.
- We look forward to meeting him
- It's very comfortable, thank you.
- I see.
- Yes, it seems very pleasant.
- It was very smooth, thank you, with no problems.
- Yes, we have heard this: people like the brand.
- We'll be very interested to see it.

2 About Bunbury Chocolate Company

Later Ron gives Mr Lal a tour of the company and tells him about the company structure. Look at the business cards below and explain to Mr Lal who the people are, what they do and what responsibilities they have.

25

Situation 1

3 Directions

After the tour Ron Nodes has to go to a meeting. Mr Lal needs to go back to the reception and so asks Ron how to get there. Carry out a role-play.

Student A is Karim Lal;
Student B is Ron Nodes.

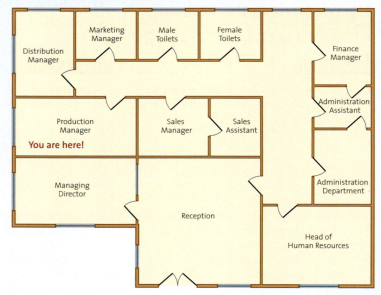

4 What's next?

Chandra Singh, the Managing Director of Shashi Foods, their company in India, has made a list of points he wants to include in an email to Karim Lal. Look at the different points and write an informal email for him.

- needed your raincoat yet?
- show Ron Nodes lates sales figures for Europe
- ask what Bunbury's sales figures for Europe are
- check who else in Britain sells chocolates to the rest of Europe
- get information about Bunbury's distribution network: how long to get foods from the factory to the airport?
- talk to some workers (factory and office): see how they like the work – and their wages
- taste some of their products
- find out how many employees they have
- look at their production line; could we do it more efficiently?
- bring back: some chocolate for my wife, for my kids too; my favourite brand of whiskey

Marketing and advertising

UNIT 3

- marketing strategies
- effective advertisements
- online advertising

1 Warm-up

Work with a partner and discuss which order you would put the various stages of the marketing process in. Say why.

a Draw up a marketing strategy
b Design the product you want to sell
c Carry out market research
d Buy advertising space to promote your product
e Design advertising
f Decide where advertising for your product will be placed

2 The marketing process

Read as Adam Collin from Pronic Digital, which manufactures digital projectors, talks to Tessa who is a trainee. Which statement (1, 2 or 3) best summarises the conversation?

Adam is talking about …
1 how the new projector developed by the company works.
2 how the company decides what sort of projectors to make and how it presents these to customers.
3 what type of customers Pronic Digital has.

Adam	Okay, so let me tell you about the Marketing Department here and how the marketing process works.
Tessa	Thanks. That would be really interesting.
Adam	Firstly, most companies base their marketing strategies around something called the four Ps. That's product, price, place and promotion. Put simply, to run an effective marketing campaign you need to get your product right. You also have to make sure you're offering it at the right price for the market. And it's really important to think about where you're going to sell it – that's place.
Tessa	Does that mean whether you sell on the internet or in shops and all that?
Adam	Exactly. The fourth P is promotion. You have to make sure that the way you promote the product is right. That means that your advertising and public relations have to contain the right messages about the product.
Tessa	I see.
Adam	Well, let's look at the first P again in more detail: product. When we're thinking about making a new projector, the first thing we do is look at what is happening in the market. We examine the projectors our competitors are making. You know, we look at the kind of features they include and how much they are being sold for. We also talk to customers and potential customers and try to evaluate from this what sort of projectors people want to buy.

27

MARKETING AND ADVERTISING

Tessa	How do you do that? With questionnaires and stuff?
Adam	Right. We often send out questionnaires to find out what customers think. Or we set up focus groups – you know, small groups of people who are brought together to be shown a product so that we can see what their reactions are. Anyway, this part of the process is called market research.
Tessa	Okay.
Adam	Now, our new digital projector, the Pronic 34RV, for example, is a light projector for business people who travel a lot. Our market research showed that business people wanted a lightweight digital projector with various different functions. So we worked closely with our Product Design staff to make sure that the Pronic 34RV was light and had all the necessary functions.
Tessa	Okay, sounds simple. You found out what the customer wanted and then tried to make it for them.
Adam	Exactly. Then once the design was complete, we had to decide how to market it. So we wrote a marketing plan. This normally helps us to make the marketing strategy clear. This plan included one or two affinity marketing ideas.
Tessa	Affinity marketing? What's that?
Adam	That's where two companies with products which appeal to similar groups of people – in this case, business people who travel a lot – tie their products together. We decided to do some affinity marketing with Fonon mobile phones because we thought their brand was cool and fresh and would work well with the Pronic brand.
Tessa	Yes, I remember seeing adverts for the two products together in a magazine.
Adam	Exactly. And that brings us onto the next important stage in the process – advertising. Now, we work with an advertising agency. They decide what the adverts for our projectors should look like and what they should say. We also have a media buying agency. They decide where the adverts should go and get us the best prices possible.
Tessa	You mean on television and in magazines for example?
Adam	Yes, that's right. And on the internet. We do a good deal of online advertising these days. Finally, the agency buys the advertising time on television or the advertising space in magazines and newspapers. And that's basically how we carry out our marketing.

3 Key marketing concepts

A Match the expressions highlighted in the text with their definitions below. There are five expressions too many. Write definitions for these in your own words.

1 the parts of newspapers and magazines which contain adverts
2 the document which lays out how to market a product
3 advertising on the internet
4 the way a company markets a product
5 companies which make and sell similar products to each other
6 the people responsible for how a product looks and what it does
7 the work carried out by Marketing staff to find out what customers want
8 the logo and name of a product or company which help customers to identify it
9 set of questions put to consumers to find out their attitudes
10 small group of people whose reactions to a product are evaluated

B Read the dialogue again and look at the order in which you put the items on the list of marketing tasks in the warm-up. Does Adam mention the tasks in the same order?

MARKETING AND ADVERTISING

UNIT 3

4 A questionnaire

A Adam shows Tessa a questionnaire which the company has developed to assess customers' attitudes to advertising. Complete the questionnaire using the words and phrases in the box.

> online • no, but I am likely to ignore it • Which type of advertising do you pay most attention to? • Do you click on advertisements on the internet? • are informative about the product's functionality • sometimes

Pronic Digital

Market Research

1 Do you buy products because of the way they're advertised?
   a never
   b ...¹
   c often

2 ...²
   a television
   b press (newspapers and magazines)
   c ...³

3 What sort of advertisements appeal to you most? Adverts which ...
   a ...⁴
   b are stylish and entertaining.
   c tell you how much a product costs.

4 ...⁵
   a never
   b sometimes
   c often

5 Do you object to receiving advertisements via SMS on your mobile phone?
   a yes
   b no
   c ...⁶

B Now complete the questionnaire, expressing your personal ideas.

C Work with a partner and take turns to explain how you answered the questions. What does the way you answered the questionnaire say about your attitudes to advertising and how you react to it?

29

UNIT 3

MARKETING AND ADVERTISING

GRAMMAR

Questions

1 **Where** do you do most of your advertising?
2 **When** did you start the market research for the product?
3 **Which** advertising agency does Gordon Bruce work for?
4 **Who** normally buys our products?
5 **What** is your plan regarding online advertising?

- Fragen mit **Vollverben** werden mit einer Form von *do* gebildet, d.h. *do/does* im *simple present* (1, 3) bzw. *did* im *simple past*. (2)
- Bei Fragen mit *to be* rückt das Verb vor das Subjekt. (5)
- Fragen nach dem **Subjekt** (mit *Who … ?* oder *What …?*) werden ohne eine Form von *do* gebildet. (4, 5)

Question words

How?	Wie?
Which?	Was? Welche/r/s?
Where?	Wo?
What?	Was?
When?	Wann?
Who?	Wer? Wen? Wem?
Whose?	Wessen?
Why?	Warum?

5 | Practice

A Use question words and the right form of either *to be* or *to do* to complete the questions.

1 … many copies of the questionnaire … we need to send out?
2 … we want to do most of our advertising: online or on television?
3 … kind of market research … you think we need to carry out?
4 … responsible for developing the marketing strategy in your company?
5 … advertising media … the Marketing Director feel will work best for this?
6 … you think the advertising campaign will start to make an impact on sales?
7 … reasons … there for continuing to spend so much on TV advertising when we know the results are unimpressive?

B The sentences below are answers to questions. What were the questions?

1 The first advert in the campaign will appear at the beginning of April.
2 Peter Wilson is Marketing Manager at our company.
3 Well, women between the ages of 25–40. That's our target market.
4 Mostly online and in a few national newspapers.
5 Garton and Brogel Advertising Ltd. They've worked for us for three years.
6 €24,000. We're going to split it equally between internet and press advertising.
7 Well, because we know that a large proportion of our target market still read a daily newspaper.

WEBCODE **BMU0301**

MARKETING AND ADVERTISING

UNIT 3

6 | The internet vs. traditional advertising media

A Adam gives Tessa an article to read about internet advertising. The parts of the article are jumbled up below. Put the paragraphs in a logical order.

It is clear then why companies advertise online. What is not clear though is how much online advertising will grow in the future. In a few years, advertising online could be even more important for companies than advertising on television. **A**

The second reason for the popularity of advertising online is that the results can be measured more accurately than with other media. If a company advertises on television, it theoretically has a large audience for its product. However, it is not possible to know how many people make a cup of coffee during the adverts and how many people actually watch them. Similarly, a newspaper may have several hundred thousand readers, but it is hard for advertisers to know if readers just turn the page when they come to their advert. **B**

So what is the attraction of internet advertising? Well, to start with, the internet is very fashionable. Companies want to see their products presented in a trendy, cool way to a young, computer-savvy audience. So they use the internet. **C**

Not long ago, few people believed that internet advertising had a future. Now the situation is very different and internet advertising is booming. **D**

Another element of online advertising which is attracting companies to the internet is 'viral marketing'. People often like to send each other funny or interesting videos that they find online. Increasing numbers of companies are becoming aware of this and are making short, eye-catching videos which feature their product in some way. They hope that these videos will circulate to people online 'virally'. Apart from being trendy, this means of spreading an advertising message online is also free. **E**

Internet advertising is different. As people have to click on adverts to see more of them, it is possible to measure how many people look at them properly. You can often buy a product by clicking on an internet advert, so companies can trace the success of their online advertising very directly. If people click on your advert – and then buy the product – you know you're doing something right. **F**

B Beantworten Sie folgende Fragen zum Text auf Deutsch. **KMK**

1 Wie hat sich in den letzten Jahren die Einstellung von Firmen zur Internetwerbung verändert?
2 Welche Zielgruppe hoffen Unternehmen über das Internet zu erreichen?
3 Warum ist es schwierig, die Wirksamkeit von Fernseh- und Zeitungswerbung zu beurteilen?
4 Wodurch ist es möglich, Erfolg oder Misserfolg von Internetwerbung zu überprüfen?
5 Wie haben Firmen es sich für ihre Internetwerbung zunutze gemacht, dass Leute sich gerne Videos online zuschicken?

UNIT 3 — MARKETING AND ADVERTISING

C Make a list of products which might be more effectively advertised online than in traditional advertising media such as TV or newspapers and vice versa and say why. Present your list to the class.

7 The advertising campaign

A Match the expressions for different types of media (1–3) to their definitions (a–c).

1. print media
2. broadcast media
3. online media

a. television and radio
b. the internet
c. newspapers and magazines

06

B Listen as Jake Reid from Pronic Digital's advertising agency talks to Adam and complete the sentences from the dialogue.

1. The market for the Pronic 34RV is business people between the ages of … and …
2. You spent a total of … per cent on broadcast media: that was … per cent on television adverts and … per cent on radio advertising.
3. Then you spent a total of … per cent on print media: … per cent on magazines and … per cent on newspapers.
4. We spent the remaining … per cent on online advertising.
5. We advise that you spend more on television adverts: … per cent in total.
6. In our opinion you should spend no more than … per cent on magazines.
7. We strongly suggest that you spend … per cent of your advertising budget online.

C Listen to the dialogue once more. Which of the sentences do you hear?

1.
   a. We'd like to propose some quite big changes for the Pronic 34RV.
   b. We'd like you to make some quite big changes for the Pronic 34RV.

2.
   a. This year we're going to suggest some big changes.
   b. This year we'd like to suggest some big changes.

3.
   a. Firstly, we recommend that you use newspaper and radio advertising.
   b. First of all, we recommend that you stop using newspaper and radio advertising.

4.
   a. Then we think that you should reduce the amount you spend on print media.
   b. Then we feel that you shouldn't reduce the amount you spend on print media.

5.
   a. We believe you should spend more than twenty per cent on magazines.
   b. In our opinion you should spend no more than twenty per cent on magazines.

> **LANGUAGE**
>
> **Making suggestions**
>
> We'd like to propose that …
> We'd like to suggest that …
> We recommend that you …
> In our opinion you should …
> We believe you should …

32

MARKETING AND ADVERTISING

8 Role-play: Which advertising media?

Sie und Ihr Partner / Ihre Partnerin wählen eine Rollenkarte. Sehen Sie sich die Produktinformationen an und führen Sie die unten stehenden Aufgaben aus. Verwenden Sie dazu Wendungen aus den Übungen und der Language Box auf Seite 32.

- Beschreiben Sie das Produkt und welcher Absatzmarkt hinsichtlich Alter usw. dafür in Frage kommt.

- Entscheiden Sie, welche deutschen Werbeträger Sie empfehlen würden und begründen Sie Ihre Auswahl.

- Überlegen Sie, welche Zeitschriften, Fernsehsender und Internetseiten Sie empfehlen würden und sagen Sie warum.

Student A

Product description:	city rucksack
Product name:	City Hiker
Product features:	internal pockets for smartphones and other devices; comes in a range of cool colours
Product price:	€30

Student B

Product description:	briefcase
Product name:	Leather Classic
Product features:	real leather, comes in brown or black
Product price:	€260

UNIT 3

MARKETING AND ADVERTISING

9 Creating effective advertisements

A Listen as Tessa tells Adam about an article about advertising she has read. Decide in what order she mentions the points below.

a strapline
b white space
c images
d subheadline
e main text
f headline

B Listen again and decide whether the statements are true or false. Correct the false statements.

1 A headline is not really necessary in an advert.
2 If you have a sub-headline, it should definitely not have anything to do with the headline.
3 It's important that the main text of an advert should not be too formal in tone.
4 The call to action tells customers what they should do once they've read the advert.
5 The strapline has to link back into the idea expressed in the headline.
6 You should avoid having white space in an advert and fill this up with photographs whenever necessary.

10 Two adverts for Pronic Digital

A The advertising agency sends Adam two adverts for the new projector. Work with a partner and think about what Tessa said about writing and designing adverts in exercise 9. What are the strengths and weaknesses of both adverts? How could the adverts be improved?

MARKETING AND ADVERTISING

UNIT 3

The first time I used the Pronic 34RV Digital Projector I thought, "Wow, why didn't I know about this before?"

Andrew Morgan, Sales Executive

Sorry, Andrew! We should have told you sooner.

The Pronic 34RV is perfect for business people who are on the move. It's the lightest digital projector you can buy. And the smallest, too.

It fits neatly into your briefcase, gives you bright, clear projection every time and is the most reliable digital projector on the market. It couldn't be simpler to use either.

Features
- 4 USB 2 ports
- 'Go to sleep' power-saving function
- Power cable
- Battery function for when no power supply is available
- Tough but cool aluminium casing
- Black business-like colouring

Okay, so it's more expensive than some other digital projectors. But that won't stop you loving it.

What are you waiting for? Be like Andrew.
Be amazed!

pronic

Introducing the new Pronic 34RV digital projector

It's the lightest, smallest digital projector on the market today.

The projector weighs just 1.7 kilos and is small enough to be slipped into your briefcase.

pronic

Order the Pronic 34RV online now:
www.pronic-digital.com

B Use elements from the two advertisements and your own ideas to design and write a new advert for the Pronic 34RV. Think about Tessa's advice from exercise 9. Then present your advert to the class.

35

KMK exam practice

11 Mediation

Die Marketing-Abteilung Ihrer Firma beauftragt Sie herauszufinden, ob eine geplante Kampagne für Sonnenschutzmittel gegen den Werbekodex verstößt. Sie finden folgenden Artikel.

Übertragen Sie den folgenden Text sinngemäß in die deutsche Sprache.

Sunburn marketing promotion "irresponsible" says Advertising Standards Authority

A competition that asked people to send in pictures of their sunburn has been banned by the Advertising Standards Authority (ASA).

The email promotion for travel comparison website Dealchecker.co.uk – which called on customers to email pictures of sunburn to likealobster@dealchecker.co.uk – offered prizes including a holiday for two for the winner and sunscreen for runners-up.

The Advertising Standards Authority received a complaint that the competition – which encouraged entrants to "earn with your burn" was irresponsible because it encouraged people to get sunburnt to win.

Parent company DMC Digital argued that the aim of the competition was to promote sun safety and said it did not believe that the text of the email "either condoned or encouraged sunburn explicitly".

The company said that a string of previous emails about the competition showed that the emphasis was on the dangers of overexposure by asking only for old sunburn photos and referring to "tanning disasters" and "sunburn nightmares".

DMC also said that during the six-week competition period there had been numerous blogposts and tweets on sun safety.

However, the ASA said that the email and homepage of the competition did not refer to sun safety or specifically ask for old photos. The watchdog also criticised the entry email address, the text "earn with your burn" and photos of sunburnt people.

The ASA banned the competition, ruling it was irresponsible and that it "could be seen to trivialise sunburn".

Source: Mark Sweney, guardian.co.uk, Wednesday 5 October 2011

Extra material

The future of marketing?

Most companies think that marketing is a straightforward business. They have a product and know which target markets they want to aim it at. They hire an advertising agency to develop an ad campaign. Then they hire a media buying agency which helps them decide where to place their ads and then buys space for them. Then they sit back and wait for customers to buy their product.

But if the previous paragraph summarises how a company understands the marketing process – and particularly the part about communicating with potential customers – it may need to think again. Why? Well, because of one or two new approaches to marketing. These are currently only being used by a few innovative companies, but will certainly become increasingly important in the future. Read on to get up to speed on the two most important new approaches to getting your message out there.

Viral marketing

A key factor behind this new type of marketing is the high costs involved in buying advertising space in traditional media such as TV and print. With the arrival of the internet, marketeers discovered people's willingness to pass on marketing messages to friends online providing the message was packaged in an interesting enough way. The savings in this for companies are clear.

Viral marketing messages can take the form of funny videos, photos or sound clips which people send on to online contacts for their entertainment value. It's often not made completely clear that these messages are actually selling a product; many people who post a viral marketing video on their social networking site would be surprised that they have passed on an advertisement. Nevertheless, the technique works and a company which markets successfully in this way will guarantee a "buzz" for its product – and hopefully increase sales.

Guerilla marketing

The idea behind guerilla marketing is to change the form in which marketing messages are presented and to get them out of conventional advertising media. The technique aims at presenting marketing messages in a form that people do not expect to see them in.

Guerilla marketing campaigns can take many forms and include, for example, putting your message on crudely produced (but cool) stickers or hiring actors to play out a scene in public which conveys your message.

Even if these approaches to marketing a sales message are too unconventional for many companies, they offer significant cost savings over more conventional approaches. For this reason alone they are certain to be used by increasing numbers of companies.

1 | Marketing methods

A What does the text say about the differences between the new methods and more traditional approaches to marketing? Make a list for each method.

B Which of these methods can you imagine working best for your company? Why?

2 | Designing a marketing concept

Work with a partner to design a viral or guerilla marketing campaign for your company. Present your ideas to the class explaining why you think it would work.

UNIT 4 Making an order on the telephone

■ telephone enquiries   ■ offers   ■ confirmation of orders

1 Warm-up

A Work with a partner. Which problems do you have when making or answering telephone calls in English? Make a list.

People sometimes speak too quietly.

I get so nervous, I forget what I want to say.

B What advice can you and your partner think of to help someone with problems on your list when telephoning in English? Present your advice to the class.

2 A telephone call

A Steve Brumford is trying to reach Garry Carlisle at Street Craze Ltd on the telephone. Read the dialogue and answer the questions.

1 Why can't Garry come to the phone?
2 When does the receptionist say he will possibly be free to speak?
3 What does the receptionist offer to do for Steve?
4 What reason does Steve give for his call?
5 What telephone number does Steve say Garry can call him back on?
6 When does Steve say he will no longer be available to take Garry's call?

Receptionist	Good afternoon. Street Craze Ltd. Sarah speaking. How can I help you?
Steve	Good afternoon. This is Steve Brumford from Manchester Guided Tours. I'd like to speak to Garry Carlisle, please.
Receptionist	Certainly. Hold on a moment, please. I'll see if I can get him for you. … Hello. Are you still there?
Steve	Yes, hello.
Receptionist	I'm sorry but I'm afraid Garry isn't in the office at the moment.
Steve	Oh, I see. That is a pity. I was hoping to catch him.
Receptionist	I'm sorry. He's out seeing one of our customers just now.
Steve	Could you tell me when he'll be back, please?

38

MAKING AN ORDER ON THE TELEPHONE

UNIT 4

Receptionist	Not really, I'm afraid. Perhaps in three or four hours. Can I take a message for him?
Steve	Yes, thank you. I would like to leave a message. Could you tell him that Steve Brumford from Manchester Guided Tours called, please?
Receptionist	OK. Sorry, I didn't catch your name. Could you spell it for me, please?
Steve	Yes, of course. It's Brumford – B–R–U–M–F–O–R–D.
Receptionist	And your calling from …?
Steve	Manchester Guided Tours.
Receptionist	OK, thank you, Mr Brumford. Can I ask what it's about?
Steve	Certainly. It's about a potential order for some of your scooters.
Receptionist	Can I get Garry to call you back?
Steve	Yes. That would be great, thanks. Can I give you my number?
Receptionist	Yes, hold on … Okay, what's the number?
Steve	Okay. It's 0161 325954.
Receptionist	Okay. I'll just repeat that. 0161 325954.
Steve	That's right.
Receptionist	Fine. I'll tell Garry you called and get him to ring you back.
Steve	Thank you very much. Could you tell him he can call anytime until 6.30 this evening?
Receptionist	No problem. Thank you. Goodbye.

TIP

Even native speakers of English sometimes don't understand what someone has said on the telephone. So don't be afraid to ask a caller to say something again. After all, it's important that you understand correctly so that you can help them fully.

Use phrases like these to get a caller to repeat what they have said:
I'm sorry but I didn't catch that. Could you say it again, please?
I'm afraid I didn't understand what you just said. Could you please repeat it?

B **Use the words in the box to complete the sentences which are similar to those in the dialogue.**

about • afraid • back (x2) • called • get • hold • leave • repeat • ring • speak • take

1 James Cannon from Healey Plc. Can I please … to Ted Brothers?
2 Sure. Please … on a second.
3 Let me just check if I can … her for you.
4 Sorry, but Sara isn't free to come to the phone right now, I'm …
5 Would it be possible for you to say when she'll be …?
6 Would you like me to … a message for her?
7 Could I … a message, please?
8 Please let her know that Ross Johnston …
9 Could you tell me what it's …?
10 Shall I ask Jane to call you …?
11 Fine. Let me just … that. 01435 83472362.
12 Okay. I'll let Brian know you called and ask him to … you back.

39

MAKING AN ORDER ON THE TELEPHONE

3 Role-play: making a phone call

Work with a partner and complete the role-play. Use phrases from exercise 2.

Student A

Antworten Sie mit Ihrem Namen. Fragen Sie, ob Sie helfen können.

Student B

Stellen Sie sich mit Ihrem Namen vor. Fragen Sie, ob Sie Peter Smith sprechen können.

Sagen Sie, dass Sie fragen werden, ob Peter Smith zu sprechen ist. Dann sagen Sie, dass er in einer Besprechung ist.

Fragen Sie, ob Sie eine Nachricht hinterlassen können.

Bejahen Sie.

Sagen Sie, dass Herr Smith wissen soll, dass Sie angerufen haben. Fragen Sie, ob Sie Ihre Telefonnummer hinterlassen können.

Sagen Sie, dass Sie Peter die Nachricht weitergeben und fragen Sie nach der Telefonnummer.

Geben Sie Ihre Telefonnummer.

Wiederholen Sie die Telefonnummer.

Bedanken und verabschieden Sie sich.

WEBCODE **BMU0401**

4 Taking a telephone order

KMK

Fertigen Sie für Ihren Abteilungsleiter eine Telefonnotiz an. Nutzen Sie dafür die Angaben im abgebildeten Formular. Sie hören die Nachricht zweimal.

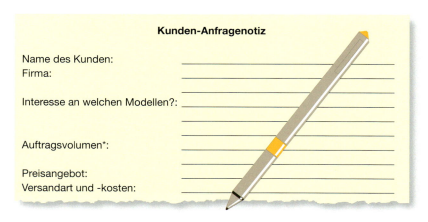

*(Geben Sie die genaue Stückzahl für jedes Produkt an.)

MAKING AN ORDER ON THE TELEPHONE

UNIT 4

5 Useful phrases

A Listen again and say in which order Garry uses these phrases during his conversation with Steve.

a Can I ask which models you've been looking at?
b Yes, I would certainly recommend you to go for one of these.
c That's no problem at all.
d Can you tell me which scooters you're interested in?
e Would you mind if I made a suggestion?
f How can I help you?
g Could you give me an idea of how many scooters you'd like to order?

B Match the phrases below to phrases in part A which have a similar meaning.

1 Could you say which models most interest you?
2 Sure, no worries.
3 Can I make a suggestion?
4 What sort of scale would you be ordering on?
5 What can I do for you?
6 Would you be able to say how big your order will be?
7 I would definitely advise you to choose that.
8 My advice would certainly be to go for that.
9 Which would be of most interest to you?
10 Which ones have you been thinking about?
11 Could I suggest something?
12 Not a problem.
13 Which models have you been considering?
14 How can I be of assistance?

C Unscramble the statements and questions that Steve uses during the telephone conversation. Listen again to check your answers.

1 returning / thank / call / for / you / my
2 help / I / you / hoping / was / there / could / me
3 just / I / best / which / be / decide / can't / would
4 you / tell / me / then / can / how / cost / that / much / will / ?
5 how / these / could / quickly / us / you / deliver / to / ?
6 much / delivery / does / how / the / cost / express / ?

UNIT 4

MAKING AN ORDER ON THE TELEPHONE

6   An email to confirm the order

A   Read the email which Garry writes to Steve to confirm his order. Correct the three mistakes he has made.

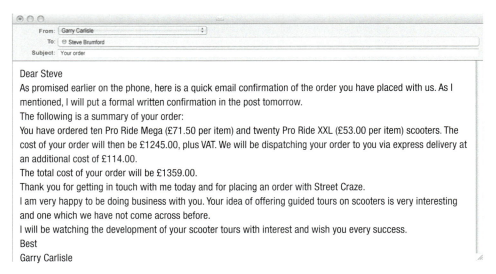

From: Garry Carlisle
To: Steve Brumford
Subject: Your order

Dear Steve
As promised earlier on the phone, here is a quick email confirmation of the order you have placed with us. As I mentioned, I will put a formal written confirmation in the post tomorrow.
The following is a summary of your order:
You have ordered ten Pro Ride Mega (£71.50 per item) and twenty Pro Ride XXL (£53.00 per item) scooters. The cost of your order will then be £1245.00, plus VAT. We will be dispatching your order to you via express delivery at an additional cost of £114.00.
The total cost of your order will be £1359.00.
Thank you for getting in touch with me today and for placing an order with Street Craze.
I am very happy to be doing business with you. Your idea of offering guided tours on scooters is very interesting and one which we have not come across before.
I will be watching the development of your scooter tours with interest and wish you every success.
Best
Garry Carlisle

B   Antworten Sie Garry mit einer E-Mail. Bedanken Sie sich für seine E-Mail, weisen Sie aber auf die Fehler darin hin.

7   Written confirmation of an order

A   A few weeks later Steve places another order for scooters. Read the letter which Garry writes to Steve to confirm the order and decide which of the statements in the speech bubbles are likely to have been said by Steve and Garry between the first and second order.

3 The scooter tour idea hasn't really been a success, but it was worth trying.

4 Manchester Guided Tours are nice guys but they're not going to be an important customer for us.

2 We should definitely not give discounts to Manchester Guided Tours as they are unlikely to become regular customers.

5 It's an interesting idea. We need to develop our business with them.

1 We need more scooters fast if we are going to keep up with demand for the tours.

6 The people that come on our tours definitely prefer the Pro Ride XXL.

Steve

Garry

42

MAKING AN ORDER ON THE TELEPHONE

UNIT 4

Mr Steve Brumford
Manchester Guided Tours
32 Selby North Road
Manchester
M4L 3SD

43 Canley Road, Coventry, CV2 6DL

13 September 20_

Re: Confirmation of your order

Dear Mr Brumford

Further to our conversation on the telephone today, I am writing to confirm your order of 40 Pro Ride XXL scooters. The price of your order will be £2603.00 including VAT which represents a 9% discount on our listed prices which we are making as a sign of our gratitude for your continued custom with us. Payment will be due within 28 days of receipt of our invoice.
As also discussed on the telephone, your order will be dispatched by means of express delivery and should arrive with you within 24 hours of your having placed it.
As a mark of our appreciation for your ongoing business, we are including express delivery at the cost of our normal delivery charges.
We very much look forward to doing business again with you soon.
If we can be of assistance to you in any way, please do not hesitate to get in contact with us.

Yours sincerely

Garry Carlisle

Garry Carlisle

B Match the expressions from a German business letter (1–7) with expressions in the letter above.

1 Sehr geehrte/r
2 Bezug nehmend auf unser Telefonat am heutigen Vormittag, bestätige ich hiermit schriftlich Ihre Bestellung von …
3 Der Rechnungsbetrag Ihrer Bestellung beläuft sich auf …
4 MwSt
5 Zahlbar innerhalb von 28 Tagen nach Erhalt unserer Rechnung.
6 Als Zeichen unserer Anerkennung für Ihre Anschlussbestellung, … wir …
7 Mit freundlichen Grüßen

C Find the formal expressions in the letter which go with the more informal expressions below.

1 All the best
2 Look forward to being able to help again.
3 About our chat on the phone this morning: I just want to let you know …
4 Hi Steve
5 Just let me know if I can do anything else for you.

D Now work in a group and discuss when you think you should use formal phrases and when you can use less formal ones.

If you already know the person quite well, it's probably OK to …

You should really be formal if …

43

MAKING AN ORDER ON THE TELEPHONE

UNIT 4

GRAMMAR

Modal verbs

1 Our new models of scooters **can** go faster than last year's models.
2 **Could** you spell your surname, please?
3 The order **must** arrive by Wednesday at the latest.
4 We will **be able to** offer more tours once we have more scooters.
5 We won't **be allowed to** use the scooters for our tours unless they meet safety standards.
6 We **should** talk about which model of scooter we want to order next time.
7 The tours were so popular that we **had to** order more scooters almost immediately.
8 The order arrived late. This **mustn't** happen again.

Modale Hilfsverben haben folgende Eigenschaften:
- Sie haben immer dieselbe Form.
- Bei der Verneinung sind Kurzformen möglich. (8)
- Alle außer *be able to, be allowed to* und *have to* werden mit dem Infinitiv ohne *to* verwendet. (1, 6, 8)
- Wenn andere Zeitformen als das Präsens nötig sind, verwendet man die Ersatzverben *be able to* (für *can*), *be allowed to* (für *may*) und *have to* (für *must*). (4, 5, 7)

Achtung: *must not* = nicht dürfen, *doesn't/don't have to* = nicht müssen.

Hilfsverb	Ersatzverb	Entsprechung
can could may	be able to	können könnten/konnten könnten
may might	be allowed to	dürfen dürfen
must	have to	müssen
shall should		sollen sollten
must not	not be allowed to	nicht dürfen
need needn't		brauchen nicht brauchen

8 Practice

Replace the German modal verb in brackets with the most suitable modal verb from the box above.

1 We … *(müssen)* to be sure that the scooter tour idea will work before we place another order.
2 As a scooter tour leader, you … *(nicht dürfen)* go too fast because it's dangerous.
3 These scooters are fantastic. They … *(können)* go almost anywhere.
4 Steve will … *(müssen)* do some advertising for the scooter tours soon.
5 They … *(dürfen)* try out some of the new scooters when they visited Street Craze last week.
6 Tell Garry he … *(nicht brauchen)* call me back until tomorrow morning.
7 … *(Könnten)* I leave a message for him along with my telephone number?

KMK exam practice

9 | Produktion

A Ihre Kollegin Susanne Peters bittet Sie, der Firma Billington per E-Mail in englischer Sprache zu bestätigen, dass ihre Bestellung bei Ihnen eingegangen ist. Frau Peters stellt Ihnen folgende Informationen zur Verfügung.

Name des Kunden:	*Ross Andrews*
Anschrift des Kunden:	*Billington Bike Market*
	47 Squires Road, Accrington, AN4 7RF
	Großbritannien
Ihre Adresse:	*Radsport Riehn*
	Freundallee 136
	13798 Berlin
	Deutschland
Angaben zur Bestellung:	Preise in Britischen Pfund
14 Dales Mountainbikes	*£6650.00*
10 Pacer Single-Speed Sporträder	*£7200.00*
Versandkosten	*£397.00*
Gesamtbestellkosten	*£14,247.00 (Preise inkl. MwSt)*

Die Bestellung wird Freitag, den 9. Februar um 10.30 Uhr an Billington Bike Market ausgeliefert.

B Verfassen Sie auf Englisch einen Brief von Billington Bike Market, in dem Sie um eine Änderung der Bestellung bitten. Verwenden Sie die folgenden Angaben in Ihrem Brief.

Zusatzauftrag:

6 Peak Pro Mountainbikes
12 Velocity BMX Räder
7 World Wide Tourenräder

Fragen Sie, wie viel die zusätzlichen Räder an Versand kosten.

Bitten Sie um Anlieferung der Bestellung am nächsten Tag.

Extra material

Blog spot - by Wordperfect

Emailing – a few dos and don'ts
Email is a great way to communicate. The fact that it's fast, easy and inexpensive explains why it has become the number one method of written business communication in the 21st century. However, email has also led to what can only be described as bad writing style. In the end, this could be bad for business. Here are a couple of basic pointers to help you get your emails right and present your company in the right light.

Formal vs. informal
In the old days, when most written communication took place via business letters, there was little need to consider the issue of how formal something should sound. Business letters were, by definition, quite formal, so the choice of being informal did not really present itself. Then along came email. There was something about the new medium which led to people being rather informal and conversational in their tone. Business people who were previously quite stiff in their writing began to open their emails with *Hi* and sign them off with *Cheers* or *Bye for now*.
This, of course, is still the case and there's a problem with it. Too much informality sounds unprofessional. So it's best to stick to a formal approach when writing email. Starting an email with *Dear* … and ending it with *Best regards* may feel old-fashioned, but it's actually good email style which won't get you – or your company – into trouble.

Good writing style
The idea that email is an informal medium has led to another idea about writing style. Before email, business people paid a lot of attention to making sure that their writing was correct. That meant that words had to be properly spelled, commas and full stops had to be in the right places and writing had to be arranged neatly in logical paragraphs. But it's unfortunately often the case that people pay little attention to this when writing email. The result is that emails often contain basic spelling errors, bad punctuation and poorly organised paragraphs. The result can be either embarrassing, difficult to read or both.
You probably want your business emails to be easy to read and to create the right impression about your professionalism. If you do, you should certainly think twice about making the mistakes in style described above.

1 True or false?

Are the statements about the text true or false? Correct the false statements.

1. The author has a negative attitude towards email in general.
2. The text states that bad email style has actually damaged businesses commercially.
3. It is suggested that the style of business letters gave people the choice of how formal to be.
4. The text suggests that emails are better if they are written formally.
5. It is claimed that people spend less time thinking about style when writing emails.

2 Do you agree?

Work in a group and carry out the tasks.

1. Make a list of the advantages of the style pointers which the author is arguing for.
2. Discuss what the argument against the author's ideas would be. Make a list of the advantages of this.
3. Present your ideas to the class.

Situation 2

Claymore Cheese is a Scottish company which has had great success in selling its various cheeses in England. Now it wishes to take its brand into Europe. Greg McGregor, the Managing Director, has asked his marketing team to hold a meeting, together with their European advisers, Cooper Bros. They brainstorm ideas and come to a decision about whether to market their cheese in Europe – and if so, how and when.

1 | The meeting

Follow the instructions on the role-play cards and act out the meeting.

Student A

Stella Murray, Head of Marketing, Claymore Cheese
(You are chairing the meeting.)
- Point out that you are worried about the budget, the potential market for Scottish cheese in Europe and the competition of other European cheeses.
- Suggest starting with Germany and waiting to see how well Claymore Cheese performs there.
- Ask for more information about what Lofty Vernon and Bob Burn plan for the media campaign.

Student B

Bob Burns, Sales & Advertising Director, Claymore Cheese
- Express that you are enthusiastic about the idea of a new European market.
- Explain that you plan to advertise the cheese through an internet, TV and newspaper campaign, starting in Northern Europe (Scandinavia, Denmark and Holland).
- Say that you want the campaign to start immediately.

Student C

Margo Campbell, Sales & Advertising Assistant, Claymore Cheese
- Support Bob's views as you are his assistant.
- Express that you think advertising through social networks like Facebook to create interest in the cheeses would be a good idea.

Student D

Lofty Vernon, Cooper Bros Consultant
- Agree with Stella that a more cautious approach is best.
- Summarise the general problems (such as transport & delivery and finding shop or supermarket outlets) and possibilities (for example, interest in Scottish cheese, as previously unknown in Europe) in marketing new brands of cheese in Europe.
- Express that you feel that a media campaign to create interest in the new cheese would be the best strategy.

Student E

Sally Warner, Cooper Bros Marketing Adviser
- Support Lofty's ideas in general as you are his assistant.
- Say that you rather like Margo's idea of using social networking media like Facebook, and that you could help to organise this.

47

Situation 2

2 The report

At the end of the meeting, Stella has to write a short report for Greg. He has asked her to make sure all sides of the argument are included. Then he can make the final decision whether to launch a European marketing campaign.

Stella sends the following email:

Dear all
Greg has just asked me to write a report about what we said at our meeting. I took notes and I know what I said, but just to make sure I don't get anything wrong, could you possibly send me a brief summary of your views on the topic?
Many thanks
Stella

A Write bullet points summarising the key aspects of what you said in exercise 1.

B Work in a group. Use the information from part A to write Stella's formal report.

TIP In general, use formal English and regular 'signposting' phrases, such as *on the contrary*; *however*; *in other words* …

Report on the Meeting held on 3rd June
to discuss the market in Europe for Claymore Cheese

By Stella Murray (Head of Marketing)

Those present: *(list)*

1 **Introduction**
Greg McGregor wanted the Marketing and Sales teams to get together with Cooper Bros in order to discuss the opportunities – and possible problems – for Claymore in Europe.

2 **The discussion**
(You should summarise the main points here.)

3 **Conclusion**
(You should give the overall view of the meeting about Claymore's decision on Europe.)

3 Answerphone messages

09

While Bob and Margo were at the meeting, several callers left messages for them. Listen to the messages and note down who called and any important information. Sort the messages into the categories business/private and important/unimportant/urgent and then decide which messages Margo should pass on to Bob.

A trade fair and an order

- meeting customers & making appointments
- orders & shipment
- payments & reminders

UNIT 5

1 Warm-up

A Work with a partner and decide what these people at a trade fair are saying.

B Write a short dialogue then role-play it for the class.

2 A visit to a trade fair stand

KMK

Hören Sie sich den Text zweimal an und beantworten Sie folgende Fragen auf Deutsch.

1. Wann hat Daniel Bach Ewan Strachan getroffen?
2. Warum besucht Daniel Ewans Messestand?
3. Wann wird Ewan zum Stand zurückkommen??
4. Was will Daniel machen, während er auf Ewan wartet?
5. Was schlägt Ben Daniel vor und was bietet er ihm an?
6. Wie nimmt Daniel seinen Kaffee?
7. Wie begründet Daniel seine Ablehnung der Werbegeschenke?

49

A TRADE FAIR AND AN ORDER

3 Key expressions

The five things in the photos are mentioned in the dialogue. What are they? Listen again to check your answers.

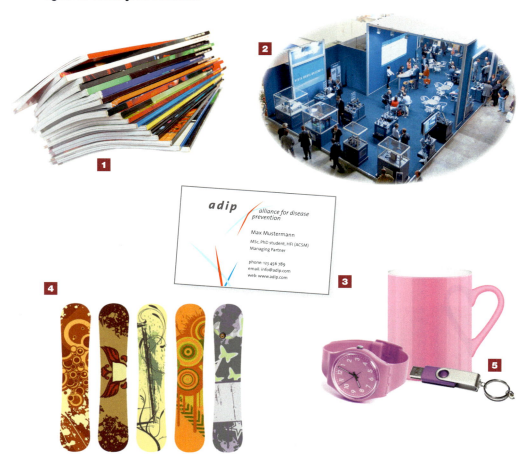

4 Key phrases

Rearrange the words to make sentences from the dialogue. Then decide in which order the sentences are used in the dialogue. Listen again to check your answers.

a   a / love / please / I'd / coffee
b   to / you / would / for / him / wait / like / ?
c   promotional / I / can / you / of / our / gifts / some / offer / ?
d   you / seat / to / take / like / would / a / ?
e   cup / I / or / offer / you / a / tea / coffee / can / of / ?
f   afraid / moment / the / Ewan / isn't / I'm / at / here
g   be / about / an / hour / back / in / half / he'll

A TRADE FAIR AND AN ORDER

UNIT 5

5 Role-play: meeting a customer

Work with a partner and carry out the role-play.

Student A

Begrüßen Sie den/die Besucher/in und fragen Sie, ob Sie behilflich sein können.

Student B

Antworten Sie und fragen Sie, ob Mr Harrington verfügbar ist.

Sagen Sie, dass er momentan nicht da ist, er aber in wenigen Minuten zurück sein wird. Bieten Sie dem/der Besucher/in einen Sitzplatz an.

Bedanken Sie sich.

Bieten Sie dem/der Besucher/in eine Tasse Kaffee oder Tee an.

Sagen Sie, dass Sie gerne einen Kaffee hätten.

Fragen Sie, ob der/die Besucher/in Milch oder Zucker nimmt.

Sagen Sie, dass Sie Milch und Zucker nehmen.

Reichen Sie dem/der Besucher/in die Tasse Kaffee.

Bedanken Sie sich.

6 A telephone call from Ewan

A After meeting Daniel at the trade fair, Ewan calls him to make an appointment. Listen to the dialogue to find out when they are going to meet.

B Complete these sentences to make useful phrases for making an appointment. Then listen to the dialogue again to check your answers.

1. Could I possibly make an … to come and see you?
2. Is there a time on either of those days that would … you?
3. How … 11 a.m. on Monday?
4. I'm … I won't be able to make that.
5. Could I … 1 p.m. on Monday afternoon?
6. No, … that won't work.
7. How … 9 o'clock on Tuesday morning be?
8. Let me see. No, sorry, that's not … either.
9. Would you be … to make 3 p.m. on Tuesday?
10. Yes. I … that would work.

51

UNIT 5 — A TRADE FAIR AND AN ORDER

7 Making an appointment

Work with a classmate. One partner looks at Diary A, the other looks at Diary B. Using the sentences from exercise 6, make an appointment to meet your partner.

Diary A

Monday	
14:00 – 16:00	Sales meeting
16:00 – 17:00	Meeting with suppliers
Tuesday	
9:00 – 12:00	Hospital appointment
13:00 – 17:00	Meeting with Managing Director
Wednesday	
9:00 – 13:00	Trip to see new factory
15:00 – 18:00	Meeting with Marketing Department
Thursday	
	Out all day on training course
Friday	
12:00 – 15:00	Team meeting
15:00 – 17:00	Write report for next Monday morning

Diary B

Monday	
	Sales meeting all day
Tuesday	
9:00 – 12:00	Dentist appointment
13:00 – 15:00	Lunch with new Sales Director
15:00 – 18:00	Write new sales strategy
Wednesday	
9:00 – 13:00	Meeting with customers
15:00 – 18:00	Present new sales strategy to Sales Director
Thursday	
9:00 – 12:00	Training with new Sales people
12:00 – 18:00	Afternoon off
Friday	
12:00 – 13:00	Lunch with Tim Berks
13:00 – 15:00	Meeting with Clara Forbes
15:00 – 17:00	Team feedback session

8 A meeting between Ewan and Daniel

A Read as Ewan visits Daniel for lunch. What does Ewan call the transportation methods shown in the photographs?

1

2

3

4

Ewan Well, Daniel. It is nice to see you again. Have you been busy since the fair?
Daniel Definitely, this is our busiest time of year. But it keeps me out of trouble!
Ewan I know what you mean! Well, shall we get down to business?
Daniel Yes, great. Well, we really liked your new Riftrider snowboard line. We'd like to place an order to try them out in our shops. Say about twenty-five snowboards.

A TRADE FAIR AND AN ORDER

UNIT 5

Ewan	Right, great.
Daniel	If we sell the snowboards quickly, we'll order more from you. So how much would that cost?
Ewan	Hm, that depends. The boards have a wholesale price of 67 euros. So that would be … let me see … 1675 euros for twenty-five boards. If I give you a small discount of 75 euros, they will cost 1600 euros.
Daniel	Okay, fine.
Ewan	Yes, but we have to remember the cost of shipping has to be added to that.
Daniel	Of course. How much will that cost?
Ewan	Well, there are a number of shipment options. Okay, sea freight is not really relevant here. So let's start with road haulage. That is certainly the cheapest way to ship the boards. But it also takes the most time. If you choose road haulage, the snowboards will take three days to arrive.
Daniel	That's quite a long time. We need them a bit faster. What are our other options?
Ewan	Well, you could transport them by rail. Rail freight is a bit more expensive, but also a bit faster. If you ship the snowboards by rail, you will get them within two days.
Daniel	That's pretty good.
Ewan	Of course, we could also send the snowboards by air. If we send the boards as air freight, you will get them within a few hours. But then it's terribly expensive.
Daniel	I don't think we need to receive them that quickly. But then I can't wait three days for them to arrive.

B **What is the significance of the numbers in the box?**

2 • 3 • 25 • 67 • 75 • 1675

9 | Key expressions

Match the German expressions (1–6) with English expressions in the box.

cost of shipping • discount • options • order • to place an order • wholesale price

1 eine Bestellung aufgeben   **4** Rabatt
2 bestellen   **5** Transportkosten
3 Großhandelspreis   **6** Möglichkeiten

10 | Key phrases

Match the sentence beginnings (1–4) to the sentence endings (a–d) to make statements about the dialogue.

1 If Daniel's shops sell the snowboards quickly,
2 If Ewan gives Daniel a small discount of 75 euros,
3 If Daniel chooses road haulage,
4 If Ewan's company ships the snowboards by rail,

a they will order more boards from Ewan.
b Daniel will get them within two days.
c the snowboards will take three days to arrive.
d the snowboards will cost 1600 euros.

53

UNIT 5

A TRADE FAIR AND AN ORDER

GRAMMAR

Conditional I & II

1. If Daniel's shops **sell** the snowboards quickly, they **will order** more boards from Ewan.
2. I **won't be able to** order more from you if you **don't increase** the size of my discount.
3. If you **ordered** more from me, I **would be able to** increase the size of your discount.
4. We'd agree to larger orders if you **gave** us a bigger discount.
5. If they **increased** the size of the discount, we **might be able to** place a larger order.

- *If*-Sätze Typ 1 drücken eine erfüllbare Bedingung aus. Beachten Sie die Zeitenfolge: Der *if*-Nebensatz steht im *simple present*, im Hauptsatz steht das *will future*. (1, 2)
- *If*-Sätze Typ 2 drücken eine möglicherweise erfüllbare Bedingung aus. Beachten Sie die Zeitenfolge: Der *if*-Nebensatz steht im *simple past*, im Hauptsatz wird *would* + Infinitiv verwendet. (3, 4) Statt *would* kann je nach Kontext auch *could*, *might* oder *should* verwendet werden. (5)
- Steht der *if*-Nebensatz an erster Stelle, wird er vom Hauptsatz durch ein Komma getrennt. (1, 3, 5)

11 Practice

A Fill the gaps with the correct form of the verb in brackets.

1. The order would arrive more quickly if you … it by rail rather than road. (ship)
2. If you decided to discount the shipping costs, I … ask my boss about this and could place the order now. (not have to)
3. You will run the risk of losing him as a future customer if you … him to pay full price for his first order. (ask)
4. If you confirm that you want us to ship your order by air, we … get it to you by tomorrow evening at the latest. (be able to)
5. If the order … on time, it could be due to the train being delayed. (not arrive)
6. I'll give you a call later if I … any other questions about placing an order. (have)

B Translate the following into English using conditional sentences.

1. Wenn Sie sich jedoch für Luftfracht entscheiden würden, müssten Sie viel höhere Versandkosten zahlen.
2. Es wird nur zwei Tage dauern, bis sie bei Ihnen ankommt, wenn Sie Luftfracht wählen.
3. Wenn Sie Seefracht wählen, dauert es etwa 10 Tage, bis die Bestellung ankommt.
4. Es wäre natürlich preiswerter, wenn Sie sich für Seefracht entschieden.

WEBCODE **BMU0501**

12 Which shipment method?

A Read Daniel's discussion with Ewan again. Which shipment method do you think Daniel should choose?

54

A TRADE FAIR AND AN ORDER

B Now listen to the end of the dialogue to check your answer. Then decide which one of the following statements is correct.

1 Ewan thinks Daniel has more than one shipping option.
2 The speed of delivery is more important than the cost.
3 Ewan offers Daniel a discount so that he can spend more money on shipping costs.
4 Ewan will place the order on Wednesday afternoon.

13 An invoice

Use the items below to complete the invoice which Ewan sends to Daniel.

account • cost • invoice • number • subtotal • within 30 days

Out There Ltd.

Mr Daniel Bach
Mountain Stars Ltd
Eschengraben 42
13089 Berlin
Germany

49 Arlington Park Avenue
Northampton
NH2 7HA

VAT ...¹: 66 -773-92845

28 August 20..

Recipients ID No: DE012345678

...² No: 118945

15 Downhill Devil snowboards	£1305.00
10 Stunt Rider snowboards	£950.00
...³	£2255.00
...⁴ of carriage	£268.00
Total	**£4778.00**

Payment should be made by money transfer ...⁵ to the following bank account:

Bank   Beaumont Bank
...⁶ number   28792085
Sorting code 43-98-86

55

UNIT 5 — A TRADE FAIR AND AN ORDER

14 A reminder

A Match the sentence beginnings (1–7) with the sentence endings (a–g) to make sentences from a first reminder.

1. We would be grateful if
2. Yours
3. Re: Our invoice no.
4. We are certain that you have simply overlooked the invoice and will clear
5. Dear
6. If you have already remitted the amount due,
7. I am writing with reference to the invoice mentioned

a. sincerely
b. above which has not been settled yet.
c. the account in the near future.
d. 165437 of 1 September
e. please ignore this letter.
f. you could settle your account in the next few days.
g. Mr Bach

B Now put the sentences into the logical order in which they would appear in a first reminder.

C Look at the extracts from reminders. Are they suitable for first, second or final reminders?

1. Despite the fact that we have already sent you two reminders, we have still to receive payment.
2. Please settle your account with us immediately or we will be forced to take legal steps against you straightaway.
3. We are left with no choice but to press you to settle the invoice within three working days.
4. We would be grateful if you could remit the amount due within one week.
5. We will give you a further four days to remit the amount due, after which time we will be passing the matter into the hands of our solicitors.
6. We are certain that you have simply overlooked our invoice and look forward to you remitting the sum due within fourteen days.
7. We must now insist that your account is cleared within the coming five days.
8. Given that we have already sent you one reminder and have still heard nothing from you, we are growing concerned about the situation regarding your payment.

D Work with a partner. Decide from the context they are used in what the terms *settle*, *remit* and *clear* mean here.

E Several weeks after the delivery of the order to Mountain Stars Ltd, Out There Ltd has not received payment for the snowboards. Write a first reminder to the company asking for payment.

KMK exam practice

15 Rezeption – Hörverstehen

Listen to the answerphone message then answer the questions.

1. When had Ewan and George arranged to meet?
2. What was the reason for the meeting and why does George feel that a meeting with his colleagues is important?
3. Why can't George's colleague attend the meeting on 6th September?
4. What date and time does George suggest as an alternative?
5. What did Ewan tell George about when they met in London?
6. What two things does George ask Ewan to do at the end of his message?

16 Interaktion

Üben Sie das Rollenspiel mit einem Partner / einer Partnerin.

Student A

Sie arbeiten für Sononic Ltd, einem Smartphone-Hersteller, und sind auf einer Messe.

Während Sie mit Besuchern Ihres Messestandes sprechen, bemerken Sie einen Besucher / eine Besucherin, der/die sich sehr für die Produkte Ihrer Firma interessiert. Unterbrechen Sie kurz Ihr Gespräch, um sich ihm/ihr vorzustellen. Bieten Sie Erfrischungen an und die Möglichkeit, ein Demonstrationsvideo anzuschauen, während Sie Ihr Gespräch mit den anderen Besuchern beenden.

Als diese gegangen sind, wenden Sie sich dem Besucher / der Besucherin zu. Machen Sie in dem Gespräch klar, dass bei Bestellung ein Rabatt möglich ist, aber in Abhängigkeit vom Auftragsvolumen. Schlagen Sie vor, einen Termin nach der Messe im Büro Ihres Besuchers / Ihrer Besucherin zu vereinbaren.

Student B

Sie arbeiten für Electro Market, einer mittelständischen Ladenkette, die elektronische Produkte vertreibt. Sie suchen auf einer Messe nach neuen Smartphone-Modellen. Am Stand eines Ihnen unbekannten Unternehmens, Sononic Ltd, finden Sie, was Sie suchen: Smartphones mit Funktionsvielfalt, aber sie sind zu teuer.

Der/Die Standmitarbeiter/in spricht mit anderen Besuchern. Er/Sie unterbricht das Gespräch und wendet sich Ihnen zu.

Sie haben Zeit und nehmen die gemachten Vorschläge an. Machen Sie in Ihrem anschließenden Gespräch klar, dass Ihnen die Smartphones gefallen, dass man Ihnen aber bei Auftragserteilung einen Rabatt gewähren müsste.

Extra material

Incoterms 2010

The Incoterms, last updated in 2010, help companies trading across international borders to agree who will cover the costs involved.

1 Key vocabulary

Match the German expressions to the highlighted words in the four Incoterms below.

Bestimmungshafen • Bestimmungsort • Export • Käufer • Spediteur • Verkäufer • Versicherung • Waren • Zollabgaben • Zollabwicklung

1. The seller is responsible for delivering the goods onto the ship. Additionally, the seller pays for transportation and insurance to the port of destination.
2. The seller is responsible for delivering the goods to the carrier. The seller additionally pays for transportation to the destination. The buyer owns the goods when they are delivered to the carrier.
3. The seller is responsible for clearing the goods for export and delivering them to the forwarding agent and for insurance up to this point. The buyer owns the goods when they are delivered to the carrier.
4. The seller is responsible for transporting the goods to the destination and pays any customs duty. The buyer owns the goods when they arrive at the destination.

2 Which Incoterms?

Match the Incoterms described in exercise 1 to the correct Incoterm in the diagram below. There are two more than you need.

58

Customer care

UNIT 6

- customer care guidelines
- customer service mistakes
- customer complaints

 1 **Warm-up**

A How customer friendly are you? Complete the questionnaire below and find out.

1   A customer comes into the shop. Do you say:
    a   What do you want?
    b   Good afternoon. How can I help you?

2   Another customer comes into the shop while you are speaking to the first customer. Do you say:
    a   Just a moment please. I'll be with you in a minute.
    b   Wait, please.

3   A customer wants to complain about a product that does not work. Do you say:
    a   I'm sorry to hear you've had problems. Let me see what I can do.
    b   What do you want me to do about it?

4   A customer comes into the shop just as you are going to take your lunch break. Do you say:
    a   I'm going to lunch.
    b   Can I get my colleague to help you? I'm going to lunch just now.

5   You ask a customer if you can help, but he says he just wants to have a look. Do you say:
    a   Okay. Just let me know if I can help.
    b   Fine.

6   A customer wants to try on a pair of shoes, but you don't have them in the correct size. Do you say:
    a   We don't have any.
    b   Sorry, but we don't seem to have the shoes in that size at the moment.

B Now work with a partner and discuss why it is better not to use the other sentences.

59

UNIT 6

CUSTOMER CARE

C Discuss the list of customer care rules below and decide which three you think are most important. Then explain your choice to the rest of the class.

If you work with customers you should …
- **a** be friendly and always say hello to customers with a smile.
- **b** help a customer as quickly as possible then go on to the next customer.
- **c** ask straight away if you can help a customer.
- **d** be friendly but firm and tell customers what is possible and what is not possible.
- **e** show customers that you have time for them.
- **f** be polite and show that you respect your customers.
- **g** give a customer time to think about what he wants before you offer to help.
- **h** (your own suggestion).

2 Customer care guidelines

Read Telco Ltd's call centre guidelines and answer the questions.

Customer Care Guidelines

1. Never use a customer's first name.

2. If you have a few minutes between incoming calls, use the time to phone a customer and ask them if they are satisfied with our service.

3. Tell new customers about our whole range of offers. The reason for this is that it is important that customers understand the quality of our full range of services. This way we can get them to choose a package which meets their needs fully and additionally maximises our revenue. We certainly want to avoid customers choosing the cheapest package that we offer.

4. When the telephone rings, answer within three rings if possible. Good customer care is fast customer care.

5. We do not give money back to customers who are having problems with the quality of service. Be friendly but firm and offer them an alternative such as some vouchers for music downloads.

6. Take time to offer good customer service and do not hurry to finish a call with a customer. Give them the impression that you have time for them. This will go a long way to guaranteeing customer satisfaction with the service we offer.

7. Customers sometimes don't understand technical problems with our service. Never make a customer feel stupid if they don't understand. This will only make it more likely that they try to cancel their contract which we want to avoid at all costs. Be friendly and explain the product to them in simple language.

8. If a customer calls to cancel their contract, ask them why they want to do this. If they have a problem with our service, offer to solve the problem for them. Do this immediately and call the customer back to say that the problem has been solved. Customer retention is important to us – every customer is valuable.

CUSTOMER CARE

UNIT 6

1 What should employees do if there are no incoming calls?
2 What reasons are given for explaining the full range of service offers?
3 How should employees react to customers who want their money back?
4 How can customer satisfaction be ensured?
5 Why is it important to explain technical issues to customers in language they understand?

3 Guideline headings

Match the parts of the guidelines (1–8) in exercise 2 to the right headings (a–h).

a Fast customer care is important!
b Take your time with customers!
c Encourage customers to buy more expensive options!
d What we can offer unhappy customers!
e Be formal and polite with customers!
f Customer satisfaction is important!
g Don't just let customers go!
h Explain things slowly and carefully to customers!

4 Word partnerships

A *Customer* can be used together with other words to form common word partnerships. How many examples can you think of? Use the guidelines in exercise 2 to help you.

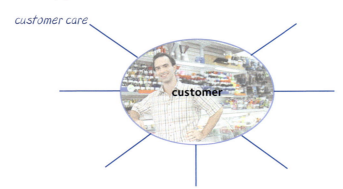

B Now use the phrases to complete the sentences.

1 The company currently has a problem with … It is losing a lot of customers at the moment.
2 … is not very good in that supermarket. You can never find anyone to help you if you have a problem.
3 I really liked the … offered by the travel company. They really looked after us and made sure we were happy.
4 … should be our priority. If customers are not happy with our service, we will lose them.

61

UNIT 6
CUSTOMER CARE

5 Customer care mistakes

Here's what not to do when you work in customer care. Listen to the three short dialogues and match the cartoons with the mistakes that you hear.

> **TIP**
>
> It's important to attend to a customer who needs help as quickly as possible. This is the case whether you're dealing with the customer face-to-face or on the telephone.
> However, it's not always possible to give a customer your immediate attention; you may, for instance, be dealing with another customer. If you have to ask a customer to wait, do so using short, polite phrases such as these.
> *Would you mind waiting? I'll be with you in a moment.*
> *Sorry, could you wait a moment. I'll be able to help shortly.*
> And don't forget to thank a customer for waiting:
> *Sorry to have kept you waiting. How can I help?*

6 Writing an article on customer care guidelines

Write an article for your company intranet emphasising the positive elements of what one should do when dealing with customers. Emphasise the benefits of acting in this way and try to offer some examples.

CUSTOMER CARE

UNIT 6

GRAMMAR

-ing form and/or infinitive

1. I **would like to help** you so please tell me what the problem is.
2. You should **avoid irritating** customers by offering them help as quickly as possible.
3. He **started working** in customer service three years ago.
4. You really only **start to understand** customers when you listen to them carefully.
5. He **stopped to take** a break after he finished the customer reports.
6. I **stopped taking** breaks for lunch after our work in the department increased.
7. Let me begin **by explaining** our warranty policy to you.

- Nach einigen Verben steht der **Infinitiv** (*to* + Infinitiv): *agree*, *choose*, *decide*, *expect*, *hope*, *learn*, *manage*, *offer*, *plan*, *prefer*, *want*, *would like*. (1)
- Nach einigen Verben steht die **-ing-Form**: *admit*, *avoid*, *dislike*, *enjoy*, *involve*, *keep*, *risk*, *suggest*. (2)
- Nach einigen Verben kann der **Infinitiv oder die -ing-Form** stehen: *begin*, *continue*, *hate*, *like*, *love*, *prefer*, *start*. (3, 4)
- Einige Verben (z. B. *forget*, *remember*, *stop*, *try*) haben **unterschiedliche Bedeutungen**, je nachem ob sie mit dem Infinitiv oder in der -ing-Form stehen, z. B: *stop to do something* = aufhören, etwas zu tun, *stop doing something* = aufhören, um etwas (anderes) zu tun. (5, 6)
- Verben, die auf eine **Präposition** folgen, stehen in der -ing-Form. (7)

7 Practice

Complete the sentences using the *-ing* form and/or the infinitive.

1. I want … (offer) you a bigger discount.
2. I prefer … (spend) my money in small shops. I hate … (give) my money to big stores.
3. She'll never forget … (make) her first phone call to England.
4. The company plans … (send) all of its staff on customer service training.
5. Can I suggest … (look) at our website? All the information is there.
6. If their prices continue … (go up), I'll have to shop somewhere else.
7. That shop keeps … (lose) customers because the staff are so rude.
8. Eddy forgot … (post) a letter to a customer.
9. I stopped … (buy) my food there because it was never fresh.
10. He offered … (call) me later in the day when I wasn't so busy.
11. Sheila loves … (shop) there because the staff are so friendly.
12. You really do risk … (annoy) customers if you offer to help them too often.
13. On my way to Paris I stopped once … (eat) something.

CUSTOMER CARE

8 Key phrases for dealing with customers

Sort the following phrases (1–12) into categories (a–d).

a   Saying hello
b   Saying you are sorry that a customer has a problem
c   Asking a customer to wait
d   Thanking a customer

1   Thanks. Goodbye now.
2   Can I help you?
3   I'll be with you in a minute.
4   I'm sorry to hear that. I'll see what I can do.
5   Good morning. What can I do for you?
6   Sorry. Do you mind waiting a moment?
7   Thank you very much. We hope to see you again soon.
8   Sorry about that. Let me see what I can do.
9   I'll be right with you.
10 Oh, dear. Let me take a look at that for you.
11 Thank you. Have a good day.
12 Hello. Would you like some help?

9 A customer complaint

A Terry is a sales assistant in one of Telco Ltd's stores. Read as a customer complains about a mobile phone that does not work. Is the customer satisfied with the service he receives?

Terry   Good morning. How can I help you?
Customer Morning. I bought a new mobile phone here about four weeks ago, but it's not working properly.
Terry   I'm sorry to hear that. Can I ask what the problem is?
Customer Yes. Well. There are two problems. The phone switches itself off after about an hour. And it won't save my text messages. It's all a bit annoying really.
Terry   Oh, I'm sorry about that. Do you have your mobile with you?
Customer Yes, of course. Here it is.
Terry   And the receipt. I need that as well.
Customer I don't seem to have it with me. I thought I put it in my jacket pocket before coming, but it doesn't seem to be there.
Terry   I'm afraid I really need to see your receipt before I can do anything.
Customer Look, I've probably just left it at home. I can bring it later. Can you help me now?
Terry   I'm not sure really. I'm not supposed to … Oh, okay. It sounds like you've got a problem with the battery. And the software probably isn't working properly.
Customer Well, that's obvious. But I don't want to talk about it. I just want my money back.
Terry   I'm sorry, but I'm afraid I can't give you a refund. It's our policy to send faulty phones back to the manufacturer for repair. We don't give money back straight away.
Customer Oh, great. And how long is that going to take?
Terry   Well. We can normally get the phone back to you within two weeks …
Customer Two weeks! And what am I supposed to do without my mobile for two weeks? I need it for my job. I'm sorry, but this just isn't acceptable. It would be okay to send it for repair if it didn't take so long. But two weeks! I want my money back.

CUSTOMER CARE

Terry	I'm terribly sorry, but I'm really not allowed to do that. I have to send your mobile back to the manufacturer for repair.
Customer	Well, this is really useless customer service, I must say. I certainly won't be coming back here again! Look, I think you should just give me my money back right now.
Terry	I'm sorry, as I have said, I'm not allowed to do that. It's our company policy to …
Customer	It seems to be your company policy to take customers for a ride. I mean, you can't just go supplying goods that don't work and then ask customers to wait forever while you supposedly sort things out.
Terry	I can see that you're upset, but if you shout, it makes it hard for me to help. I'm only doing my job here.
Customer	Well, if I may say so, you're not doing a terribly good job. I mean really …
Terry	I'm really sorry that you've had problems. But please, calm down. Look, I probably should have told you this earlier, but I can offer you a replacement phone while your own mobile is being repaired.
Customer	Sorry, what?
Terry	I can offer a replacement while your phone is away for repair.
Customer	Ah, okay. Well … That's not ideal. But it's better than nothing, I suppose.
Terry	So, if I can just show you the three models of phone you can choose the replacement from, then I can get your phone off for repair.
Customer	Well, okay. That sounds fine, I suppose.

B **Choose between a, b and c to complete the sentences correctly.**

1 The customer's problem is that …
a his phone switches itself off when he wants to send a text message.
b his phone won't let him send text messages and switches itself off.
c his mobile turns itself off and loses his text messages.

2 Terry thinks the problem is that …
a there is no software on the phone.
b the battery and software do not work properly.
c the customer doesn't understand how the software works.

3 The customer wants Terry to …
a give him his money back.
b send the mobile for repair.
c give him a new mobile.

4 Terry says that the company normally …
a gives customers their money back.
b sends mobiles away to be repaired.
c offers customers a better mobile to replace the phone that doesn't work.

5 The customer does not find the offer acceptable because …
a he wants a new phone.
b he's away for two weeks.
c two weeks is too long for him to wait for his phone to be repaired.

6 Terry offers …
a his own mobile while the customer's is being replaced.
b another mobile while his is being repaired.
c to repair the customer's mobile himself.

WEBCODE **BMU0601**

65

UNIT 6
CUSTOMER CARE

10 Assessing Terry's performance

Work with a partner and discuss the following questions.

1. How polite was Terry with the customer?
2. Which mistakes did Terry make in his handling of the customer? Use the flowchart below, which was designed by Telco Ltd to assist its employees deal with this problem, to help you.
3. What could Terry learn about how to deal with customer complaints?

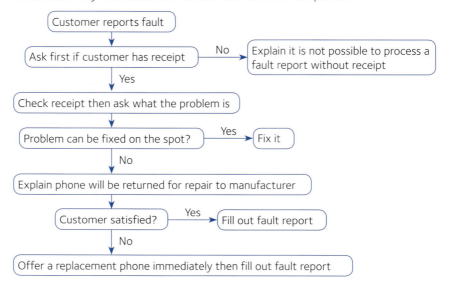

11 Role-play: a customer complaint

Work with a partner and carry out the role-play.

Student A	Student B
Sie haben eine Kamera gekauft, aber sie funktioniert nicht einwandfrei. Sie verlangen auf der Stelle eine Ersatzkamera. Wenn man Ihnen dies abschlägt, möchten Sie ihr Geld zurück.	Sie arbeiten in einem Fotogeschäft. Hat ein Kunde eine nicht einwandfrei funktionierende Kamera gekauft, können Sie anbieten, sie zur Reparatur einzuschicken. Dies dauert 10 Tage. Sie können eine Ersatzkamera und kostenlose Fotodrucke anbieten, aber Sie können kein Geld erstatten.

LANGUAGE

Offering a customer help
How can I help?
Hello, would you like some assistance?

Apologising for the customer's problem
I'm really sorry that you've had problems.
Sorry to hear that you've got a problem.

Asking an angry customer to calm down
If you shout, it makes it hard for me to help.
Please, calm down.

KMK exam practice

12 Produktion

Sie sind zuständig für den Kundenservice einer Firma, die andere Firmen mit Fotokopierern beliefert. Lesen Sie diese Beschwerde-E-Mail einer verärgerten Kundin und lösen Sie die nachfolgenden Aufgaben.

Dear Sir or Madam

Several members of my department have had problems with our photocopiers in the last three days. However, when they called your hotline number for support, nobody answered the phone. When one of my colleagues did finally manage to speak to a member of your staff, he assured my colleague that he would call back but never did.

Could you please let me know why we are experiencing these difficulties? Our service contract with you states that you will deal with our requests for help within a maximum of one hour. You are currently not fulfilling the terms of the contract. If this situation continues, I will have to consider making a formal complaint.

I look forward to hearing from you soon.

Best
Carol Bennie

A Entwerfen Sie eine E-Mail, die folgende Punkte beinhaltet:

- Entschuldigen Sie sich, indem Sie sich auf die Aspekte beziehen, die Grund für die Beschwerde liefern. Entschuldigen Sie sich für jeden einzelnen Punkt.
- Versichern Sie der Kundin, dass Sie sie als Kundin wertschätzen und dass die Geschäftsbeziehungen Ihrer Firma wichtig sind.
- Informieren Sie die Kundin über die Gründe für die Ausfälle im Kundendienst – hier: eine Krankheitswelle unter den Kundendienstberatern und Mitarbeitern des technischen Kundendienstes.
- Bieten Sie zwei kostenlose Tonerkartuschen für Fotokopierer an, um für die Kundendienstpanne zu entschädigen.
- Versichern Sie, dass Sie sich mit der Kundin so schnell wie möglich in Verbindung setzen, um einen Termin für einen Technikerbesuch abzustimmen.

B Schreiben Sie eine weitere E-Mail an ihre Teamkollegen.

- Geben Sie den Teammitgliedern eine Zusammenfassung der Probleme, die aus der Krankheitswelle unter den Mitarbeitern resultierte.
- Bitten Sie sie, in den nächsten Tagen die Zeit zwischen Anrufen dafür zu nutzen, die Anruflisten zu überprüfen und Kunden zurückzurufen, die bisher noch kein Feedback bekommen haben.
- Die Teamkollegen sollen sich bei diesen Kunden entschuldigen, die Gründe für den Kundendienstausfall erklären und erfragen, wie sie dem Kunden jetzt behilflich sein können.

Extra material

Customer retention

It's not just winning new customers – customer acquisition – which is important to companies. Keeping existing customers – customer retention – is also a priority.

The reason that customer retention is regarded as important is due to the fact that it costs so much to acquire a customer in the first place. A customer only becomes profitable for a company after they have spent a certain
5 amount on the company's products or services. If customers go to the competition before having done enough business with a company, the company basically makes a loss – and not a profit – on them.

That's why companies have thought up many different ways of keeping their customers.

Good customer service is clearly a big factor in customer retention. But that alone is not always enough. Companies often take additional action to try to hold onto their customers. Different kinds of company have
10 different methods of customer retention. Here are some examples.

1 **Food retail** – Supermarkets frequently use customer loyalty cards to hold onto customers. Customers are given a loyalty card which they use every time they buy something. They then build up points on the card which they can use to pay for goods. Loyalty cards have been on offer for years in Britain and the US and they are used to offer customers quite large discounts on what they buy.
15 2 **Telecoms companies** – Mobile phone companies have enormous problems with customer retention because customers often change company when their contract finishes. Mobile companies try to prevent this by offering customers cheaper tariffs and better phones if they stay with the company.
3 **Online retailers** – The internet offers ways for companies to hold onto customers – involving the customer in evaluating products. The most well-known company to do this is Amazon, the online book retailer. Customers
20 can write long book reviews for Amazon – for which they receive small payments – or short comments about books saying why they liked or disliked them. In theory at least, this is supposed to give customers the feeling that they are important – and to make them come back and buy more.

---

1 Understanding the text

A Write a more interesting headline for the text which summarises what it says.

B Now complete the following tasks.

1 Explain why companies see customer retention as important.
2 Describe what companies risk if customers go to their competition.
3 Give details of how supermarket loyalty cards work.
4 Describe mobile telecoms companies' strategy to retain customers.
5 Give reasons for the approach to customer retention taken by online retailers such as Amazon.

---

2 Group task

Work with a group to complete the following tasks.

1 Discuss the ways your company tries to retain its customers. Make notes about this.
2 Brainstorm and note down ideas about further methods your company could use to hold onto customers.
3 Write a short presentation about the methods your company uses and could use to retain customers. Explain what you regard as the benefits of these methods of customer retention.
4 Give your presentation to the class.

Situation 3

Every January in Birmingham sellers and buyers of sports goods meet at the annual sports fair to do business. Todd Sloan of Hard Ace has come from Melbourne in Australia to sell his company's tennis equipment. Christine Mortimer runs a small tennis school in Surrey, England, and she has come to the fair to look for new equipment to use at her school the following summer.

1 At the stand

Todd and Christine meet at the Hard Ace stand. Christine has only a few minutes as she is meeting her sister for lunch in Birmingham. Look at the cards and carry out the role-play.

Todd
- greets
- describes his company
- begins to show Hard Ace's goods
- asks when they can meet
- only free after 4 p.m.; can meet here?
- asks her to take their brochure and look at it before the meeting

Christine
- responds
- talks a little about her tennis-school
- explains she has no time now
- suggests the next day at 11
- not convenient, as catching train at 5 p.m. but okay if no other option
- thanks Todd, and promises she will do so

2 An order

After studying the brochure, Christine fills in the form below and orders the following items for her tennis school.

The Hard Ace Tennis Company

Menzies Road
Melbourne • Victor a
Australia

ORDER FORM

Please complete the order form below, indicating the items and the number you wish to receive:

	ITEM	QUANTITY
Racquets	child's	
	junior	10
	full-size	12
	senior	
Other equipment	mini-nets	
	full-size nets	3
	tennis shirts	
	tennis caps	
	ball hoppers (to collect balls in)	3
	umpire's chair	
	ball machine (to hold 100 balls)	1
	tennis line marker	
DVDs	The Roger Federer Way to Play Tennis	
	The John McEnroe Way to Play Tennis	
	The Lleyton Hewitt Way to Play Tennis	1

69

Situation 3

After 6 weeks, Christine receives a shipment of the following items sent by Hard Ace in Melbourne, together with this invoice.

Compare the invoice Christine has just received with the order she sent. What errors have been made in the shipment?

The Hard Ace Tennis Company

Menzies Road
Melbourne • Victoria
Australia

Christine Trueman
Surrey Road, Epsom
Great Britain

INVOICE

Order dated 21/01/2012

	Price (in Euro)
• 14 full-size racquets	1960,00
• 12 junior racquets	480,00
• 3 ball hoppers	93,00
• 13 Hard Ace tennis nets	949,00
• 1 DVD of The John McEnroe Way to Play Tennis	12,00
Total	3494,00

3 A complaint

As you have found, there are various things wrong with the shipment Christine has received. Christine calls Todd to complain. Look at the role cards below and carry out the role-play.

Christine

Include the following points:
- Thank him for correct items.
- Explain which items are wrong or missing.
- Complain politely about errors.
- Ask for discount on remaining unsent items.

Todd

Include the following points:
- Apologise for errors.
- Mention that you haven't received payment yet.
- Ask whether Christine wants to keep and pay for extra items not on original order (specify these).
- Say you can't give discount, but will allow Christine to keep extra items without payment.
- Argue (humorously) that McEnroe is better tennis player than Hewitt and has made better DVD.

4 An email

After the phone call write Christine an email from Todd apologising for the problems again and confirming what you agreed on the phone.

Business travel

UNIT 7

- a business trip
- airport & hotel
- small talk

1 Warm-up

Work with a partner. Discuss which of the four items shown in the pictures would be the most important to take on a business trip? Explain why to the rest of the class.

2 Arranging a business trip

A Read the dialogue and make notes about Mark's flight details. When is he arriving in and leaving Frankfurt?

Phillip Good morning. Flair Business Travel. Phillip speaking. How can I help?
Mark Morning, Phillip. Mark Harkleroad from Good Foods here. How are you this morning?
Phillip Oh, hi Mark. Fine, thanks. And you?
Mark Very well, thank you. Listen, Phillip. I'd like to fly to Frankfurt on Tuesday next week with three colleagues. Could you organise travel and accommodation for us please?

71

UNIT 7

BUSINESS TRAVEL

Phillip	Certainly, Mark. No problem at all.
Mark	Splendid. Right, so as I said, we're going on Tuesday.
Phillip	That's Tuesday 4 June, right?
Mark	Yes, that's right. But we need to be in Frankfurt for a meeting at three in the afternoon.
Phillip	Right. Well, I know that there's a flight from London Stansted which arrives in Frankfurt at 12.10. That should give you enough time to get to your meeting, shouldn't it?
Mark	Yes, that sounds about right. What time does it leave?
Phillip	Hm, one second, please. Yes, it departs Stansted at 9.50.
Mark	That sounds good. And how much does it cost?
Phillip	It'll be … let me see … £113 including airport tax.
Mark	Fine. I'd like you to book that then, please.
Phillip	Okay. How long are you staying in Frankfurt for, Mark?
Mark	We're coming back on Thursday afternoon. At about four o'clock, I suppose.
Phillip	Right. There's a flight back to Stansted at seven in the evening.
Mark	That's a bit late really. Isn't there anything earlier?
Phillip	Yes … There's a flight which leaves Frankfurt at 4.20. But it flies to London Heathrow.
Mark	Ah. That's probably going to be more expensive, isn't it?
Phillip	Let me take a look. Hm, funnily enough it's just £123. Not that much more expensive at all.
Mark	That's a surprise. Does that include airport tax?
Phillip	Yes, it does.
Mark	Okay. Could you book that too, please?

B   **Complete the sentences using information from the dialogue.**

1   Mark would like Phillip to …
2   He and his colleagues need to be in Frankfurt by …
3   Phillip tells Mark about a flight from London Stansted which …
4   Mark wants to come back on …
5   He does not want to fly back to Stansted because …
6   Mark is surprised about the flight to Heathrow because …

C   **Find words in the dialogue which mean the same as the German words below.**

1	abfliegen	**3**	Flug	**5**	Reisen
2	ankommen	**4**	Flughafengebühr	**6**	Unterkunft

3 | At the airport

A   **Look at the airport plan on the next page. Where do you do the following things? Sometimes there may be more than one answer.**

a   collect your bags and suitcases after the flight
b   wait to get on to your flight
c   see what time your flight leaves
d   get your bags checked for dangerous objects
e   show your passport
f   see if flights are coming in on time
g   show your ticket and get your boarding card
h   say if you are bringing a lot of goods such as alcohol or cigarettes into the country

72

BUSINESS TRAVEL

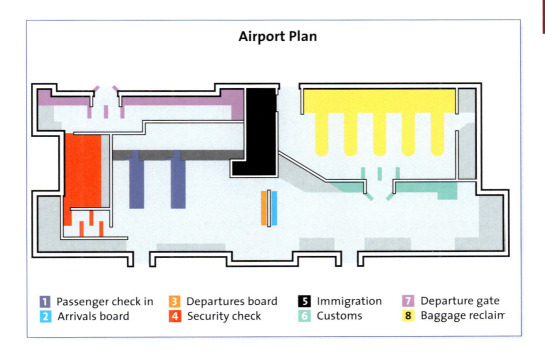

Airport Plan

1. Passenger check in
2. Arrivals board
3. Departures board
4. Security check
5. Immigration
6. Customs
7. Departure gate
8. Baggage reclaim

B Work with a partner and decide which of the phrases can be used for asking directions and which for giving directions. Then take turns to ask how to get from one part of the airport to another.

1. Can you tell me how I can get to … ?
2. No problem. It's just down the …
3. Could you please tell me where the … is?
4. Go along here past the … It's on the right-/left-hand side.
5. Sure. It's opposite / next to / beside the …
6. Of course. It's between … and …
7. Excuse me. Where can I find the …?

15

C Listen to the airport announcements and decide what you should do when you hear each one.

D Use the words in the box to complete the sentences.

bag • board • boarding • call • immediately • luggage • passport • suitcase • ticket

1. You can take your … onto the plane as hand …, but you're not allowed to take your … It's too big.
2. Thank you, sir. Here's your … card. Please have it ready when you … your flight.
3. Here's the immigration desk. I need to show them my …
4. Your flight leaves in fifteen minutes. Please proceed … to gate 6.
5. Could you tell me how much a … from Stansted to Munich costs?
6. There was a final … for our flight while you were in the toilet. We have to hurry up.

WEBCODE **BMU0701**

73

BUSINESS TRAVEL

4 Booking a hotel

A Mark now has to book a hotel for his trip. Match these symbols to the descriptions of the hotel facilities mentioned in the dialogue.

B Now listen again. Which of these facilities is Mark interested in using?

5 A presentation

A Your boss asks you to find a suitable hotel for a business trip. You find the following hotel on the internet. Prepare a short presentation for your boss to inform him of what you've found. Then give the presentation.

KMK

THE ROYAL BRIGHTON HOTEL ★★★★

Where it's a pleasure to do business

The Royal Brighton offers first-class, modern accommodation and business facilities. Its accommodation comprises 3 suites, 14 single rooms and 22 double rooms all fully-equipped with satellite TV and en-suite bathrooms.
The Royal Brighton also offers three large conference rooms, each of which can accommodate up to 60 participants, as well as 8 meeting rooms. Our conference and meeting rooms are fully equipped with the latest presentation technology such as digital projectors and cordless microphones. These facilities are complemented by our business centre which offers fax, printing and photocopying services as well as secure internet access.

Click here for prices.

It's not all business!
The hotel also offers a full range of leisure facilities to help you unwind after you've completed your business.

Dining at the Royal Brighton
Guests at the hotel are spoilt for choice when it comes to dining. Visit our three eateries which can offer you anything from a snack to a five course meal.

BUSINESS TRAVEL

UNIT 7

B Now work with a partner and brainstorm which additional information you would need before making a decision about which hotel to book. Tell the class what's on your list.

6 Arriving at the hotel

A Mark arrives at the hotel reception in Frankfurt. Read the sentences and decide who said them: Mark or the receptionist?

1. Thank you. And enjoy your stay.
2. Yes, of course. How can I help you, sir?
3. Thank you. Can I have an early morning call at 6.30 tomorrow, please?
4. Ah, yes. Mr Harkleroad. Welcome to the Sud Hotel.
5. Yes, of course.
6. Okay, great. Room number 342. Here's your key, sir.
7. Yes, certainly. I'll just put that into my computer. No problem.
8. What name is the reservation under?
9. Harkleroad.
10. Sorry. Do you speak English? I don't speak German.
11. Guten Tag. Was kann ich für Sie tun?
12. My colleagues and I have reserved two rooms for the next three nights.
13. Could I just ask you to fill in a reservation form, please?
14. Thanks.

B Listen to the dialogue to check your answers to exercise A.

C Now work with a partner and complete the following role-play.

Student A

Begrüßen Sie Ihren Gast.

Fragen Sie, auf welchen Namen die Reservierung lautet.

Bitten Sie den Gast, ein Formular auszufüllen.

Sagen Sie die Zimmernummer und geben Sie dem Gast den Schlüssel.

Sagen Sie, dass es Frühstück ab 6.30 gibt. Wünschen Sie Ihrem Gast einen angenehmen Aufenthalt.

Student B

Sagen Sie, dass Sie zwei Zimmer für zwei Nächte gebucht haben.

Sagen Sie Ihren Namen.

Sagen Sie, dass Sie das Formular gerne ausfüllen.

Bedanken Sie sich und fragen Sie, ab wann es Frühstück gibt.

Bedanken Sie sich.

75

BUSINESS TRAVEL

GRAMMAR

Future with the simple present and present continuous

1 He's **staying** at the North Brays Hotel.
2 There's a big conference and exhibition in May.
3 Your flight **departs** at 13.00.
4 The meeting **starts** at 9.00 a.m.

- Das *present continuous* und das *simple present* können für künftige Ereignisse verwendet werden, für die ein Plan, eine Verabredung oder ein Programm vorliegt. (1–4) Dies gilt insbesondere, wenn durch eine Zeitangabe ausgeschlossen ist, dass es sich um ein gegenwärtiges Ereignis handelt. (2–4)
- Mit dem Vollverb *be* ist in diesem Zusammenhang nur das *simple present* möglich. (2)
- Mit anderen Verben wird das *simple present* verwendet, wenn die zukünftigen Ereignisse als feststehend betrachtet werden, z. B. wenn es sich um Fahrpläne oder Stundenpläne handelt. (3, 4)

7 Practice

A Use the simple present or the present continuous to express these sentences in English.

1 Jörgs Präsentation beginnt um 11 Uhr.
2 Er nimmt den Flug um 15.30.
3 Christoph und Jörg sind nächste Woche auf einer Konferenz in Aberdeen.
4 Ich treffe am Montag einen neuen Kunden in Bristol.
5 Die Ausstellung endet am 24. März.
6 Ihr Taxi wird Sie um 4.15 abholen.

B Use the simple present and the present continuous to write sentences expressing when the events below will take place. The first example has been done for you.

1 4th August. 10 a.m. – meeting with Bob Norman *(entry in Tim Scott's diary)*
   Tim Scott is meeting Bob Norman on 4th August at 10 a.m.
2 Flight no. NG 4386 – scheduled arrival time: 21.42 *(on an airport information board)*
3 International Water Quality Conference, 13th June 20.., *(diary entry)*
4 9.15 – Opening presentation – The importance of clean energy for your business – Mike Boyd, Enercor Ltd *(from a conference programme)*
5 Lunch: 1 p.m. – 2 p.m. *(from a meeting agenda)*

8 Small talk

A Mark geht mit einem seiner deutschen Geschäftspartner nach einem Meeting zum Essen. Hören Sie ihr Gespräch an und beantworten Sie die Fragen auf Deutsch.

1 In welcher Phase des Essens findet das Gespräch zwischen Mark und Werner statt?
2 Wie bringt Mark zum Ausdruck, wie sehr ihm der Nachtisch schmeckt?
3 Wie erklärt Mark die Beliebtheit indischer Speisen in Großbritannien?
4 Was macht Mark am nächsten Samstag und warum?
5 Was hat Werner am kommenden Wochenende vor und warum ist ihm dies wichtig?
6 Warum geht Mark zurzeit an Samstagnachmittagen mit seiner Freundin einkaufen?
7 Wie begründet Mark, dass er keinen Kaffee im Restaurant trinken möchte?

BUSINESS TRAVEL

UNIT 7

B Look at the sentences and decide whether they would be used before or after Mark and Werner's conversation in the restaurant. Then put the sentences into a logical order.

    a I'll start with a green salad. Then I'd like the fish, please.
    b Could we have the bill, please?
    c I'd like to try the *Kalter Hund*, please.
    d Yes, thank you. Everything was absolutely delicious.
    e Can I pay with my credit card?
    f Could we have a look at the wine list, please?
    g Could we have a table away from the door, please?
    h Good evening. I've reserved a table for two under the name of Niemann.

> **TIP**
>
> **Making small talk**
>
> If you're making small talk with business partners, it's best to talk about 'safe' subjects such as holidays and pastimes, and not subjects such as politics and religion.
> It's also important to have a few questions ready to keep your conversation moving. It may be a good idea to prepare these questions in advance of meeting a business contact. You can also use short phrases – *Ah, that's interesting*, for instance – to let your conversation partner know that you're interested in what they're saying.

C Work with a partner and say which topics Mark and Werner talk about during their conversation. Which questions do they use to start conversation about these topics? Note down questions like those you remember them using. Now listen again and compare the questions you noted with the questions they used.

D Work with a partner to carry out the following tasks.

    1 Spend a few minutes making a note of some small talk questions which you could ask someone to keep the conversation going. Choose to ask about things like hobbies, sports and food.
    2 Imagine that they are a business contact and that you are going to make some small talk with them. During the conversation answer your partner's questions with real information about yourself.
    3 Don't forget to use phrases for letting your partner know that you are interested in what they are saying.

> **LANGUAGE**
>
> **Making small talk**
>
> **Questions**
> What do you do in your spare time?
> Do you have any hobbies outside of work?
> What do you get up to when you're not working?
> How often do you …?
> Do you like …?
> Have you been to …?
>
> **Letting someone know you're interested**
> That's nice.
> Oh, really? That's interesting.
> That sounds great.
> Sounds good.

77

KMK exam practice

9 Rezeption – Leseverstehen

Da die Bedeutung der interkulturellen Kommunikation im Zuge der Globalisierung immer mehr zunimmt, sollen Sie für Mitarbeiter Ihrer Firma einem Artikel wichtige Aspekte interkultureller Kommunikation entnehmen.

Erstellen Sie eine auf den Aussagen des Textes basierende Liste von Ratschlägen zur interkulturellen Kommunikation in der globalen Geschäftswelt. Berücksichtigen Sie die folgenden Punkte:

- Wirklich erfolgreiche Unternehmen
- Sprachtraining
- Kulturelle Missverständnisse
- Gesellschaftliche Ebene
- Informationen sammeln
- Stereotypen
- Kosten
- Aufgeschlossenheit

Get fit for doing business globally
Increase your intercultural awareness

Business has gone global and companies which used to concentrate on markets in neighbouring countries are now doing deals on the other side of the world. The companies which do this most successfully pay attention to the cultures of the other countries they're doing business in. Read on and find out how to maximise your global business through better cultural understanding.

In the past, companies often tended to think that all they needed to do business successfully in far flung parts of the world was make sure that their key executives could speak the right languages. That's where Simon Darby came in. He ran a large business language consultancy which provided international businesses with training.

"Then, about ten years ago, we started to realise from the stories that our customers were telling us that language alone isn't enough. It seemed clear to us that quite a lot of deals we were hearing about were not being signed due to problems arising from cultural misunderstandings," explains Darby. He decided to change the direction of his business and now specialises in providing intercultural training.

"If you want to do business successfully with someone from another culture, you have to understand what makes them tick. Not as an individual person but at a social level. You can only do this by getting inside their culture."

Darby goes on: "Problems arise for business people when they make mistakes in the way they communicate due to the fact that there's something they don't know about another culture. The classic example is business cards in Japan. If you want to make the right impression on Japanese negotiating partners you better be prepared to spend what's regarded as the right amount of time examining your partner's business card. This is a simple mark of respect. If you don't do it, you create some very bad vibes right from the word go."

So, what else does Darby advise business globetrotters to do?

"The main thing is, be prepared to do your homework into the culture you're going to be doing business with. You can do this on the internet but you have to be careful with some of the free advice which is available online. It can tend to be a bit shallow and make you stereotype the people you will be working with."

"A better idea may be to ask one of the several specialist consultancies which are out there these days to provide you with some insight and training. That doesn't tend to come cheap, but it's money well invested if it means that you're going to close a deal successfully thanks to the training.

"Basically, you have to be open," concludes Darby. "There's no point in assuming that your way of seeing something is the best or only way. That's just not going to be true. And if you don't realise this, your business will suffer."

Extra material

Cutting the costs of business travel

In some respects, life was more exciting for business people back in the 1970s and early 1980s. Air travel was relatively new and business people flew around the world first class, their companies gaining in status because they could afford to move their executives about in this manner.

However, these days first-class air travel is expensive and companies everywhere are attempting to spend less on air travel to bring down their costs. This is being made possible by the development of communication technology. Conferencing over the internet makes it possible for business people from different countries to 'meet' without leaving their offices.

There can be some initial costs as well as disadvantages in this. To start with, webcam technology has to be paid for. Additionally, some users complain that it is not as easy to communicate effectively with someone on a computer monitor as it is face-to-face. Companies can train their staff to overcome these communication difficulties; however, there are also some additional costs here. These costs, however, aren't as great as those involved in sending someone halfway around the world. So, in the end the cost-cutting argument in favour of communication technology is clear.

Of course, there are occasions when business people just have to travel. What can you expect, then, if you are a business traveller these days? Well, flying first class is no longer normal. Companies will simply not pay for this. Business travellers either have to sit in standard class or travel on budget airlines. The same logic applies to hotels. Companies are not prepared to book their staff into upmarket hotels. This is why there are growing numbers of hotels which offer relatively cheap accommodation for business people.

So, the glamour has rather gone out of the lives of business executives in recent years. They no longer get the chance to stretch their legs in first class while sipping champagne on the way to meetings. Instead, they often have to hold their meetings over the internet. On the other hand, though, they do get to be home in time for dinner: for most, a definite advantage!

1 Summarising the article

Read the article and decide which statement summarises it best.

1 Travel has become expensive and companies are cutting their costs in this area by investing heavily in webcam conferencing technology.
2 Companies regard low-cost airlines and hotels together with webcam conferencing technology as means of cutting the cost of business travel.
3 Air travel has become expensive since webcam conferencing technology has reduced demand for it among business people.

2 Advantages and disadvantages of webcam conferencing

Work with a partner and make notes on what the article says about the advantages and disadvantages of webcam conferencing.

- Can you think of further advantages and disadvantages?
- What advice can you and your partner offer to overcome any communication problems which could arise when using webcam conferencing?
- Report the results of your discussion to the class

UNIT 8

Presentations

■ audio-visual equipment   ■ preparing presentations   ■ presentation strategies

1 Warm-up

A Work with a partner to match the names of the audio-visual equipment with the pictures.

> digital projector • flipchart • interactive whiteboard • laptop •
> marker pens • microphone • TV and DVD • whiteboard

B Now discuss the advantages and disadvantages of each piece of equipment. What equipment would you use for a presentation?

80

PRESENTATIONS

UNIT 8

2 A telephone call to arrange audio-visual equipment

Read the email that Mark Harkleroad sends his assistant Claire about his trip to Frankfurt. Then listen as she telephones Julia Schwarz. What does she forget to ask Julia for? What mistakes does she make?

From: MHarkleroad@goodfoods.co.uk
To: CGrogan@goodfoods.co.uk
Subject: audio visual equipment for Frankfurt

Hi Claire
As I mentioned last week, I'd like you to phone Julia Schwarz at Starkling Lebensmittel GmbH in Frankfurt and arrange some audio-visual equipment for our trip to Frankfurt. She has offered to provide it for us so that we do not need to carry as much.

Here's what I would like:
a digital projector
a whiteboard
a flipchart

About the email I sent you last week: we no longer require loudspeakers, so please just forget about that. We will also need an extra laptop although I am planning to take mine as well. Would you be able to take care of the audio-visual equipment this afternoon? That would be great.

Thanks
Mark

---

3 Role-play: booking audio-visual equipment   KMK

Üben Sie das Rollenspiel mit einem Partner / einer Partnerin.

Student A

Ihre Firma hat in einem Hotel in Paris einen Konferenzraum für ein Meeting Donnerstag, den 24. April gebucht. Ihr Chef braucht dafür audiovisuelle Geräte. Rufen Sie das Hotel an und bitten Sie um Bereitstellung folgender Geräte bzw. Geräte, die den gleichen Zweck erfüllen. Erfragen Sie, wie viel es kostet, die Geräte für den Tag zu nutzen.
Sie brauchen:
- einen digitalen Projektor
- einen Laptop
- ein Flipchart

Student B

Sie arbeiten im Business Centre eines Hotels in Paris. Sie bekommen einen Anruf von einer Firma, die einen Konferenzraum in dem Hotel für ein Meeting gebucht hat. Die Firma bittet um Bereitstellung audiovisueller Geräte für das Meeting.
Lassen Sie sich das Datum der Buchung bestätigen.
Die Kosten für die Nutzung der Geräte sind:
- digitaler Projektor: €23
- Laptop: €19
- Whiteboard: €11

Weisen Sie darauf hin, dass Sie kein Flipchart, dafür aber ein Whiteboard anbieten können.

81

PRESENTATIONS

4 Preparing for the presentation

Mark is preparing himself for the presentation he has to make in Frankfurt. Match the pictures (1–4) he finds online about what to do and not to do when presenting with the descriptions (a–d).

a   too informal for the audience
b   using too many slides and boring the audience
c   unprepared and disorganised
d   body language reveals nervousness

TIP: Preparing for presentations

It's important to spend time preparing for a presentation to make sure that you have got the content right. It's also important to try to ensure that you have got your approach to the subject and audience right to make the most of your presentation.

You can do this by doing your homework about your audience. How big will it be? What sort of people will be sitting in front of you? Will they appreciate an informal or more formal approach? It may well be possible to get some answers to questions like this from the organisation or company you will be making the presentation to. Once you can answer some of these questions, you'll be in a position to use the right tone and approach to suit your audience.

5 Making the presentation

20

A Mark is giving his presentation in Frankfurt. Listen to his introduction and identify the order in which he is going to talk about these points.

a   what Good Foods hope to sell
b   how long the companies will work together
c   the company history
d   why the company wants to work with Starkling Lebensmittel

PRESENTATIONS

UNIT 8

B Als Mitarbeiter der Firma Starkling Lebensmittel hören Sie Mark Harkleroads Vortrag. Da Ihr Abteilungsleiter noch nicht anwesend ist, schreiben Sie stichpunktartig auf, worüber Mark sprechen wird.

- Redner: Mark Harkleroad
- Firma
- Job
- Struktur des Vortrags

C Put these phrases and sentences into the order Mark uses them in his presentation.

1 Then, thirdly, I'm going to talk in detail about …
2 Thank you very much for the opportunity to talk to you this afternoon.
3 Good afternoon, everybody.
4 I'll be happy to answer any questions at the end of the presentation.
5 Now, to begin with, I'd like to talk about the structure of my presentation.
6 First, I'm going to tell you about …
7 Finally, I'm going to explain …
8 The second section of my presentation will focus on …
9 My name's …
10 I'm the …

D Now match the phrases and sentences (1–10) above with the phrases and sentences which can be used in the same way (a–j).

a To end with, I'm going to talk about …
b Secondly, I'm going to look at …
c I'd like to thank you for the chance to talk to you today.
d Right. To start with, I'd like to give you an outline of my presentation.
e I work as the …
f Firstly, I'm going to talk about …
g Please feel free to ask me questions during the presentation.
h I'm …
i Good morning, ladies and gentlemen.
j The third thing I'm going to discuss is …

6 Key expressions from the presentation

A Match the German expressions (1–8) to the English equivalents (a–h) used by Mark in his presentation.

1 beeindruckt   a develop
2 einsatzbereit   b experience
3 entwickeln   c impressed
4 Erfahrung   d in place
5 Partnerschaft   e partnership
6 sich spezialisieren auf   f section
7 Teil; Abschnitt   g specialise in
8 Zeitrahmen   h time frame

83

PRESENTATIONS

UNIT 8

B **Now use five of the words from part A to complete these sentences.**

1 The final … of my presentation is about our newest products.
2 I think the … will work well. Both companies work in a similar way.
3 Now I'm going to discuss the project's … There is a lot to do in the next six months.
4 Now I'm going to tell you about the … we have gathered in working in China.
5 Finally, I'm going to tell you about the kind of services we … providing to manufacturing companies.

GRAMMAR

The future with *will* and *going to*

1 **I'll be** in Paris to make a presentation at a conference on Monday.
2 **I'll make** another appointment with you and I can tell you how the conference was.
3 My colleague Steven **is going to come** with me to the meeting in Frankfurt.
4 He's **going to leave** for a two-day business trip on Sunday evening.
5 **I'm going to go** back to the office now and write to the Starkling management team
   with a new proposal.
6 **I'm going to start** my presentation this morning by looking at our company history.
   Then, **I'll go on** to examine the way we want to develop our business in the future.

- Das *will future* wird mit dem Hilfsverb *will* und dem Infinitiv (ohne *to*) gebildet.
  Das *will future* wird oft verwendet, wenn man ganz allgemein über die Zukunft spricht. (1)
  Es wird manchmal auch verwendet, wenn etwas im Moment des Sprechens entschieden
  wird. (2)
- Das *going to future* wird mit *am/is/are* + *going to* + Infinitiv (ohne *to*) gebildet.
  Das *going to future* wird für Absichten oder Pläne verwendet. (3, 4)
- Man sollte jedoch beachten, dass dies keine starren Regeln sind! Muttersprachler
  verwenden das *will future* und das *going to future* gelegentlich in anderen Sprach-
  situationen. So wird das *going to future* manchmal anstelle des *will future* verwendet,
  wenn man eine gewisse Entschlossenheit unterstreichen möchte. (5)
- Das *will* und *going to future* können aber auch abwechselnd benutzt werden, um auf-
  einanderfolgende Handlungen zu beschreiben, z. B. zu Beginn einer Präsentation. (6)

---

7 | Practice

**Look at your diary and think about what you are going to do in the coming week.
Then write sentences describing your plans using the *will* and *going to future*. Use the
example below to help you.**

Example: Monday – 9.30: meeting with training manager – talk about performance during
last three month

| Mo | *I'm going to meet my company's training manager on Monday at 9.30.*
We'll discuss my performance at work during the last three months. |

84

PRESENTATIONS

UNIT 8

8 Presentation visuals

A During his presentation, Mark uses some PowerPoint slides. Match four of the titles (a–f) with the slides (1–4). Two titles do not match.

a Why customers like our products
b Starkling Lebensmittel GmbH – strong points
c Our plans for the future
d A history of Good Foods Ltd
e Our share in the UK healthy snacks market
f One of our most popular products

The Quix
- A healthy, sweet snack which is low in fat and sugar
- Comes in three varieties:
  • nut and raisin
  • chocolate and nut
  • banana and apple
- Costs a little more than other similar sweet snacks

1

- Company started in 1971
- Built a new factory in 1978
- Won The Queen's Award for Industry in 1982
- Currently employ 430 staff at our factory and headquarters in Hammersmith, West London

2

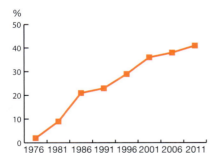

3

- Popular products which are well marketed
- A solid base in the Central and Eastern European market
- Excellent logistics networks
- First class staff who speak English!

4

B Now work with a partner and write slides for the two titles you didn't match.

9 Referring to visuals

🔊 21

A Mark refers to six slides during his presentation including the four shown in exercise 8. In which excerpts from his presentation does he refer to these four slides?

85

PRESENTATIONS

B **Rearrange the phrases to make sentences from the presentation. Listen again to check your answers.**

1   what our company's strong points are / you can see that it summarises / so, if you look at my next slide,

2   between the UK and / that our sales are split / this slide / fairly equally / Western Europe / you'll note from the pie chart on

3   refers to / of the market / the growth in our share / the line graph here

4   to this next slide, / if I can direct your attention / the key events in our development / you'll get an overview of

5   has proved so popular / about why this product / which provides a few details / now, on to my next slide

6   for the same period / while the table details / the chart depicts our sales growth / net profits

---

LANGUAGE

Giving presentations

Introductions
Good morning, ladies and gentlemen.
Hello, everybody.
I'm … and I'm responsible for … at …
My name's … and I'm the … at …
I'm going to tell you about …
Today, I want to describe to you …

Describing the structure of the presentation
Firstly, I'm going to talk about …
Then, I'll move on to …
My next point will be about …
Finally, I'll show you how …

Referring to visuals
If I can direct your attention to this slide, you'll see that it depicts …
You'll note from this line graph, which describes our sales growth, that …
Look at the pie chart on this slide. You'll note that it shows …

---

10 | Preparing an introduction to a presentation

Prepare the introduction to a presentation using sentences and phrases from the unit. Write one or two slides for the introduction of the presentation. Choose one of the following topics:

- A profile of my company and its products/services
- A profile of the department I work in and why it is important for my company

Make the introduction to the presentation for the class.

WEBCODE **BMU0801**

KMK exam practice

11 | Mediation

Als Mitarbeiter der Firma Starkling Lebensmittel GmbH haben Sie sich Mark Harkleroads Präsentation angehört. Da Ihr Abteilungsleiter einen anderen Termin wahrnehmen muss, kann er sich das Ende der Präsentation nicht mehr anhören und bittet Sie, ihm am nächsten Tag eine Zusammenfassung auf Deutsch zu geben. Herr Harkleroad stellt Ihnen seine Unterlagen zur Verfügung, sodass Sie den folgenden Teil der Präsentation vorliegen haben.

So, ladies and gentlemen, I want to turn now to the final section of my presentation today. What I'm going to do in this section is explain what I think the benefits of the deal we're offering will be to Starkling Lebensmittel and to Good Foods. Now, you hear this a lot in business, and sometimes it's just not
5   true, but what's on offer here is a real win-win deal for both our companies. There will be no losers here: both companies will stand to profit a great deal from what we're putting on the table.

So what will the benefits of the deal be to us, to Good Foods? Well, firstly, we're almost guaranteed to secure the growth we're aiming at by increasing our
10   sales in Central and Eastern Europe (CEE). As I've explained, it's absolutely crucial to our business and the development we've planned for it that we secure at least 10% growth in sales next year. So this deal will help us hit one of our most important current business aims.

A further point to our benefit: The deal will enable us to cement a working
15   partnership with Starkling Lebensmittel which both companies can develop in the future. We've only been talking about CEE today, however, there are other regions of Europe new to both our companies which we will be able to take on together as a result of the experience we will gain here.

And what about Starkling Lebensmittel? What benefits can your company
20   expect to get out of this deal? Well, firstly, you've admitted that some of your products are no longer selling as well as they could be in CEE. The deal will give you some new products to strengthen your product range thanks to the joint branding that we're offering.

And, of course, not least among the benefits to yourself will be the fact that
25   you can keep your new distribution centre in Carlsbad open. Your falling sales in the region will mean that you have to close this, losing the investment that you poured into it. This deal will give you the cash flow to keep the distribution centre open.

So, ladies and gentlemen, it's exactly for these reasons that I believe this is
30   going to be a win-win deal for both of us.

Extra material

1 Presentation body language

A Read the article and match the headlines to the four appropriate sections.

a Don't jump about
b Get on your feet!
c Keep your audience in view
d No funny expressions, please

Presentations will succeed or fail on the basis of its contents. But the same can also be true of how a presenter behaves in front of an audience. Read our top five tips to find out how to get your body language right.

1 ...
You should only look away from your audience to check your notes quickly or look briefly at a presentation visual. You should certainly not be standing with your eyes turned down as though you are reading your presentation. Maintain eye contact with the people who have come to hear you speak. This helps you connect and makes people feel that you can be trusted.

2 ...
Keep your hands as still as possible because lots of hand movement just distracts people. It also makes you look nervous. In fact, if you want to avoid the latter, you should certainly not be running your fingers through your hair or pulling on your chin. Unless you are pointing to a presentation visual or making a gesture to emphasise something, keep your hands down at your side.

3 ...
Stand up to make your presentation. Sitting will make it look like you're lacking in energy. It can also appear lazy and give an audience the impression that you're not very committed to what you're saying.

4 ...
Okay, you might feel nervous, but you don't need to give this away by moving about frantically. Try to stand on the spot, perhaps taking only a couple of paces to either side occasionally so that you can make eye contact with other members of the audience.

5 ...
We can all make strange facial gestures when we're under pressure, but do avoid them since they can make you appear quite strange. So no biting on your lips, sucking in your cheeks or puckering your mouth, please. And while we're talking about it, do be aware of what your eyes are doing. You should certainly not roll them, especially when answering questions from the audience. This makes you look impatient and unfriendly.

B Now write a headline for the section of the text which does not already have one.

2 Most important tip

Work with a partner and discuss which tip you think is most important and why? Can you think of any further tips about good presentation body language which are not mentioned in the text? What are they? Tell the class about your discussion.

3 Poster

Work with a small group of students. Design a poster which conveys the advice given in the text, as well as additional pieces of advice you have thought of. Use cartoons, as well as keywords and phrases. Present your poster to the class.

Situation 4

Annie Lombard is going to Dubrovnik, Croatia, for an international conference on the cost of marriage. She asks her travel agent, Tiger Travel, to book a suitable hotel. Her requirements are:

- 3 nights, May 18–21
- not far from conference centre
- swimming pool
- in a quiet area
- internet access
- vegetarian food

1 Finding a hotel

Annie's travel agent rings the Adriatica Hotel to ask the necessary questions and make a booking. Look at the role cards and carry out the role-play.

Tiger Travel	Adriatica Hotel
▪ 3 nights, May 18–21? ▪ location? ▪ quiet? ▪ swimming pool? ▪ internet? ▪ vegetarian food?	▪ rooms available in May ▪ hotel close to conference centre ▪ quiet location in side street ▪ small swimming pool ▪ Wi-Fi in every room ▪ range of food, including vegetarian options

2 A complaint

After two nights at the Adriatica Hotel Annie is not completely happy and decides to make notes so that she can write something about the hotel in the internet guide, TravelPlanner, when she gets back home.

Write Annie's entry to the internet hotel guide. Make sure you use full sentences and mention all the points from her notes.

GOOD	OKAY	BAD
– staff very nice – speak English (a bit) – Wi-Fi works, but … →	– room cleaning – quiet – BUT near nightclub! – have to pay for internet access!	– vegetarian food: where?! – TINY pool! – not all computers in business centre work
– fitness centre very good – lovely city! but … →	– bit far to walk into centre	

Situation 4

3 | Preparing a presentation

On the third day of the conference, Annie has to give her presentation on how to reduce the cost of marriage in Britain. Look at the notes Annie made when she planned her presentation and decide in groups which part of her talk the topics should go in.

1 Introduction
2 Section 1: why does it cost so much?
3 Section 2: solutions
4 Conclusion

- people want 'dream' wedding
- use alternative to champagne
- average cost of wedding £21,000
- reduce number of guests
- main aim should be a dream marriage
- go for civil not church wedding
- the future for marriages?
- buy wedding dress in charity shop
- get friends and family to help with invitations, decorations, etc.
- marriage at lowest level since 1862
- my own view
- ask friend to take photos
- peak of weddings in 1940
- agree on your upper and lower cost limits
- you could save thousands
- use of expensive hotels
- reason: number of couples living together increasing
- avoid high season (May–Oct)

4 | The presentation

In your groups use your answers to exercise 3 to give a 3-minute version of Annie's presentation. One group member will give the introduction, one will talk about section 1, another about section 2 and a fourth member will provide the conclusion.

Begin the presentation like this: *"Good afternoon, everybody. I'm going to talk to you about how to reduce the cost of marriage in Britain. Now to begin with, I'd like to give you the structure of my presentation ..."*

Logistics

UNIT 9

- the logistics process
- safety rules & regulations
- just-in-time production

1 Warm-up

A Work with a partner and make a flowchart with the stages in the logistics process in the right order.

- **a** Production call-up – Parts needed in production are requested by the Production Department
- **b** Packing and storage – Finished products are covered in protective materials before being stored in the warehouse
- **c** Procurement – Parts needed in production are bought from suppliers
- **d** Shipment – Finished products are transported to the customer
- **e** Delivery – Parts are shipped to the factory and stored in the warehouse
- **f** Inspection – Finished products are checked to ensure they meet quality standards
- **g** Production – Products are assembled from parts called up from the warehouse

B Discuss with your partner how the terms highlighted in the text are expressed in German.

C Discuss and make a note of any differences between your flowchart and the logistics process in your company. Tell the class about these.

91

LOGISTICS

2 An email from the Logistics Manager

Stefan Nordling from Germany is doing a work experience placement in the Logistics Department at Upland Mountainbikes Ltd in England. His manager, Alex Fenton, is away on business when Stefan arrives. On his first day, he finds an email from Alex welcoming him to the company.

Read the email and answer the questions.

1 Why has Alex written an email to Stefan instead of welcoming him in person?
2 Which processes does Alex say logistics is made up of?
3 What is Alex's main responsibility as Logistics Manager?
4 What reason does Alex give for not being in the office to welcome Stefan?
5 What other development in the work of the Logistics Department does Alex mention?
6 Which role will Stefan have during his work experience placement?
7 What should Stefan do today and why?

From: Alex Fenton
To: Stefan Nordling
Subject: Welcome to Upland

Dear Stefan

Welcome to my department at Upland Mountainbikes. I'm delighted that you're going to be doing some work experience with us. Unfortunately, I have to be out of the office today and tomorrow, but I'm looking forward to welcoming you in person on Wednesday.
5   In the meantime, I want to give you an overview of the work of the Logistics Department and some of the tasks you're going to be involved in.
Let's start by defining what our work's about. Logistics is basically the management of all the processes in the company related to receiving raw materials and components we need for production from suppliers, storing these and delivering them to the production
10 line when they're needed. The logistics process also involves storing finished products – our mountain bikes – and shipping them to customers.
My central aim as the Logistics Manager is to organise all of this so that it happens in the most efficient and cost-effective way.
We're currently negotiating delivery terms with some new suppliers – that's why I'm out of
15 the office at the moment. And we have recently introduced some new enterprise resource planning (ERP) software which links together information about, for instance, orders from customers and how many components we have in the warehouse so that we can co-ordinate this better.
I'm going to get you involved in monitoring how successful our new suppliers are in
20 making their deliveries in the times that we've agreed. I'll also be asking you to help us develop some training packages in the new software for our warehouse staff.
I'd like you to get in touch with Ken Forbes, our Warehouse Manager, today and get him to take you through some basic safety information. You'll need this when you're out and about in the warehouse and on the production line.
25 Looking forward to seeing you on Wednesday.

Best
Alex

LOGISTICS UNIT 9

3 Safety clothing and equipment

A Listen as Stefan is given a tour of the warehouse. In which order are the items of safety clothing and equipment mentioned?

1 protective gloves
2 hard hat
3 work boots
4 safety harnesses

B Match English words in the dialogue to the German words below. Listen again to check your answers.

1 Einzelteile
2 Lagergestell
3 Lagerregal
4 Leiter des Warenlagers
5 Personalsicherheit
6 Sicherheitsmaßnahmen

C Decide which statements about the dialogue are true.

1   a   Stefan has come to see Ken to tell him about the warehouse.
    b   Stefan has come to see Ken to learn something about the warehouse.

2   a   Stefan needs to sign in because of safety measures.
    b   He needs to sign in because there are expensive things in the warehouse.

3   a   Staff safety in the warehouse is very important for the company.
    b   The company thinks that staff are responsible for their own safety.

4   a   The staff use safety harnesses when they work on the storage racks.
    b   The staff use harnesses so that they don't have to work on the storage racks

5   a   The company's warehouse is bigger than any other bicycle companies' in Britain.
    b   It is as big as any other British bicycle companies' warehouse.

4 Safety rules

A Listen as Ken describes the company's warehouse safety rules to Stefan. In which order does he mention the safety signs below?

93

LOGISTICS

B Use the words in the box to complete the sentences about the safety warnings. Listen again to check your answers.

> allowed • fire • flames • flammable • generally • voltage

1. This means that there are highly … materials in storage.
2. This sign says that there is high … electricity in the area.
3. If you see this sign, it means that this area is … dangerous.
4. This one here means that you are not … to smoke.
5. This one means no naked …
6. This sign means that you should not try to put out a … with water.

C Ken gives Stefan a leaflet about what employees should do if a colleague has an accident. Match the sentence beginnings (1–5) to the endings (a–e) to make statements from the leaflet.

1. Quickly tell other people
2. If the person has a serious
3. Make the injured person as
4. If you think the person has a head
5. Get the first-aid kit so that you can give the injured person

a. basic medical help.
b. comfortable as possible.
c. that an accident has taken place.
d. or neck injury, do not try to move them.
e. injury, call an ambulance.

TIP: Phrases to use in the event of an accident

If a colleague has an accident and injures themselves, it's important that you use the right phrases to take control of the situation as quickly as possible.
The first thing you have to do is raise the alarm. You can do this using phrases like:
John has had an accident. Can someone quickly call an ambulance, please?
Next, you need to give your attention to your injured colleague. If they are seriously injured, you should tell them to keep still:
Please, don't try to move. Just stay as still as possible.
You should also reassure your colleague and try to keep them calm:
Don't worry. An ambulance is on its way. It'll be here soon.

D Work with a partner and look at the pictures below of the injuries the people have suffered. Decide what you should do and say in each case.

LOGISTICS

UNIT 9

5 In the warehouse

A **Work with a partner and brainstorm the tasks which are carried out in a warehouse. Think of as many as possible.**

B **Read as Alex explains the tasks that are carried out in the warehouse when she returns to the office. Which of the tasks that you thought of does she mention?**

Alex	Okay, so here we are in the warehouse. Hard hat on, please.
Stefan	Oh, yeah, okay.
Alex	So, the warehouse is a really important part of our logistics process. You could say that it's like the hub – or centre – of it. Let me run you through the tasks that are carried out here and how that fits into the company's supply chain.
Stefan	Right.
Alex	Firstly, everything we need to make our bikes is stored here. You can see the components we have in stock on those racks over there. But we don't just store components. We also receive incoming deliveries from our suppliers here in the warehouse. If you look over there, you can see two delivery bays. That's where the trucks unload their goods. Then we deal with the paperwork that comes with the deliveries – they're called delivery notes. We check that we get what is written on the documents.
Stefan	Ah, I see. You check everything in case the suppliers have made a mistake.
Alex	That's right. Once the delivery notes have been checked by Ken Forbes and his staff they come up to us in the Logistics Department. We file them and keep them so we have a record of deliveries.
Stefan	Okay, I see.
Alex	Now, we have a lot of different components here so it's important that they can all be found quickly and easily when they're needed in production. Ken's staff are responsible for storing everything in the correct places.
Stefan	So, there's a system showing what components are stored where?
Alex	Oh, yes. That's really important. For example, wheel components are stored just here in Row B, Shelf 6. Another big job that Ken and his guys are involved in is stocktaking.
Stefan	What's that?
Alex	We have to make sure that we actually have the components that we think we have. If we have less of a component than we think, this can lead to delays in production. When we take deliveries, we use barcodes and scanners to check components into the new ERP software system I was telling you about. But sometimes our suppliers can make mistakes when they pack components for delivery, so we do regular stocktaking manually.
Stefan	Ah, okay. So you count what you've got and check it against a list of what there should be in the warehouse?
Alex	Exactly. And the other important task done here is picking out components when they are called up by the Production Department and then delivering them to the production line. We do this every day.
Stefan	Wow. Then you really do a lot more than just store things in the warehouse.
Alex	That's right. The guys here have lots to do and they're always busy. Now, if we go through this passageway here, we'll be on the production line. It makes sense to show you it this way since this is the route that components take after they've been called up. We'll go through here, then come back into the warehouse later to see the final stages of the logistics process.

95

LOGISTICS

C Stefan tries to prepare his own list of tasks carried out in a warehouse. Do the list for him.

Tasks carried out ...

1 _____
... _____

D Match the words from the dialogue (1–10) to their definitions (a–j).

1 logistics process
2 delivery
3 supply chain
4 delivery bays
5 paperwork
6 delivery note
7 stocktaking
8 barcodes and scanners
9 components
10 warehouse

a the series of systems that come together to ensure that a company has what it needs for production
b the area of a warehouse where deliveries are made
c the listing, counting and checking of goods held in a warehouse
d the system a company uses to move raw materials from delivery to production
e goods given from the seller to a buyer
f the general word used to describe documents used in business
g the document which comes with the goods a supplier sends
h the equipment used to record raw materials in the logistics software system
i the parts required in the assembly of a product
j the area in which components, raw materials and finished products are stored

GRAMMAR

The passive

1 The bicycle components **are stored** in the warehouse before they are used.
2 **Have** all these bikes **been ordered** by customers in the UK?
3 The warehouse **was built** five years ago to provide more floor space.
4 Safety regulations in the warehouse and on the production line must **be followed** at all times.

- Das Passiv wird mit einer Form von *to be* und dem *past participle* (3. Form des Verbs) gebildet. (1–4)
- In technischen Texten und Prozessbeschreibungen wird im Englischen häufig das Passiv verwendet, um Handlungen zu beschreiben, ohne deren Urheber zu nennen, z. B. wenn der Urheber keine Rolle für die Aussage des Satzes spielt. (1, 3)
- Wenn man hervorheben will, von wem etwas getan wird oder wodurch etwas geschieht, fügt man diese Information mit der Präposition *by* an. (2)

LOGISTICS

UNIT 9

6 Practice

Complete these sentences about work in the warehouse using the passive form of the verbs in brackets.

1. The delivery note … (sign) by Brian Roberts as soon as the delivery arrived.
2. These components … (not/record) in the computer system correctly.
3. All our goods … (store) in the company warehouse.
4. The components … (deliver) next Tuesday.
5. In the past, delivery notes … (process) by the Administration Department, but now it … (do) by the warehouse staff.
6. Normally our goods … (order) a few days before they … (need).
7. The delivery … (send) out two hours ago. It should be there by now!
8. Some more components … (need) for production tomorrow. They … (pick up) later today.

7 Just-in-time production

A Listen as Alex explains how production logistics is organised at Upland Mountainbikes and answer the questions.

1. Why does Alex describe the production methods in use as 'relatively old-fashioned'?
2. Why does the company prefer to build bikes by hand?
3. What are the details of the system for bringing components from the warehouse to the production line explained by Alex?
4. What advantages are there for the company in this system?
5. What is Mike's role in production?
6. What happens to the bikes after they have left the production line and are taken back into the warehouse?

B Match the words in the box to the words below to make word partnerships used in the dialogue. Listen again to check your answers.

| packaging • assembly • manual • customer • production • contractor • quality |

1. … assembly
2. automated …
3. … line
4. … orders
5. … control
6. … area
7. haulage …

C Work with a partner and take turns explaining what the word partnerships mean.

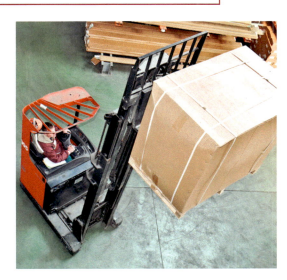

UNIT 9 LOGISTICS

8 A delivery note

Alex shows Stefan a delivery note. Read it and find the sections which provide the following information.

Delivery note

Delivery No. 49382372B89
Recipient:

Upland Mountainbikes Ltd

Recipients Address:
32 Stonewall Road
Gliberton Industrial Estate
Coventry
CV3 4AL

Delivery date: 25 May 20..

Delivery details:

Product No.	Product Name	Quantity
RR 287	Downhill Race	80
RR 298	Smooth Street	140

Driver   Recipient

Roughrider Tyre Company Ltd. • 142 Uppington Avenue • Leamington Spa, CV21 7BD

a   supplier's name
b   where the supplier is based
c   name of company receiving delivery
d   where the company taking the delivery is based
e   signature of the person making the delivery
f   signature of the person receiving the delivery
g   number of goods/ products supplied
h   day the goods were delivered
i   item number

WEBCODE **BMU0901**

9 Logistics in your company

Work with a partner to discuss and make notes about the logistics process in your company. Then describe the process to the class.

> **LANGUAGE**
>
> ### Talking about stages in a process
>
> **Signposting a description**
> First, …
> Secondly, …
> Then, …
> Next, …
> Finally, …
> To end with, …
>
> **Describing processes**
> Firstly, parts are brought to the …
> Next, the components are mounted to the …
> Then, the finished product is taken to …
> Finally, the product is … before it's …

98

KMK exam practice

10 Produktion

One of Upland Mountainbikes' new suppliers, Simlon Cycling Componentry Ltd, makes a delivery. Unfortunately, when the warehouse staff open the boxes to sort the components into the right areas of the warehouse, they discover differences between the order and what was contained in the delivery.

Schreiben Sie auf Englisch eine E-Mail an Simlon, in der Sie auf jeden einzelnen Fehler der Lieferung hinweisen. Bitten Sie Simlon außerdem, die überschüssig gelieferten und die fehlenden Bauteile baldmöglichst abzuholen bzw. zu liefern. Geben Sie exakt an, welche Bauteile fehlen, sodass keine neuerlichen Fehler gemacht werden.

Order No: 83663XX2C
Delivery date: 3 July 20..
Order details:

Product No.	Product Name	Quantity
783628	Gripper brake blocks	160
346743	Gripper brake levers	24
6554446	Stylex gear changer	46
4553677	Stylex chainset	50

Upland Mountainbikes Ltd
32 Stonewall Road
Gliberton Industrial Estate
Coventry
CV3 4AL

192 Upper North Street
Milton Keynes · MK4 5BU

Delivery Note

Order No. 83663XX2C

Delivery No. 25130688X

Delivery date: 4 July 20XX

Delivery details:

Product No.	Product Name	Quantity
783628	Gripper brake blocks	140
346743	Gripper brake levers	48
7389105	Speedex chainset	50

Driver   Recipient

Simlon Cycling Componentry Ltd · 192 Upper North Street · Milton Keynes · MK4 5BU

Extra material

How companies ensure quality in production

You hear a lot these days about 'quality'. But what does this actually mean in practice? We asked Simon Donaldson, who has 20 years' experience as a quality consultant.

Q: Why is quality such an important issue for companies?
Simon Donaldson: Well, basically it's an issue of protecting your reputation as a business. If you don't have good systems to ensure quality and sell products which are faulty, you could damage your reputation. That means losing customers. This is a situation companies obviously want to avoid.
Q: So they put in place measures to ensure quality. But what are these measures?
Simon Donaldson: Most companies use a two-sided strategy: quality assurance and quality control.
Q: That's interesting. I thought that these were two names for the same thing.
Simon Donaldson: That's a common misunderstanding. No, QA and QC are two quite different things, though they can be used together.
Q: So, what's the difference?
Simon Donaldson: Well, QA is used before a product has been manufactured. It's about the activities that go into ensuring that it's possible to make a product of the right quality standard in the first place. For example, QA includes ensuring that raw materials at the right quality are available and that machinery is set up so that it can produce at the level of quality aimed at.
Alternatively, QC is about checking that finished products are up to standard. This is done by inspecting products as they come off the production line. Manufacturers' approaches differ depending on what they make. A company which mass produces something like TVs will test a sample of products; for example, every tenth TV. Manufacturers which use small batch production may inspect each individual product.
Q: You said that QA and QC can be linked together. How is this done?
Simon Donaldson: The best way to guarantee quality is to use both systems. Then part of a QA programme would include the setting up of the monitoring processes which take place under QC.

1 Quality control or quality assurance?

A Read what these people who work for a manufacturing company say and decide whether their work contributes to quality control or quality assurance.

1 I train staff to make sure that their work meets our quality standards.

2 I make sure that finishing on our products meets quality standards before they are sent to customers.

3 I decide the best way to inspect products to make sure they are up to standard.

4 I write reports about the faults discovered by our product inspectors.

B What measures for guaranteeing quality are used in your company?

C How do they differ from the approaches described in the text?

Applying for a job

UNIT 10

- career planning
- applying for a job
- a job interview

1 Warm-up

A Look at the text below with a partner. What sort of questions do you think you are asked when you do a career planner test? Why do you think tests like these might be useful?

If you don't know what job is for you or what your next career step should be, a career test could help you. There are many free career tests available on the internet, but some of these aren't scientifically validated. However, try one or several of them and see if they are of any use to you. A good example is the Career Planner Quiz. Or take the fun Career Interest Game by the University of Missouri. Additionally quizzes such as the Job Security Test and the Office Character Test which test attitudes to specific aspects of work could be useful.

B Now carry out one of the online tests.

UNIT 10

APPLYING FOR A JOB

2 Skills questionnaire

A Complete the questionnaire below. Rate on a scale of one to five how highly developed your skills and personal qualities are in the areas mentioned. Try to be as honest as possible.

SKILLS QUESTIONNAIRE

1 = not very well developed   2–3 = quite well developed   4–5 = highly developed

		1	2	3	4	5
1	hard-working	■	■	■	■	■
2	fast learner	■	■	■	■	
3	pay attention to detail	■	■	■	■	
4	ambitious	■	■	■	■	
5	good communicator	■	■	■		■
6	self-motivated	■	■	■		■
7	team player	■	■	■		■
8	can take responsibility	■	■		■	■
9	numerate	■	■		■	■
10	can work under pressure	■	■		■	■
11	well organised	■	■		■	■
12	calm under pressure	■		■	■	■

B Now work with a partner and tell them about how you rated yourself. Suggest jobs to your partner which might suit their skills and personal qualities.

3 Job advertisements

A Discuss with your partner which of the following factors are most important to you when you apply for a job. Are there other things which are important to you? Tell your partner about these.

1 How much money you get paid
2 Where the job is
3 How much holiday you get
4 What you do in the job
5 What the company does

B Read the job advertisements on the next page and answer the questions.

In which job/s …
1 do you need to have specific experience?
2 would you need to be able to drive a car?
3 is it important to have good arithmetic and well-developed skills with numbers?
4 do you have contact with people in and outside the company?
5 might you need to have studied further after leaving school?
6 will you be selling directly to customers?

102

APPLYING FOR A JOB

Administrative Support Assistant (Sales)

Salary in the region of £14,750 + benefits (according to age and experience)

PlayList Ltd is a successful company which specialises in the development of internet audio software. We are looking for a motivated Administrative Support Assistant with a background in sales to support the team in our headquarters in Milton Keynes. As the successful candidate, you'll have to demonstrate your understanding of the internet and the online sales environment. You will be able to work on your own as well as help us to plan our busy work schedule in the sales office so it goes without saying that you're highly organised. You should be a good team player who is able to provide support to the Sales Manager and solve problems. You'll be helping to compile sales reports and maintain our customer database so you'll have proven skills with a PC. Additionally, you must be able to work under pressure and communicate effectively between our sales staff and customers.

Requirements:
- a college qualification in business administration, plus work experience
- experience of modern office systems
- a driving licence
- Fluency in at least one European language.

Closing date for your application: 30 July 20..

To apply for the job send your CV together with a covering letter and the names of two referees to:

Kevin Anderson, HR Assistant. PlayList Ltd . Central Way West, Milton Keynes. MK3 8BU

Customer Services Agent

Swift Sportswear Ltd is a rapidly expanding company which is looking to develop its team of customer service agents. If you think you're up to speed on the following skills, apply now.

You'll need:

Proven communications skills on the telephone – We talk to our customers across the world on the phone 24/7. To take part in this exciting conversation you'll need to be able to show patience, humour and the power to persuade and convince new customers to buy from us

Customer service values – Our customers are the most important people we know! You'll have to show that you value customers as much as we do and that you go out of your way to help them.

Computer skills – We're a 21st century business with computer systems to back this up. That's why your skills with a PC will be as important as anything else.

Salary in the region of £14,000 plus bonuses (depending on performance)

Interested?
Then email our HR Manager right now:
michael.thwaite@swiftsport.co.uk

Marketing Assistant

Salary circa £15,300

Hazel Lee Organic Foods Ltd makes tasty and healthy organic meals for our customers to enjoy at home. We're growing fast and are looking for a Marketing Assistant to help us. Are you the right person for the job?

Here's who we're looking for:

Since you'll be involved with collecting market research data and writing reports, you'll need to be good with figures and details will be important to you. You'll also need to show creativity in your ability to find market data. As you'll be working closely with the Marketing Manager to develop presentations for senior management about developments in the market for our products, your skills with PowerPoint will come in very handy. Additionally, as well as being able to contribute fully to the work of the marketing team, you'll be able to work independently and organise your own workload.

Although we are not looking for someone with specific experience of working in marketing, you'll need to be able to demonstrate your interest in working in the field and show us that you have the potential to be trained for the role.

If you're interested, download the application form **here** and email it back to us by 18 May 20..

APPLYING FOR A JOB

C Read the job advertisements again and match the expressions (1–8) to the definitions (a–h).

1	application form	a	a company's main offices
2	candidate	b	the money you will earn
3	salary	c	what you have done before
4	background	d	something you receive from school or college
5	headquarters	e	the letter you send with your application for a job
6	qualification	f	numbers
7	covering letter	g	the document which some companies ask people to fill in to apply for a job
8	figures	h	a person applying for a job

D Aufgrund eines Mangels an qualifizierten Bewerbern in Deutschland, möchte ihr Chef Arbeitskräfte aus Großbritannien anwerben. Erstellen Sie für ihn auf der Grundlage der drei Stellenangebote (auf Seite 103) eine Übersicht der Konditionen, die Arbeitskräften in Großbritannien angeboten werden. Ihre auf Deutsch verfasste Übersicht soll auch Qualifikationen, Kenntnisse und Erfahrungen enthalten, die britische Arbeitgeber verlangen. **KMK**

E Work with a partner and read the personal profiles of two people who saw the job advertisements on page 103. Which of the jobs do you think they should apply for and why?

Urs Schmidt
Education   Berufliches Gymnasium
Skills   very good with people, very calm, current driving license, very organised, can motivate himself well at work
Aims   wants to work closely with other people including customers, would like a job which offers him the chance to develop his career

Sue Brightspear
Education   Secondary school
Skills   good at working on her own, not so much a 'team player', good at maths, organised and self-motivated, current driving license
Aims   doesn't have much work experience, but looking for a job where she can 'learn by doing', would like to develop her abilities as a team player

APPLYING FOR A JOB

4 | A covering letter

Urs applies for the job with PlayList. Complete his covering letter to Kevin Anderson with the words in the box.

application • apply • Dear • details • enclose • experience • hearing •
improve • interesting • organised • sincerely • skills

...[1] Mr Anderson

...[2] **for the position of Administrative Support Assistant with PlayList Ltd**

I am writing to ...[3] for the position of Administrative Support Assistant which I saw advertised on the internet. I would like to be considered for the job and ...[4] my CV for your further information.

I have just completed my Abitur (equivalent to A Levels) and am looking for a job. I would like to work in Great Britain to gain ...[5] of working in the country. Also, although my English is good, I would like to ...[6] it by using it at work every day.

I find the job with PlayList very ...[7] as I am interested in music on the internet and electronic products. I developed this interest whilst working part-time as a Sales Assistant at MediaCentre while I was still at school.

I am sure that I can offer you the right ...[8] and personal qualities for the job. I like working with other people and feel that I am a good communicator. I am also well ...[9] and have experience of working on my own.

I have tried to include all the information you need, but if you require further ...[10], please do not hesitate to contact me.

I look forward to ...[11] from you.

Yours ...[12]

Urs Schmidt

APPLYING FOR A JOB

5 English language CVs

A Urs writes to a friend in England for advice about how to write an English language CV. Read Tim's email and match the German words to the English words he uses.

1	Arbeitserfahrung	6	Praktikum
2	Bildung	7	Qualifikationen
3	Fertigkeiten	8	Referenzgeber
4	Führerschein	9	Zertifikat
5	Lebenslauf	10	Zeugnis

Hi Urs

Good to hear from you! I'd love to help you with your curriculum vitae. It would be great if you got a job over here – it's been a long time since we last saw each other in Mainz.

Right, so a British CV should be no longer than two pages long (that's really important) and has around five sections. The first is usually called Personal information. Here you give information about yourself like your full name, your date of birth, your address and your nationality.

Then there's a section called Education and training. Here you list which schools you went to and what qualifications you have. You start with your most recent school and then work backwards.

Next comes Work experience – you list all the jobs you have had, with which companies and when. Again, you start with your most recent job. The next section is generally called Personal skills and competences, that's experience from other places – I mean not at school or in a specific job. You could list your computer skills here, your driving licence or any experience you got during work experience.

Finally, you have Additional information. This is where you tell the company what you do in your spare time. It's only a short section and it shouldn't take up very much space, but companies like to know what sort of person you are outside of work.

Oh, and you need to put the names and contact details of two referees at the end. The company might get in touch with them to ask what sort of person you are. One should be your current or last employer; the other should be a professional who knows you well like a teacher. You don't need to include a photo or sign the CV. And don't send copies of certificates and qualifications – companies will ask for these if they need them.

Actually, I've heard about a new online CV offered by the European Union called Europass. It offers a kind of standardised CV for the whole of Europe. Perhaps you should look it up online.

Anyway, I think that was everything. Let me know if you need any more help.

Hope to see you soon!
Tim

B Identify the three things which are different from German CVs.

APPLYING FOR A JOB

C   Sie werden gebeten, einen Artikel für Ihre Schülerzeitung darüber zu schreiben, wie man einen englischen Lebenslauf verfasst. Verwenden Sie dafür die Informationen in Tims E-Mail.

6 Urs' curriculum vitae

A   Put the different pieces of information from Urs' CV (1–12) under the correct Europass CV headings (a–e).

   a   Work experience
   b   Personal information
   c   Education and training
   d   Additional information
   e   Personal skills and competences

   1   Member of the Mainz Youth Football Team
   2   05 June 1991
   3   Life guard and First Aid certificate (2007)
   4   Mainzer Weg 34 B
   5   Skilled user of MS Office; basic understanding of programming languages
   6   Sales Assistant in the electronics department at MediaCentre (Saturday job)
   7   Berufliches Gymnasium Halsenbach, 2004–2011
   8   Full, current driving license
   9   Ehrenbach Grundschule, 1996–2001
   10 Abitur (equivalent to A Levels)
   11 Member of the local carnival club
   12 Assistant at Albi Supermarket (summer job 2007)

B   Fill out your Europass CV online (http://europass.cedefop.europa.eu/en/documents/curriculum-vitae) and then print it out and present it to the class.

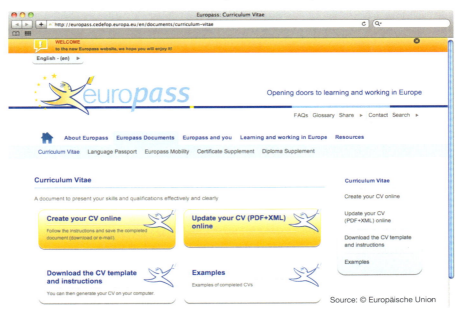

Source: © Europäische Union

APPLYING FOR A JOB

> **GRAMMAR**
>
> ### Simple past and present perfect
>
> 1 I **worked** part-time at a book shop during the summer holidays.
> 4 He **met** many people during his traineeship in London.
> 2 I've really **developed** my organisational skills since starting my current job.
> 3 She's **improved** her English so much since starting her course at college.
>
> - Das *simple past* wird mit dem Infinitiv + *-ed* gebildet. Man verwendet es, um zu sagen, was zu einem bestimmten Zeitpunkt in der Vergangenheit abgeschlossen wurde. (1) Unregelmäßige Verben haben eigene Formen, z. B. *write – wrote – written*. (2)
> - Das *present perfect* wird mit dem Hilfsverb *have* und dem Partizip Perfekt (3. Form des Verbs) gebildet. Man verwendet es, um zu sagen, dass etwas irgendwann in der Zeit bis zum Moment des Sprechens Gültigkeit hat. Es wird oft mit Signalwörtern wie *since*, *for* und *ever* gebraucht. (3, 4).

7 Practice

Complete the sentences with the correct form of the verb in brackets.

1 Sandra … (write) a lot of job applications since she left school.
2 I … (gain) a lot of experience in my current job.
3 Simon … (apply) for a job in Germany last month, but didn't get it.
4 I … (study) English, Geography and Chemistry at school.
5 Fred … (have) a summer job last year after he left college.
6 We … (receive) a lot of applications so far for the job we advertised last week.
7 He … (study) Business Administration for two years now.
8 Jo … (want) to work in sales after school, but now he … (decide) R&D is better.

WEBCODE **BMU1001**

8 The job interview

25

A What would you expect to be asked at a job interview? Make a list. Then listen to Urs' interview at PlayList. Which of your ideas does the interviewer use?

B Work with a partner and carry out the role-play.

> **Student A**
>
> Sie sind Personalleiter/in in einem großen Reiseunternehmen. Sie suchen Customer Service Agents, die Kunden am Telefon betreuen.
>
> Bewerber/innen sollten folgende Qualifikationen haben:
> PC-Kenntnisse – in der Lage sein, Daten genauestens einzugeben
> Organisationstalentiert – Arbeiten selbstständig organisieren und Multitaskingfähigkeit
>
> Sie suchen Bewerber/innen mit folgenden persönlichen Eigenschaften:
> Fleiß und freundlicher, geduldiger und höflicher Umgang mit Kunden
> Dynamische Einstellung im Hinblick auf den beruflichen Werdegang
>
> Führen Sie ein Bewerbungsgespräch mit dem/der Bewerber/in und erfragen Sie, ob er/sie die gesuchten Fähigkeiten und Eigenschaften hat. Fragen Sie nach entsprechenden beruflichen Erfahrungen.

APPLYING FOR A JOB

UNIT 10

Student B

Sie haben sich um die Stelle als Customer Service Agent in einem großen Reiseunternehmer beworben und sind zu einem Bewerbungsgespräch eingeladen worden.

Verwenden Sie die folgenden Angaben zur Beantwortung der Ihnen gestellten Fragen.

Berufserfahrung:

1,5 Jahre als Telefonkundenbetreuer/in in einer Bank
Erfahrung mit selbstständiger Arbeitsorganisation wie beispielsweise der Beschaffung der nötigen Informationen für Kunden mit einem Problem, bevor Sie sie zurückrufen, um das Problem zu lösen
Erfahrung im Umgang mit Kundendatenbanken sowie mit der üblichen MS Office Software.

Ihre persönlichen Eigenschaften:

Sie haben die Stelle bei der Bank aufgegeben, weil Sie nicht genügend Möglichkeiten für Ihre berufliche Entwicklung sahen. Sie suchen nach einer Möglichkeit, Ihre Chancen auf einen besseren Arbeitsplatz in der Zukunft zu steigern.
Sie sind fleißig und möchen Kunden zufriedenstellen.
Während Ihrer Arbeit bei der Bank bekamen Sie eine Auszeichnung für Ihre positive Einstellung zu Ihrer Arbeit mit Kunden.

---

9 | Questions for the interviewer

The following sentences are answers to questions asked by a job candidate in an interview. Work with a partner and decide what the questions were.

1 Well, there are currently six people in the team. With this new job it will be seven.
2 I would say that, within six months, we would expect you to take on your own small projects.
3 Yes, sure. We'll be giving you additional training in the software we use as well as our office systems.
4 It's very possible. The last assistant we took on in the department is now a team leader.
5 You'll report to Nora Clairmont, our Customer Services Manager.

TIP

Usually the point will come in an interview when you are asked if you would like to ask any questions. It pays to have thought about this beforehand and to have prepared a few questions in advance.

It's also a good idea not to concentrate too much on things like pay at this point. Instead, plan to ask questions which show your interest in other aspects of the job:

Will I be given the opportunity to take responsibility for my own work?
How long will it be before I can take on my own projects?

109

KMK exam practice

10 Rezeption – Hörverstehen

A Sie haben sich auf Stellenanzeigen in Großbritannien beworben. Als Vorbereitung auf mögliche Bewerbungsgespräche hören Sie sich einen Radiobeitrag zu verschiedenen Bewerbungsgesprächsmethoden von Firmen an. Notieren Sie dazu Antworten auf folgende Fragen.

1. Was sollte man dem Bericht nach vor einem Bewerbungsgespräch machen?
2. Wie sind Telefoninterviews bisher eingesetzt worden?
3. Welche neuen Entwicklungen hat es bei Telefoninterviews gegeben und was sind die Gründe dafür?
4. Welche Vorteile haben Videopräsentationen und Telefoninterviews für Firmen?
5. Welche Vorteile haben Videopräsentationen für Bewerber/innen?
6. Woher kommt der Begriff *elevator pitch*?
7. Was wird mit *elevator pitches* bezweckt?
8. Wie werden *elevator pitches* mit Videopräsentationen kombiniert?

11 Interaktion

Sie sollen eine dreiminütige Videopräsentation auf Englisch für folgenden Arbeitsplatz erstellen. Diskutieren Sie mit Ihrem Partner / Ihrer Partnerin, wie Sie die Präsentation erstellen und was Sie sagen wollen. Tragen Sie Ihre Präsentation der Klasse vor.

Stellenbezeichnung: Verwaltungsassistent/in

Aufgabenschwerpunkte:

- Archivieren von Abteilungsdaten
- Mitwirkung bei der Erschafffung eines neuen Archivierungssystems
- Anrufe entgegennehmen und Kunden und Kollegen in anderen Abteilungen mit Informationen versorgen
- Bestellen von Bürobedarfsartikeln
- Übernahme der allgemeinen Büroorganisation bei Abwesenheit des Büroleiters

Extra material

Assessment centres

Recruiting and training new members of staff can be time-consuming and expensive for companies. Many businesses are finding out that the conventional interview situation just isn't enough when it comes to finding the right candidate. After all, candidates can 'talk up' their abilities at interview but not be much use when it comes to actually doing something. This is why assessment centres have become so popular.

So what is an assessment centre? Well, it's a one or two day programme of activities at which candidates get the chance to actually show what they can do.

At the centre you are given tasks which are closely related to the ones you will perform in the job. You may be asked to research something and write a report, respond in writing to customer complaints or design a website.

You will probably be asked to work with other candidates as well: your potential employer wants to see how you work as part of a team as well as on your own initiative. Companies will be on the look out for candidates who have difficulties working in a team setting as well as those who display leadership qualities.

The assessment may also include social events where employers can assess how well you relate to other people in a non-working environment.

According to Trent Crawford, a Human Resources Manager at Stretch Graphic Technology Ltd, the most important thing is to be yourself and not to panic.

"Some candidates try to act how they think the potential employer wants them to. But recruitment managers are not stupid and they can generally see when a candidate is not acting naturally. My advice is to relax. You should feel confident. After all, potential employers would not have invited you to the centre if they were not impressed and wanted to find out more."

---

1 | The right headline

Which of these headlines best summarises what the text says?

1 Why the growth in assessment centres? Because they're cheaper, that's why
2 Assessment centres – help companies get a more complete picture of candidates

---

2 | Understanding the text

Complete these sentences about the text in your own words.

1 These days, potential employers are …
2 The difference between an interview and an assessment centre is …
3 At an assessment centre you can expect …
4 You should relax about being invited to an assessment centre because …

---

3 | Group work

Work in a small group and brainstorm all the things a job candidate can do to prepare for an interview. Then write a webpage for job candidates giving them advice about preparing for interviews.

111

Situation 5

Bob Appleyard is looking for a job. He has had several short-term jobs since leaving university, but hasn't had a 'proper' one yet. One day in November, as he is looking in the newspaper for possible jobs, he sees the following advertisement.

BOSWORTHS Department Store requires

Accounts Assistant to support sales and purchase activities and liaise with suppliers.

Must …
- have previous experience
- be familiar with Word and Excel
- show attention to detail
- be patient, friendly and diplomatic

Salary: £25,000 p.a.

Further details from www.bosworths.co.uk

---

1 The application

Bob decides to apply for the job. Look at the notes he has made and then write his application letter for him. Only use the relevant information.

- graduated in Accounting & Finance
- not worked for last 2 months
- Boy Scout from ages 7–14
- use Word and internet a lot
- parents say I'm very patient & diplomatic
- worked for last 3 summers at Garden Centre (selling, stock-taking)
- have biggest collection of model planes in the Midlands
- often shop at Bosworths
- have used Excel a few times
- have set up own website to buy, sell & exchange model planes
- father is an accountant

2 The interview

Bob is invited for an interview by Bosworths. He is interviewed by John Wardle, the Chief Accountant. Look at the role cards and carry out the role-play.

Bob	John
Prepare for the interview by … • reading what you wrote in your application • thinking of all the skills you might need to be an Accounts Assistant (e.g. care and attention) • re-reading the Bosworths advertisement	During the interview you want to find out about Bob's … • personal qualities • work experience • possible attitude to clients/ customers

Situation 5

3   A delivery note

27

Bob is happy: he has got the job. One of his first tasks is to order new office furniture for his boss. You work for Dodge & Co. Office Supplies, who Bob calls to make an order for furniture. Listen to Bob's order and copy and complete the delivery note for the delivery.

Dodge & Co. Office Supplies Ltd

14–18 Rugby Road
Leicester
LE2 4DD

Delivery No: 6538920

Recipient: …

Recipient's address: …

Delivery date: …

Delivery details

Item	Quantity
…	…

4   An accident

A few days later, while the office is being reorganised, Bob has an accident and an accident report has to be written. Look at the notes that Diana Dore, the Personnel Manager has made and then copy and complete the report for the Health & Safety officer.

ACCIDENT REPORT

Name of investigator:
Date and time of accident:
Injury details:
First aid given (and name of first-aider):
Medical treatment given (if any):
Description of the accident:
Actual or possible causes:
Involvement of equipment, objects, other people:
Witnesses (if any), names and addresses:
Action to be taken to prevent a similar accident:

- 13/12, approx. 3.15 p.m.
- Bob Appleyard, Accounts Assistant
- in office no. 2.13
- present: John Wardle (Chief Acc.)
- head hurt + mild shock
- no damage to desk, wiring, office
- Bob A.: not bad – felt OK after sit-down
- first aid: J. Wardle (gave brandy)
- taken to hospital for treatment
- no serious injury found – home after 2 hrs
- cause: moving furniture, tripped over wires
- action: wireless computers? Neater wiring?

113

KMK mock exam

Schriftliche Prüfung

Zeit: 90 Minuten
Hilfsmittel: allgemeines zweisprachiges Wörterbuch
Maximale Punktzahl: 100 Punkte

Im Rahmen der schriftlichen Prüfung werden die Aufgabenanteile für die drei Kompetenzbereiche wie folgt gewichtet:
- Rezeption – Hörverstehen 30 %
- Rezeption – Leseverstehen 20 %
- Produktion 30 %
- Mediation 20 %

Im Folgenden werden vier Aufgaben vorgelegt, die Sie bearbeiten sollen. Die erste und die zweite Aufgabe beziehen sich auf Ihre Fähigkeit, englische Texte (gesprochene und geschriebene) zu verstehen = **Rezeption**. Bei der dritten Aufgabe sollen Sie ein Schriftstück erstellen = **Produktion** eines englischen Textes. Bei der vierten Aufgabe wird von Ihnen erwartet, dass Sie Texte von der deutschen oder englischen in die jeweils andere Sprache übertragen = **Mediation**.

Die Prüfung beginnt mit der Hörverständnisaufgabe.
Alle weiteren Aufgaben können in beliebiger Reihenfolge bearbeitet werden.

Rezeption I (Hörverstehen)

KMK-Stufe II (B1, Threshold)

28

Situation: Sie sind Auszubildende/r bei der Firma TransTech, die innerhalb des kommenden Jahres Kontakte in Europa, Asien und Südamerika ausbauen möchte.

Aufgabe: Um sich zu informieren, was es für Sie künftig bedeuten würde, in einer global aufgestellten Firma zu arbeiten, hören Sie sich ein Interview unter dem Motto *Going Global* an, in dem über unterschiedliche Erfahrungen berichtet wird. Fassen Sie die Aussagen von Nicola, Derek und Heike stichwortartig für Ihre Kollegen auf Deutsch zusammen.

Nicola:
1. Standort der Firma (1 Punkt)
2. Organisationsform (1 Punkt)
3. Produkt (1 Punkt)
4. Welche Entwicklung hat sich für die Firma vor zwei Jahren in Bezug auf Expansion ergeben? (3 Punkte)
5. Warum kann Nicola von sich sagen, dass er zur richtigen Zeit am richtigen Ort war? (3 Punkte)

Derek Chalmers:
1. Größe der Firma: (1 Punkt)
2. Standort: (1 Punkt)
3. Was ist mit Dereks Firma AKZ Engineering nach 1990 passiert? (4 Punkte)
4. Auswirkungen der Veränderungen auf den Umsatz? (1 Punkt)
5. Welche Absatzmärkte nennt Derek? (3 Punkte)

Heike Zweibel:
Was wird über Heikes Firma ausgesagt in Bezug auf …
1. … das Produkt? (3 Punkte)
2. … die Größe der Firma? (3 Punkte)
3. Warum ist sie nicht so sehr an einer Expansion ihres Unternehmens interessiert? (3 Punkte)
4. Welche Schlussfolgerung wird aus den drei Interviews gezogen? (2 Punkte)

KMK mock exam

Rezeption II (Leseverstehen)

KMK-Stufe II (B1, Threshold)

Situation: Bevor Ihr Chef einen Geschäftskontakt im asiatischen Raum aufbaut, möchte er Informationen zu asiatischer Firmenkultur einholen.

Aufgabe: Ihr Chef bittet Sie, folgenden Text zu lesen und festzustellen, ob es Unterschiede zwischen Deutschland und China bei Geschäftstreffen gibt. Halten Sie sowohl Unterschiede a s auch Gleiches stichwortartig auf Deutsch fest.

Generelle Aussage über das Verhalten bei Geschäftstreffen (3 Punkte)		
	China	Deutschland
Pünktlichkeit (3 Punkte)	…	…
Begrüßung (3 Punkte)	…	…
Visitenkarten (3 Punkte)	…	…
Geschäftsessen (3 Punkte)	…	…
Sitzordnung (5 Punkte)	…	…

Business culture in Europe and Asia – some guidelines

How we react to other cultures is shaped by our own culture. To communicate effectively with people from other cultures, we need to understand their own cultural attitudes. Let's look at meetings as an example.

To have successful meetings with people from other cultures, we need to know what makes them tick in this setting. It pays to find out how you should greet your business partner so that you can create the right impression. Then, you'll need to understand how meetings are conducted in the culture in question so that you can stick to the rules.

1 **Punctuality** – Being on time is regarded as important in Europe and Asia. Arriving late is seen as a waste of time and an insult. When travelling to a meeting, there can be delays: planes can arrive late and traffic can delay the drive into town. If you're late, call to explain the reason and when you expect to arrive.

2 **Greetings** – In Europe shaking hands is normal and expected. Offer your hand confidently without waiting for your business partner to do so. In China, however, the shaking of hands is not common. Business people generally greet one another with a nod rather than a bow. If your business partner offers their hand, shake it confidently. However, wait for them to initiate this.

3 **Business cards** – All business people are familiar with exchanging business cards. In Europe this is done casually. In Asia, it is common to offer your card using both hands. Also, be sure to spend some moments studying your business partner's card; this is a mark of respect.

4 **Mixing business and pleasure** – Business lunches have been common in Europe for decades and now it's not uncommon to meet over breakfast! However, while Asian business people have adopted the business lunch, they are not used to doing business over breakfast so it's probably not a good idea to suggest this.

5 **Seating arrangements** – European business people take a relaxed attitude to who sits where, but in Chinese culture there are more set ideas about this. The person hosting the meeting sits in the middle facing the door with the most senior guest of importance on their left. Other participants seat themselves in descending order according to their status.

KMK mock exam

Produktion

KMK-Stufe II (B1, Threshold)

Situation: Ihr Chef Peter Meier möchte in der kommenden Woche eine Geschäftsreise nach Beijing antreten. Erste Kontakte sind mit der chinesischen Firma bereits geknüpft worden.

Aufgabe: Herr Meier bittet Sie, an den künftigen Geschäftspartner Wing eine E-Mail in englischer Sprache vorzubereiten. In dem Schreiben sollen Sie ihm mitteilen, dass …

- Herr Meier sich für die Einladung nach Beijing bedankt, die Herr Wing im letzten Telefonat in der vergangenen Woche ausgesprochen hat.
- er nächsten Mittwoch (Datum angeben) von Frankfurt aus direkt nach Beijing (Bejing Capital International Airport) fliegen und um 17:00 Uhr landen wird.
- Vom Flughafen zum Hotel Utani wird er ein Taxi nehmen.
- Er bittet allerdings darum, gegen 19:00 Uhr von Herrn Wing oder einem Fahrer abgeholt zu werden, damit er rechtzeitig zum Geschäftsessen im erwähnten Restaurant erscheinen kann.
- Er hofft, dass erste Kontakte geknüpft werden können und freut sich auf das Treffen.

Mediation

KMK-Stufe II (B1, Threshold)

Situation: Ihre Firma hat eine Einladung zu einem Forum mit dem Titel *The Europass Mobility – an advantage for companies and applicants* erhalten. Ihre Personalabteilung möchte wissen, was sich hinter dem Begriff *Europass Mobility* verbirgt.

Aufgabe: Übertragen Sie für die Personalabteilung den folgenden Text ins Deutsche.

The Europass Mobility

What is it?

The Europass Mobility is a record of any organised period of time (called Europass Mobility experience) that a person spends in another European country for the purpose of learning or training.
This includes for example:
    a work placement in a company; […]
The mobility experience is monitored by two partner organisations, the first in the country of origin and the second in the host country. Both partners agree on the purpose, content and duration of the experience; a mentor is identified in the host country. The partners may be […] training centres, companies, […] etc.

Who is it for?

The Europass Mobility is intended for any person undergoing a mobility experience in a European country, whatever their age or level of education.

Who is responsible for completing it?

The Europass Mobility is completed by the home and host organisations involved in the mobility project in a language agreed between both organisations and the person concerned. […]

Where can it be obtained?

Please contact the organisation sending you abroad and ask them to contact their National Europass Centre.

Source: © Europäische Union –
http://europass.cedefop.europa.eu

KMK mock exam

Mündliche Prüfung Teil I

Die Prüfung ist eine Gruppenprüfung, bei der Sie Gespräche persönlichen und fachlichen Inhalts in der Fremdsprache führen sollen. Es wird von Ihnen erwartet, dass Sie der vorgegebenen Situation entsprechend sprachlich agieren und reagieren. Es kommt dabei vor allem darauf an, dass Sie sich spontan äußern, dass Sie versuchen, sich verständlich zu machen, und dass Sie gut zuhören.

Die Prüfung besteht aus zwei Teilen (ggf. noch einer dritten Zusatzaufgabe) und dauert insgesamt ca. 20 Minuten. Zur Vorbereitung haben Sie 20 Minuten Zeit.

Im ersten Teil der mündlichen Prüfung werden Sie gebeten, sich zu persönlichen oder beruflichen Themen zu äußern.

Im zweiten Teil sollen Sie zusammen mit einem anderen Kandidaten ein Rollenspiel durchführen. Dazu erhalten Sie vom Prüfer Rollenkarten, auf denen eine Situation beschrieben ist, die Sie vorspielen sollen. Eventuell nehmen Sie in einem dritten Teil zu einer vorgegebenen Situation Stellung.

Hilfsmittel: allgemeines zweisprachiges Wörterbuch.

Mündliche Prüfung Teil II

KMK-Stufe II (B1, Threshold)

Kandidat/in A

Situation: Sie sind bei der Firma TransTech beschäftigt, die technische Geräte produziert.

Aufgabe: Führen Sie ein Gespräch mit einem Transporteur, da Sie eine Transportmöglichkeit für Ihre empfindlichen technischen Geräte nach Beijing benötigen.
- Sie eröffnen das Gespräch und begrüßen die Mitarbeiterin / den Mitarbeiter der Spedition.
- Fragen Sie nach der schnellstmöglichen Versendungsmöglichkeit.
- Reagieren Sie auf den Vorschlag, indem Sie nach dem Preis fragen.
- Reagieren Sie erschrocken und fragen Sie nach Alternativen.
- Fragen Sie auch danach, wie der Transport vom Flughafen zur Firma ca. 30 km außerhalb Beijings erfolgt.
- Fällen Sie eine Entscheidung.

KMK mock exam

Kandidat/in B

Situation: Sie sind bei der Spedition Easy-Logistics beschäftigt.

Aufgabe: Führen Sie ein Gespräch mit einem Mitarbeiter / einer Mitarbeiterin der Firma TransTech.

- Ihr Gesprächspartner eröffnet das Gespräch.
- Die Kundin / Der Kunde der Firma TransTech fragt, welche schnellstmögliche Transport-möglichkeit nach Beijing Sie für empfindliche technische Geräte anbieten können.
- Sie schlagen den Versand mit dem Flugzeug vor.
- Sie teilen Ihrem Kunden / Ihrer Kundin mit, dass bei Versand von empfindlicher Ware mit dem Flugzeug mit mindestens 50 % höheren Kosten im Vergleich zu anderen Transport-möglichkeiten gerechnet werden muss.
- Als Alternative bieten Sie den Transport mit dem Schiff an, der selbstverständlich länger dauert.
- Teilen Sie mit, dass der Transport vom Flughafen zur Firma ca. 30 km außerhalb Beijings mit einem LKW erfolgt, der nur für diese Fracht zur Verfügung gestellt wird und damit garantiert ist, dass die Ware sicher und schnellstmöglich ankommt.
- Reagieren Sie auf die Entscheidung Ihrer Kundin / Ihres Kunden.

Mündliche Prüfung Teil III (didaktische Reserve)

Situation: Your company is considering offering its trainees the opportunity of attending a placement abroad.

Aufgabe: You are a member of the committee which will decide if this plan should be discussed.

With your partner(s) discuss …

- what could be the advantages of spending a period of time abroad for apprentices,
- how the company can benefit from it,
- how the success of the internship could be evaluated.

Incoterms® 2010

In international trade the eleven Incoterms® 2010 Rules (international commercial terms) are used in contracts of sale to define the rights and obligations of the buyer and seller as regards risk, transport, insurance, packing, customs duty and documentation. They are terms of delivery.

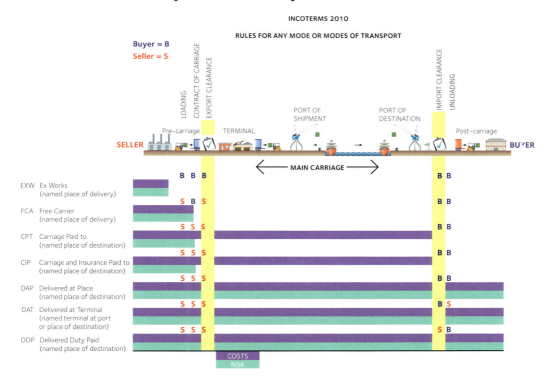

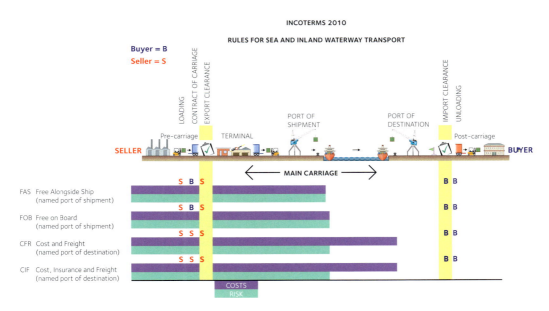

Incoterms® 2010

Rules for any mode or modes of transport

EXW – EX WORKS (... named place of delivery)
The seller makes the goods available at his premises in the customary packing. The seller assists the buyer in obtaining any documentation needed at the buyer's expense. The buyer is responsible for loading the goods, transporting them to their destination, customs clearance and insurance.

FCA – FREE CARRIER (... named place of delivery) Multimodal transport
The seller is not responsible for the main carriage of the goods. The seller delivers the goods at his own expense and risk, in the customary packing, cleared for export to the carrier nominated by the buyer. The seller provides the commercial invoice and, if requested, a certificate of origin at the buyer's expense. If the goods are collected at the seller's premises, the seller loads the goods. The seller bears the risks until the goods are in the custody of the first carrier. After that the buyer bears all the costs and risks of transporting the goods to their destination.

CPT – CARRIAGE PAID TO (... named place of destination) Multimodal transport
The seller pays for the main carriage of the goods. The seller delivers the goods, in the customary packing, cleared for export to the carrier which he nominates. The seller bears the risk until the goods have been delivered into the custody of the first carrier. The seller pays the transport costs for the goods, excluding transport insurance, up to the named destination. The buyer is responsible for insuring the goods for the main carriage and pays all import duties and taxes.

CIP – COST AND INSURANCE PAID TO (... named place of destination) Multimodal transport
The seller pays for the main carriage of the goods. The seller delivers the goods in the customary packing, cleared for export to the carrier which he nominates. The seller bears the risk until the goods have been delivered into the custody of the first carrier. The seller pays the transport costs for the goods, including transport insurance, up to the named destination. The buyer pays all import duties and taxes.

DAP – DELIVERED AT PLACE (... named place of destination) Multimodal transport
The seller is responsible for the carriage of the goods in the customary packing, cleared for export to the named terminal at the destination by the carrier which he nominates. He bears the risk until the goods have been delivered to the named terminal. The buyer is responsible for unloading the goods at the place of destination and pays all import duties and taxes.

DAT – DELIVERED AT TERMINAL (... named terminal at port or place of destination) Multimodal transport
The seller is responsible for the carriage of the goods in the customary packing, cleared for export to the named terminal at the destination by the carrier which he nominates. He bears the risk until the goods have been delivered to the named terminal. The seller is responsible for unloading the goods at the place of destination. The buyer pays all import duties and taxes.

DDP – DELIVERED DUTY PAID (... named place of destination) Multimodal transport
The seller is responsible for the carriage of the goods in the customary packing, cleared for export to the named terminal at the destination by the carrier which he nominates. He bears the risk until the goods have been delivered to the named destination. The seller pays all import duties and taxes. The buyer is responsible for unloading the goods at the place of destination.

Incoterms® 2010

Rules for sea and inland waterway transport

FAS – FREE ALONGSIDE SHIP (... named port of shipment)
The seller is not responsible for the main carriage of the goods. The seller delivers the goods at his own expense and risk, in the customary packing, cleared for export, alongside the vessel selected by the buyer at the named port of shipment. Thereafter, the buyer bears all the costs and risks of transporting the goods to their destination.

FOB – FREE ON BOARD (... named port of shipment)
The seller is not responsible for the main carriage of the goods. The seller delivers the goods at his own expense and risk, in the customary packing, cleared for export, on board the vessel selected by the buyer unless otherwise agreed, at the named port of shipment. Thereafter, the buyer bears all the costs and risks of transporting the goods to their destination.

CFR – COST AND FREIGHT (... named port of destination)
The seller pays for the main carriage of the goods. The seller delivers the goods at his own expense and risk, in the customary packing, cleared for export, on board the vessel selected by the buyer, at the named port of shipment. The seller pays the transport costs for the goods, excluding transport insurance, up to the named port of destination. The buyer is responsible for insuring the goods for the main carriage and pays all import duties and taxes.

CIF – COST INSURANCE FREIGHT (... named port of destination)
The seller pays for the main carriage of the goods. The seller delivers the goods at his own expense and risk, in the customary packing, cleared for export, on board the vessel selected by the buyer, at the named port of shipment. The seller pays the transport costs for the goods, including transport insurance, up to the named port of destination. The buyer pays all import duties and taxes.

Terms of payment

payment in advance	Vorauszahlung/Vorkasse
cash with order (CWO)	Barzahlung bei Auftragserteilung
payment by irrevocable and confirmed documentary (letter of) credit	Zahlung durch unwiderrufliches und bestätigtes Dokumentenakkreditiv
documents against payment (D/P) / cash against documents (CAD)	Kasse gegen Dokumente
cash on delivery (COD)	gegen Nachnahme
1/3 with order, 1/3 on delivery, 1/3 within 30 days after delivery	1/3 bei Auftragserteilung, 1/3 bei Lieferung, 1/3 innerhalb von 30 Tagen nach Lieferung
payment within 60 days from date of invoice	Zahlung innerhalb von 60 Tagen nach Rechnungsdatum
10 days 2%, 30 days net	Zahlung innerhalb 10 Tagen abzüglich 2 % Skonto oder innerhalb 30 Tagen netto
payment on receipt of goods	Zahlung bei Erhalt der Waren
payment on receipt of invoice	Zahlung bei Rechnungserhalt
documents against (three months') acceptance (D/A)	Dokumente gegen (Dreimonats-)Akzept
open account terms with monthly/quarterly settlement	offenes Zahlungsziel mit monatlicher/ vierteljährlicher Abrechnung

Useful phrases

A visit to a new company
Unit 1

Finding out what you can do for someone

- Can I help you? / How can I help you? / Can I be of any assistance?
- Kann ich Ihnen helfen? / Wie kann ich Ihnen helfen? / Kann ich Ihnen behilflich sein?

Explaining the reason for your visit

- I have an appointment with / would like to see … (name).
- Ich habe einen Termin mit / möchte gern … zu (Name).

- I am here for an interview.
- Ich bin zu einem Vorstellungsgespräch da.

Saying that someone is sorry for not being there

- … (name) is in a meeting at the moment.
- … (Name) ist gerade in einer Besprechung.

Saying that you're happy to meet someone

- Pleased/Nice to meet you.
- Schön/Nett, Sie kennenzulernen.

- Good to see you again.
- Es freut mich, Sie wiederzusehen.

- Great to meet you in person at last.
- Es freut mich, Sie endlich persönlich kennenzulernen.

Introducing people who have never met

- Can/May I introduce you to … (name)?
- Kann/Darf ich Ihnen … (Name) vorstellen?

- This is … (name) from … (department).
- Dies ist … (Name) von … (Abteilung).

- … (name) will introduce you to … (name) who is our … (function).
- … (Name) wird Sie … (Name) vorstellen. Er/Sie ist unser/e … (Funktion).

Describing jobs and responsibilities
Unit 1

Saying where you work

- I work / am a trainee / at the company headquarters / production facility / distribution centre / in the … department.
- Ich arbeite / bin Auszubildende(r) / in der Hauptfiliale / Produktionsanlage / im Vertriebszentrum / in der … -Abteilung.

Saying what you are responsible for

- I'm responsible for / in charge of sales / customer relations / looking after our trainees.
- Ich bin für den Verkauf / die Kundenbetreuung / unsere Auszubildenden verantwortlich/zuständig.

Saying where you and your team are in the company hierarchy

- I work for/with/alongside the other staff / employees / in the … department.
- Ich arbeite für/mit den anderen Mitarbeitern/ Angestellten der … -Abteilung.

- I liaise/communicate/cooperate with …
- Ich arbeite zusammen / kommuniziere/kooperiere mit …

- I have a team of … (number) staff who report to me.
- Mir untersteht ein Team von … (Anzahl) Mitarbeitern.

- The team I work in/with reports directly to the head of department / chief executive officer.
- Das Team, in/mit dem ich arbeite, untersteht direkt dem (der) Abteilungsleiter(in)/Geschäftsführer(in).

Talking about your department or team

- The department's/team's job is incredibly important.
- Die Rolle der Abteilung / des Teams ist äußerst wichtig.

- Basically, our job is to sell/advertise our products.
- Im Wesentlichen ist es unsere Aufgabe, unsere Produkte zu verkaufen/bewerben.

- The department looks at / monitors/analyses the market.
- Die Abteilung beobachtet/analysiert den Markt.

- This is very important because … (reason).
- Dies ist sehr wichtig, weil … (Grund).

- The department/team also looks after our staff / workers and makes sure that they are doing their work properly / get paid on time.
- Die Abteilung / Das Team kümmert sich auch um unsere Angestellten/Mitarbeiter und sorgt dafür, dass sie Ihre Arbeit ordnungsgemäß ausführen / rechtzeitig bezahlt werden.

122

Useful phrases

Directions
Unit 1

Asking for directions

- Excuse me. Can you tell me how to get / how do you get to the ... department, please?
- Can you tell me how to find / give me directions to the canteen / staff café / kitchen / conference / photocopier room?

- Entschuldigen Sie. Können Sie mir bitte sagen, wie ich zur Abteilung ... komme?
- Können Sie mir bitte sagen, wie ich zur Kantine / Cafeteria / zum Tagungsraum / Kopiererraum komme?

Giving directions

- Go up/along the corridor. Take the second turning on the right/left. It's the first door on the right/left just after the conference room / stationery cupboard.

- Gehen Sie den Gang entlang. Nehmen Sie den zweiten Gang rechts/links. Es ist die erste Tür rechts/links gleich hinter dem Tagungsraum/ Bürobedarfschrank.

Asking for and offering help and giving instructions
Unit 2

Asking for help

- I'm stuck. Could you help me with this, please?
- Could you tell me what to do / how to do it, please?

- Ich komme nicht weiter. Könnten Sie mir bitte helfen?
- Könnten Sie mir bitte sagen, was ich tun / wie ich das machen soll?

Offering help

- I'll explain/show / tell you what you have to do. Is that OK?

- Ich erkläre/zeige/sage Ihnen, was Sie machen müssen. Ist das in Ordnung?

Asking what the next step is

- What should I do next? / And then / now what do I do?
- What is the next step?

- Und was mache ich jetzt/dann?
- Welches ist der nächste Schritt?

Instructions

- Before you begin, make sure you have disconnected the cable from the socket / turned off the electricity.
- So, first of all you have to ...
- After that / Then you need to ...
- Once / After you have ..., you should ...
- Just carefully remove the broken component/part/ old printer cartridge and then ...
- ... seal it in a plastic bag before disposing of it.
- You need to remove the new/replacement part from the packaging ...
- ... and then put it in the ... (tool/machine).

- Bevor Sie beginnen, stellen Sie sicher, dass Sie das Kabel aus der Steckdose gezogen / den Strom abgeschaltet haben.
- Also, zuerst müssen Sie ...
- Dann/Danach müssen Sie ...
- Nachdem Sie ..., sollten Sie ...
- Entfernen Sie sorgfältig das kaputte Geräteteil/Teil / die alte Druckerpatrone und dann ...
- ... verschließen Sie es/sie/ihn in einer Plastiktüte, bevor Sie es/sie/ihn entsorgen.
- Sie müssen das neue Teil/Ersatzteil aus der Verpackung nehmen ...
- ... und setzen Sie es in ... (Werkzeug/Gerät).

Making suggestions
Unit 3

- We'd like to propose/suggest that ...
- We recommend that you ...
- In our opinion you should ...
- We believe you should ...
- Perhaps you might consider ...
- May I suggest ...?
- Have you thought about ...?

- Wir möchten vorschlagen, dass ...
- Wir empfehlen, dass Sie ...
- Unserer Meinung nach sollten Sie ...
- Wir glauben, dass Sie ...
- Vielleicht ziehen Sie in Betracht, ...
- Darf ich vorschlagen ...?
- Haben Sie schon daran gedacht, ...?

Making a telephone call
Unit 4

Answering the telephone

- Good morning/afternoon/evening. ... (name) speaking. / This is ... (name). / How can/may I help / be of assistance?

- Guten Morgen/Tag/Abend. ... (Name) am Apparat. / Hier spricht ... (Name). Wie kann ich Ihnen helfen / Ihnen behilflich sein?

123

Useful phrases

Saying who you are and who you want to speak to

- This is … *(name)* from … *(company/organisation)*. I'd like to speak to … *(name)*, please.
- *Hier spricht … (Name) von … (Firma/Organisation). Ich möchte … (Name) sprechen, bitte.*

Asking someone to hold

- Hold on a moment please. I'll see if I can get him/her for you.
- *Einen Moment, bitte. Ich schaue mal, ob er/sie da ist.*
- Are you still there?
- *Sind Sie noch dran?*

Apologising that someone is not there and asking when they will be back

- I'm sorry but I'm afraid … *(name)* isn't in the office/is out at the moment/seeing one of our customers just now.
- *Es tut mir leid, aber … (Name) ist gerade nicht im Büro/Haus/im Kundengespräch.*
- Sorry, but … *(name)* isn't free to come to the phone right now.
- *Leider kann … (Name) gerade nicht ans Telefon kommen.*
- Could you tell me when he/she will be back, please?
- *Könnten Sie mir bitte sagen, wann er/sie wieder da ist?*

Taking a message

- Can I take a message for him/her?
- *Kann ich eine Nachricht für ihn/sie hinterlassen?*
- Could you tell him/her that … *(name)* from … *(company/organisation)* called, please?
- *Könnten Sie ihm/ihr bitte sagen, dass … (Name) von … (Firma/Organisation) angerufen hat?*
- Sorry, I didn't catch your name. Could you spell it for me, please?
- *Ihren Namen habe ich leider (akustisch) nicht verstanden. Könnten Sie ihn mir bitte buchstabieren?*

Asking why someone is calling

- May/Can I ask what it's about?
- *Darf ich fragen, worum es geht?*
- Could you tell me what it's about?
- *Könnten Sie mir sagen, worum es geht?*
- It's about a potential order/repeat order for some of your … *(product)*.
- *Es geht um eine mögliche Bestellung/Nachbestellung Ihres … (Produkt).*

Calling someone back later

- Can I get … *(name)* to call you back?
- *Kann … (Name) Sie zurückrufen?*
- I'll let … *(name)* know you called.
- *Ich sage … (Name), dass Sie angerufen haben.*
- Thank you very much. Could you tell him/her he/she can call anytime until … *(time)* this evening?
- *Vielen Dank. Könnten Sie ihm/ihr sagen, dass er/sie jederzeit bis… (Uhrzeit) heute Abend anrufen kann?*
- Thanks for your call/for calling/returning my call.
- *Vielen Dank für Ihren Anruf/Rückruf.*

Ending a telephone call

- Have a nice day/evening/weekend. Goodbye/Bye.
- *Ich wünsche Ihnen einen schönen Tag/Abend. Auf Wiederhören/Tschüs.*

Making an order   Unit 4

Talking about specific products

- I was looking at some of your … *(products)* on your website/in your brochure and am really interested in …
- *Ich habe mir einige Ihrer … (Produkte) auf Ihrer Website/in Ihrer Broschüre angesehen und bin sehr an … interessiert.*
- Can you tell me which models you have been considering/ which product/model you're interested in?
- *Könnten Sie mir sagen, welche Modelle Sie in Betracht ziehen/für welches Produkt/Modell Sie sich interessieren?*
- Which model would be of most interest to you?
- *Welches Modell finden Sie am interessantesten?*
- We want to offer/provide … *(service)* so we need something which is suitable for that.
- *Wir möchten … (Service) anbieten und brauchen deshalb dafür etwas Passendes.*
- The two/ones which seem to be most interesting are …
- *Die zwei/Diejenigen, die am interessantesten zu sein scheinen, sind …*

Making a suggestion and offering advice

- Can I make a suggestion?/Could I suggest something?
- *Darf ich Ihnen einen Vorschlag machen?*
- I would definitely advise you to choose that./My advice would certainly be to go for that.
- *Ich würde Ihnen auf jeden Fall raten, sich dafür zu entscheiden.*

Useful phrases

Size of the order

- What sort of scale would you be ordering on?/Would you be able to say how big your order will be?

- I'd like to order/I think only about … *(number/ amount)* at first.

- If the … *(service)* is popular then we'll buy/order more.

- *In welcher Größenordnung bewegt sich Ihre Bestellung?/Könnten Sie mir sagen, wie groß Ihre Bestellung sein wird?*

- *Ich möchte zunächst nur … (Anzahl/Menge) bestellen.*

- *Wenn … (Service) gut ankommt, werden wir mehr kaufen/bestellen.*

Prices

- Can you tell me how much that will cost then?

- So, the … *(product)* costs … *(price)* and the … *(product)* costs … *(price)*. That will come to/makes … *(price)* including VAT.

- *Könnten Sie mir sagen, wie viel das dann kosten wird?*

- *Also, … (Produkt) kostet … (Preis) und … (Produkt) kostet … (Preis). Zuzüglich Mehrwertsteuer kostet/ macht das … (Preis).*

Discussing delivery

- How quickly could you deliver these to us?

- If we confirm your order and how you'd like to pay now, I can get it/them to you by normal delivery for … *(date)*.

- I could do an express delivery to you this evening/ tomorrow/next week, but that would cost a bit more/requires a surcharge.

- I'd like/I'll just go for the normal/standard/express delivery, please.

- *Wie schnell könnten Sie uns diese liefern?*

- *Wenn wir Ihre Bestellung und Zahlweise jetzt bestätigen, würden Sie es/sie/ihn am … (Datum) erhalten.*

- *Ich könnte Ihnen eine Expresslieferung bis heute Abend/Morgen/nächste Woche anbieten, allerdings kostet das etwas mehr/ist das mit einem Aufpreis verbunden.*

- *Ich entscheide mich für die Normal-/Express- zustellung.*

Meeting customers at trade fairs   Unit 5

Introducing yourself and asking to see someone

- Good morning/afternoon. My name's … Is … *(name)* here?

- *Guten Morgen/Tag. Mein Name ist … Ist … (Name zu sprechen?*

Apologising that someone isn't there and offering to help

- I'm afraid … *(name)* isn't here at the moment. He'll/ She'll be back in about/around half an hour/at … *(time)*. I'm … *(name)*, one of his/her colleagues. Could I help you maybe?

- *Es tut mir leid, aber … (Name) ist gerade nicht da. Er/Sie sollte in etwa einer halben Stunde/um … (Uhrzeit) wieder da sein. Ich bin … (Name), ein Kollege von ihm/ihr. Kann ich Ihnen vielleicht helfen?*

Saying what you are interested in

- I'm very interested in some of/would like to find out about the company's new … *(product)*. Would you be able to tell me something about them?

- *Ich bin sehr an einigen der neuen … (Produkte) Ihrer Firma interessiert. Könnten Sie mir etwas darüber sagen?*

Asking someone to wait

- … *(name)* would be the best person for/knows most about that. Would you like to wait for him/her?

- Would you like to take a seat?

- Can I offer you a cup of tea or coffee?

- You can watch a video/presentation showing our latest models/products/range while you wait.

- Can I offer you some of our promotional gifts/free samples?

- *… (Name) wäre da Ihr(e) Ansprechpartner(in)/weiß darüber am besten Bescheid. Möchten Sie auf ihn/ sie warten?*

- *Möchten Sie sich setzen?*

- *Kann ich Ihnen eine Tasse Tee oder Kaffee anbieten?*

- *Sie können sich ein Video/eine Präsentation über unsere neuesten Modelle/Produkte/ neueste Angebotspalette ansehen, während Sie warten.*

- *Kann ich Ihnen einige unserer Werbegeschenke/ kostenlosen Proben/Muster anbieten?*

Making an appointment   Unit 5

Introducing yourself

- Good morning/afternoon. My name is … *(name)* from … *(company)*.

- *Guten Morgen/Tag. Ich bin … (Name) von … (Firma).*

125

Useful phrases

Saying what you want to talk about

- I'd like to meet you again to talk about/discuss the order we talked about at the trade fair/conference last month.
- Ich möchte mich erneut mit Ihnen treffen, um die Bestellung zu besprechen, die wir auf der Messe/Konferenz im letzten Monat vereinbart haben.

Asking for an appointment

- Could I possibly make an appointment to come and see you?
- Könnte ich bitte einen Termin mit Ihnen vereinbaren?

- I'm going to be at the company/trade fair on … (day) and … (day). Is there a time on either of those days that would suit you?
- Ich werde am … (Tag) und … (Tag) in der Firma/auf der Messe sein. Würde Ihnen ein Zeitpunkt an einem dieser beide Tage passen?

Suggesting a time

- How about/Are you free at … (time) on … (day)?
- Wie sieht es mit/Haben Sie am … (Tag) um … (Uhrzeit) Zeit?

Saying you can't make that time

- No, I'm afraid/sorry that won't work.
- Nein, das geht leider nicht.

- I won't be able to make that, unfortunately.
- Das werde ich leider nicht schaffen.

- I'm sorry but I have a plane/train to catch/am meeting a client/have another appointment then.
- Es tut mir leid, aber ich muss meinen Flug/Zug erreichen/mich mit einem Kunden treffen/habe einen anderen Termin.

Making an alternative suggestion

- Could I suggest … (time) on … (day) instead?
- Kann ich stattdessen … (Tag) um … (Uhrzeit) vorschlagen?

- Would you be able to make … (time) on … (day)?
- Könnten Sie am … (Tag) um … (Uhrzeit)?

- Why don't we meet at … (time) on … (day) for lunch?
- Wir wäre es, wenn wir uns am … (Tag) um … (Uhrzeit) zum Mittagessen treffen?

Agreeing to the suggestion

- I think that would/should work/I can make that. I look forward to seeing you then. See you on … (day/date).
- Ich denke, das klappt/passt. Ich freue mich darauf, Sie dann zu sehen. Bis … (Tag/Datum).

Shipment

Unit 5

Placing an order

- We really liked your new … (products) and would like to order/place an order for … (number) of … (products).
- Uns gefallen Ihre neuen … (Produkte) sehr und wir möchten eine Bestellung über … (Anzahl, Produkte) aufgeben.

Discussing prices

- So how much would that cost?
- Wie viel wird das kosten?

- What does that come to altogether?
- Was macht das insgesamt?

- The … (products) have a wholesale price of … So that makes/would be … (price) for … (number). But shipping costs have to be added to that.
- Die … (Produkte) haben einen Großhandelspreis von … Es beläuft sich also auf … (Preis) für … (Anzahl). Aber Transportkosten müssen hinzugerechnet werden.

Describing shipping options

- There are a number of shipment options.
- Es stehen mehrere Versandmöglichkeiten zur Auswahl.

- So let's start with road haulage. That is certainly the cheapest way to ship the … (products). But it also takes the most time.
- Beginnen wir also mit Straßentransport. Dies ist sicherlich die günstigste Möglichkeit, die … (Produkte) zu transportieren. Aber es dauert auch am längsten.

- If you choose road haulage, the … (products) will take … (number) days/weeks to arrive.
- Wenn Sie sich für Straßentransport entscheiden, kommen die … (Produkte) innerhalb von … (Anzahl) Tagen/Wochen an.

- Rail freight is slightly/a bit more expensive, but also a bit/much faster. If you ship the … (products) by rail, you will get them within … (number) days/weeks.
- Bahnfracht ist etwas teurer, dafür aber ein wenig/viel schneller. Wenn Sie die … (Produkte) per Bahn versenden, bekommen Sie sie innerhalb von … (Anzahl) Tagen/Wochen.

126

Useful phrases

- Of course, we could also send the … (products) by air. If we send the … (products) as air freight, you will get them within a few hours. But then it's terribly/really expensive.

- Wir können die … (Produkte) natürlich auch auf dem Luftweg versenden. Wenn wir die … (Produkte) als Luftfracht versenden, bekommen Sie sie innerhalb weniger Stunden. Aber dann ist es wirklich/sehr teuer.

Writing reminders
Unit 5

First reminder

- I am writing with reference to the invoice mentioned above which has as yet not been settled.

- Ich schreibe bezüglich der oben genannten Rechnung, die bisher noch nicht beglichen wurde.

- We would be grateful if you could settle your account in the next few days.

- Wir wären Ihnen dankbar, wenn Sie diese Rechnung in den nächsten Tagen begleichen würden.

- We would be grateful if you could remit the amount due within one week.

- Wir wären Ihnen dankbar, wenn Sie den offenen Betrag innerhalb einer Woche überweisen könnten.

- We are certain that you have simply overlooked the invoice and will clear the account in the near future.

- Wir sind sicher, dass Sie die Rechnung einfach übersehen haben und dass Sie den offenen Betrag in naher Zukunft begleichen werden.

- If you have already remitted the amount due, please ignore this letter.

- Falls Sie den ausstehenden Betrag bereits überwiesen haben, können Sie dieses Schreiben als gegenstandslos betrachten.

Further and final reminders

- Given that we have already sent you one reminder and have still heard nothing from you, we are growing concerned about the situation regarding your payment.

- Da wir Ihnen bereits eine Zahlungserinnerung gesendet und bislang nichts von Ihnen gehört haben, machen wir uns zunehmend Sorgen bezüglich Ihrer Zahlung.

- Despite the fact that we have already sent you … (number) reminders, we have still to receive payment.

- Obwohl wir Ihnen bereits … (Anzahl) Mahnungen gesendet haben, ist die Zahlung bei uns noch immer nicht eingegangen.

- We must now insist that your account is cleared within the coming … (number) days.

- Wir bestehen nun darauf, dass der offene Betrag innerhalb der nächsten … (Anzahl) Tage beglichen wird.

- We are left with no choice, but to press you to settle the invoice within … (number) working days.

- Uns bleibt nichts anderes übrig, als Sie zur Zahlung innerhalb von … (Anzahl) Werktagen aufzufordern.

Threatening legal action

- Please settle your account with us immediately or we will be forced to take legal steps against you straightaway.

- Bitte begleichen Sie sofort den Betrag, sonst sehen wir uns dazu gezwungen, umgehend rechtliche Schritte gegen Sie einzuleiten.

- We will give you a further … (number) days to remit the amount due, after which time we will be passing the matter into the hands of our solicitors.

- Sie haben noch … (Anzahl) Tage Zeit, den ausstehenden Betrag zu begleichen, dann werden wir diese Angelegenheit unseren Anwälten übergeben.

Dealing with customers
Unit 6

Offering help

- What can I do for you?

- Wie kann ich Ihnen helfen / behilflich sein?

- Would you like some help/assistance?

- Brauchen Sie Hilfe?

Saying you are sorry that a customer has a problem

- Oh dear. I'm sorry to hear that.

- Oje. Es tut mir leid, das zu hören.

- Let me / I'll see what I can do.

- Ich werde schauen, was ich für Sie tun kann.

- Let me take a look at that for you.

- Lassen Sie mich das einmal anschauen.

- I'm really sorry that you've had problems.

- Es tut mir wirklich leid, dass Sie Probleme hatten.

Asking a customer to wait

- I'll be right with you / with you in a minute.

- Ich bin gleich bei Ihnen.

- Sorry. Do you mind waiting a moment?

- Entschuldigung. Könnten Sie bitte einen Moment warten?

127

Useful phrases

Thanking a customer

- Thanks / Thank you very much. Goodbye now.
- We hope to see you again soon.

- *Vielen Dank. Auf Wiedersehen.*
- *Wir hoffen, Sie bald wieder bei uns begrüßen zu dürfen.*

Customer complaints
Unit 6

Talking about a problem

- I bought a … *(product)* here recently, but it's broken / not working properly.
- I'm sorry about / to hear that. Can I ask what the problem is?
- Do you have your … with you? And the receipt. I need that as well.

- *Ich habe hier neulich ein … (Produkt) gekauft, aber es ist kaputt / funktioniert nicht richtig.*
- *Das tut mir leid. Darf ich fragen, was das Problem ist?*
- *Haben Sie Ihr … dabei? Und der Kassenbon. Den bräuchte ich auch.*

Asking for help

- Can you help me with my problem, please?
- Can you fix/mend my …, please?

- *Könnten Sie mir bitte mit meinem Problem helfen?*
- *Könnten Sie bitte mein … reparieren?*

Asking for a refund

- I'd like a refund, please.
- Could you give me a refund?
- I want my money back.

- *Ich hätte gern den Kaufpreis erstattet.*
- *Könnten Sie mir den Kaufpreis erstatten?*
- *Ich will mein Geld zurück.*

Talking about company policy

- I'm sorry, but I'm afraid I can't give you a refund.
- It's company policy to send … *(product)* back to the manufacturer for repair.
- We don't give money back straight away.
- I'm not allowed to do that.
- We can normally send/get the … *(product)* back to you within … *(number)* days/weeks.

- *Es tut mir leid, aber ich kann Ihnen den Kaufpreis nicht erstatten.*
- *Es ist Firmenpolitik, … (Produkt) an den Hersteller zur Reparatur zurückzuschicken.*
- *Wir können den Kaufpreis nicht sofort erstatten.*
- *Das darf ich nicht.*
- *Im Normalfall bekommen Sie … (Produkt) innerhalb von … (Anzahl) Tagen/Wochen wieder.*

Complaining about customer service

- I'm sorry but this just isn't acceptable.
- This is really useless/terrible customer service.
- I certainly won't be coming back here again.

- *Es tut mir leid, aber das ist völlig inakzeptabel.*
- *Ihr Kundenservice ist wirklich nutzlos/schlecht.*
- *Ich komme mit Sicherheit nicht mehr hierher.*

Asking an angry customer to calm down

- I can see that you're upset/angry, but if you shout, it makes it hard for me to help. I'm only doing my job here.
- Please, calm down.

- *Ich sehe, dass Sie aufgebracht/wütend sind, aber wenn Sie schreien, kann ich Ihnen schlecht weiterhelfen. Ich mache ich hier nur meine Arbeit.*
- *Bitte beruhigen Sie sich.*

Making the customer an offer

- I can offer a replacement while your … *(product)* is being repaired / away for repair.

- *Ich kann Ihnen einen Ersatz anbieten, während … (Produkt) repariert wird.*

Arranging a business trip
Unit 7

Booking flights

- I'd like to fly to … *(place)* on … *(day)* next week with … *(number)* colleagues. Could you organise travel and accommodation for us, please?
- We need to be in … *(place)* for a meeting at … *(time)*. We're coming back on … *(date)* afternoon/morning.

- Business/first/economy class, please.
- Is that a direct flight?
- Are there any available/free seats on these flights?

- *Am … (Tag) nächster Woche möchte ich mit … (Anzahl) Kollegen nach … (Ort) fliegen. Könnten Sie bitte für uns Flug und Unterkunft organisieren?*
- *Wir müssen um … (Zeit) bei einer Besprechung in … (Ort) sein. Wir kommen am … (Datum) am Nachmittag/Vormittag zurück.*
- *Business Class / erste Klasse / Economy Class, bitte.*
- *Ist das ein Direktflug?*
- *Sind noch freie Plätze / Plätze verfügbar auf diesen Flügen?*

Useful phrases

- That's a bit late/early really. Isn't there anything earlier/later?
- How much do the flights cost?

- Das ist eigentlich ein bisschen zu spat/früh. Gibt es eine frühere/ spätere Verbindung?
- Wie viel kosten die Flüge?

Describing hotel facilities

- Let me tell you a bit about the hotel. Well, the first thing is that all the staff speak English.

- It offers first-class/high-quality, modern accommodation and business facilities.
- Its accommodation comprises … suites, … single rooms and … double rooms …
- … all fully-equipped with a telephone, satellite TV and en-suite bathrooms.
- The hotel also has a business centre with fax, printing and photocopying services and secure internet access …
- … and conference rooms for meetings with the latest presentation technology such as digital projectors and cordless microphones.
- The hotel also offers a full range of leisure facilities. There's a sauna, steam room and massage service.

- Guests can take advantage of free internet access via WLAN in all the rooms.
- Room and laundry services are available 24 hours a day and there is a car park.

- Lassen Sie mich Ihnen ein wenig über das Hotel erzählen. Also, erstens spricht das ganze Personal Englisch.
- Es bietet erstklassige/hochklassige, moderne Unterkünfte und Geschäftseinrichtungen.
- Die Unterkünfte umfassen … Suiten, … Einzelzimmer und … Doppelzimmer …,
- … die mit Telefon, Satellitenfernseher und eigenem Bad ausgestattet sind.
- Zudem verfügt das Hotel über ein Business-Center mit Fax-, Drucker- und Kopierservice und sicherem Internetzugang …
- … sowie Tagungsräume für Besprechungen mit den neusten Präsentationstechnologien wie Beamer und schnurlosen Mikrofonen.
- Darüber hinaus bietet das Hotel eine ganze Reihe an Freizeiteinrichtungen. Es gibt eine Sauna, ein Dampfbad und einen Massageservice.
- Gäste können kostenlosen WLAN-Internetzugang in allen Zimmern nutzen.
- Ein Zimmer- und Wäscheservice ist rund um die Uhr verfügbar und es gibt einen Parkplatz.

Booking a hotel

- I'd like to book the … (name of hotel) for … (number) people/colleagues for … (number) nights.
- How much does a single/double room cost?

- Ich möchte das … (Name des Hotels) für … (Anzahl) Personen/Kollegen für … (Anzahl) Nächte buchen.
- Wie viel kostet ein Einzel-/Doppelzimmer?

Checking in to the hotel

- Welcome to the … (name of hotel).
- How can I help you, sir/madam?
- My colleagues and I have reserved … (number) rooms for the next … (number) nights.
- What name is the reservation under?
- Could I just ask you to fill in a reservation form, please?
- Can I have an early morning call at … (time) tomorrow, please?
- Enjoy your stay.

- Willkommen bei … (Name des Hotels).
- Wie kann ich Ihnen behilflich sein?
- Meine Kollegen und ich haben … (Anzahl) Zimmer für die kommenden … (Anzahl) Nächte gebucht.
- Unter welchem Namen läuft die Reservierung?
- Darf ich Sie bitten, ein Reservierungsformular auszufüllen?
- Könnte ich morgen bitte einen Weckanruf um … (Uhrzeit) bekommen?
- Einen schönen Aufenthalt.

Small talk in a restaurant   Unit 7

Questions

- What do you do in your spare/free time?
- What else do you get up to when you're not working?
- How often do you …?
- Do you like …?
- Have you been to …?
- And what about you?

- Was machen Sie in Ihrer Freizeit?
- Was machen Sie noch so, wenn Sie nicht arbeiten?
- Wie oft machen Sie …?
- Mögen Sie …?
- Waren Sie schon in …?
- Und Sie?

Useful phrases

Letting someone know you're interested

- That's nice. It's good that you find the time to …
- Oh, really? Is that true? That's interesting.
- I know exactly what you mean.
- That sounds great.
- Sounds good.

- *Das ist schön. Es ist gut, dass Sie die Zeit finden, um zu …*
- *Ach, wirklich? Ist das wahr? Das ist ja interessant.*
- *Ich weiß genau, was Sie meinen.*
- *Das klingt großartig.*
- *Klingt gut.*

Presentations and visual aids   Unit 8

Introductions

- Good morning, ladies and gentlemen.
- Hello, everybody.
- I'm … *(name)* and I'm responsible for … *(function)* at … *(company)*. Thank you very much for the opportunity to talk to you this afternoon.

- I'm going to tell you about …
- Today, I want to describe to you …

- *Guten Morgen, meine Damen und Herren.*
- *Hallo allerseits.*
- *Ich heiße … (Name) und bin bei … (Firma) für … (Funktion) zuständig. Ich möchte mich herzlich bei Ihnen bedanken, hier heute Nachmittag vor Ihnen sprechen zu dürfen.*
- *Ich werde über … sprechen.*
- *Heute möchte ich Ihnen … beschreiben.*

Describing the structure of the presentation

- I'd like to talk about the structure of my presentation.
- To begin with / firstly, I'm going to talk about …
- The second section of my presentation will focus on …
- Then, I'll move on to …
- My next point will be about …
- Finally, I'll show you how …

- *Ich möchte über den Aufbau meiner Präsentation sprechen.*
- *Zuerst werde ich über … sprechen.*
- *Der zweite Teil meines Vortrags beschäftigt sich mit …*
- *Dann werde ich mich mit … befassen.*
- *Als Nächstes geht es um …*
- *Zuletzt zeige ich Ihnen, wie …*

Getting started

- Right, let's get started. I have a lot to talk about in the next … minutes and I think you will find it very interesting.
- I'll be happy to answer any questions at the end of the presentation.
- I'm going to start now by looking at my first topic …

- *Also, beginnen wir. Ich habe in den nächsten … Minuten über vieles zu sprechen und ich denke, es wird sehr interessant für Sie sein.*
- *Zum Schluss meiner Präsentation werde ich gern Ihre Fragen beantworten.*
- *Ich beginne nun mit dem ersten Thema …*

Referring to visuals

- If you look at my first slide, you can see that it summarises …
- If I can direct your attention to this slide, you'll see that it depicts/shows …
- You'll note from this line graph/pie chart, which describes our sales growth, that …

- Look at the pie chart on this slide. You'll note that it shows …
- The line graph here refers to … As the graph demonstrates …
- Now, on to my next slide which provides a few details/an overview about …

- *Wenn Sie sich die erste Folie anschauen, sehen Sie eine Zusammenfassung von …*
- *Wenn ich Ihre Aufmerksamkeit auf diese Folie lenken darf, werden Sie sehen, dass sie … darstellt.*
- *Bei diesem Linien-/Tortendiagramm, das unser Umsatzwachstum darstellt, werden Sie feststellen, dass …*
- *Sehen Sie sich das Tortendiagramm auf dieser Folie an. Sie werden bemerken, dass es … zeigt.*
- *Dieses Liniendiagramm bezieht sich auf … Wie aus dem Diagramm ersichtlich ist …*
- *Meine nächste Folie zeigt einige Details über/eine Übersicht der …*

Talking about stages in a process   Unit 9

Signposting a description

- First, …
- Secondly, …
- Then, …
- Next, …

- *Erstens …*
- *Zweitens …*
- *Dann …*
- *Als Nächstes …*

130

Useful phrases

- Finally/Lastly, …
- And then, …
- To end with, …

- *Zuletzt/Schließlich …*
- *Und dann …*
- *Zum Schluss …*

Describing processes

- Firstly, parts are brought to the …
- Next, the components are mounted to the …
- Then, the finished product is taken to …
- Finally, the product is … before it's …

- *Zuerst werden die Teile zum … gebracht.*
- *Dann werden die Bauteile an … montiert.*
- *Dann wird das fertige Produkt zum … gebracht.*
- *Schließlich wird das Produkt …, bevor es …*

Writing a covering letter
Unit 10

Opening phrases

- Dear Sir or Madam,
- I am writing to apply for the position of … which I saw advertised on the internet.
- In reply to/With reference to your advertisement in … *(newspaper, etc)* of … *(date)* …
- I see that you are looking for a…
- I wish to apply for the above-mentioned position of …
- I would like to be considered for the job and enclose my CV for your further information.

- *Sehr geehrte Damen und Herren,*
- *Hiermit bewerbe ich mich für die Stelle als …, die im Internet ausgeschrieben ist.*
- *Bezug nehmend auf Ihre Stellenanzeige in … (Zeitung usw.) vom … (Datum) …*
- *Wie ich sehe, suchen Sie eine/einen …*
- *Hiermit möchte ich mich für die oben genannte Stelle als … bewerben.*
- *Ich würde gerne bei der Stellenvergabe bedacht werden und füge zu Ihrer Information meinen Lebenslauf bei.*

Saying why you are applying for the job

- I would like to work in … *(country)* to gain experience of working abroad/in the country.
- Although my English is good, I would like to improve it by using it at work every day.

- I find the job with … very interesting as I am interested in …
- I developed this interest whilst working as a …

- *Ich möchte in … (Land) arbeiten, um Auslandserfahrungen zu sammeln.*
- *Obwohl ich bereits über gute Englischkenntnisse verfüge, würde ich sie gerne verbessern, indem ich die Sprache täglich bei der Arbeit verwende.*
- *Ich bin an der Stelle bei … sehr interessiert, weil ich mich für … interessiere.*
- *Dieses Interesse habe ich entwickelt, während ich als … arbeitete.*

Saying what you can offer your potential employer

- I am sure that I can offer you the right skills and personal qualities for the job.

- I like working with other people and feel that I am a good communicator.
- I am also well organised and have experience of working in a team/on my own.

- *Ich bin sicher, dass ich die von Ihnen gewünschten Fähigkeiten und Eigenschaften für den Posten mitbringe.*
- *Ich arbeite gern mit anderen zusammen und betrachte mich als sehr kommunikativen Menscher.*
- *Ich bin sehr gut organisiert und habe Erfahrungen mit Team-/Einzelarbeit.*

Education/training; present employment

- I attended … *(school/college)* for …
- I studied … at university/vocational school in … *(place)* from … to …
- At present I am working for … as a …

- *Von … bis … besuchte ich … (Schule)*
- *Ich besuchte die Universität/Berufsschule in … (Ort) von … bis …*
- *Zurzeit arbeite ich bei … als …*

131

Useful phrases

Closing paragraph

- I enclose my CV and a list of my qualifications and experience.
- I have tried to include all the information you need, but if you require further information, please do not hesitate to contact me.
- I hope you will consider my application favourably and …
- I look forward to hearing from you in the near future/ soon.
- I am available for interview at your earliest convenience.

- *Anbei finden Sie meinen Lebenslauf und eine Übersicht meiner Qualifikationen und Erfahrungen.*
- *Ich habe versucht, alle für Sie notwendigen Informationen beizufügen, sollten Sie aber weitere Informationen benötigen, können Sie mich gern jederzeit kontaktieren.*
- *Ich hoffe, Sie werden meine Bewerbung wohlwollen prüfen und …*
- *Ich freue mich, bald von Ihnen zu hören.*

- *Für ein Vorstellungsgespräch stehe ich Ihnen jederzeit gern zur Verfügung.*

Interviews

Unit 10

Talking about work experience

- I think I've got some quite relevant experience. While I was at school, I worked part-time in the … department at … I learned a lot there.

- It was really good because I've always been interested in … So that was the ideal job for me really.

- *Ich denke, ich verfüge über durchaus relevante Arbeitserfahrungen. Während meiner Schulzeit arbeitete ich Teilzeit in der … -Abteilung bei … Dort habe ich viel gelernt.*

- *Es war sehr gut, weil ich mich schon immer für … interessiere. Das war also für mich der ideale Job.*

Describing strengths and personal qualities

- First of all, I think I'm a hard worker. I like to finish a job and can concentrate on it until it is done properly.

- I'm also a fast learner. It doesn't take me long to understand new tasks and I like learning new things.

- I would also say that I am a good communicator which I think would be important in this job.

- And I'm self-motivated. And ambitious. I'd like to do well in this job and then get a better one as soon as I'm ready.

- *Zuerst einmal möchte ich sagen, dass ich mit großem persönlichem Einsatz arbeite. Ich führe Aufgaben gern bis zum Ende durch und kann mich darauf konzentrieren, bis sie vollständig erledigt sind.*

- *Zudem lerne ich schnell. Ich erfasse neue Aufgaben innerhalb kurzer Zeit und nehme gerne neue Herausforderungen an.*

- *Ich würde von mir auch behaupten, ein sehr kommunikativer Mensch zu sein, was meines Erachtens in diesem Beruf sehr wichtig ist.*

- *Und ich bin motiviert. Und ambitioniert. Ich möchte in dieser Position gute Arbeit leisten und dann möglichst eine bessere erlangen, sobald ich dafür die Fähigkeiten erworben habe.*

Describing weaknesses

- One of my weaknesses is that I sometimes think that I can't let go of a task. I have to keep working at it until I've got the perfect result. That can be a problem when you have lots of others things to get on with.

- *Eine meiner Schwächen liegt darin, dass ich manchmal eine Aufgabe nicht loslassen kann. Ich muss weiter daran arbeiten, bis ich das perfekte Ergebnis habe. Das kann problematisch sein, wenn man auch viel anderes zu erledigen hat.*

Questions for the interviewer

- How many people are in the team?
- When will I be able to take on/manage my own projects?
- Can I receive additional training for software and office systems?
- What promotion possibilities are there?
- Will I be able to gain some management experience?

- Who will I report to?

- *Wie viele arbeiten im Team?*
- *Ab wann werde ich eigene Projekte übernehmen dürfen?*
- *Besteht die Möglichkeit zur Weiterbildung im Bereich Software und Büroabläufe?*
- *Welche Aufstiegsmöglichkeiten gibt es?*
- *Werde ich Managementerfahrungen sammeln können?*

- *Wer wird mein Vorgesetzter?*

Basic word list

Dieses Liste enthält Grundwörter, die in *Business Matters* als bekannt vorausgesetzt werden.

A

able, to be ~ können, in der Lage sein
about über, etwa
above über, oben (stehend), oben genannt
absolutely absolut, völlig
accept annehmen, akzeptieren
across (quer) über
active aktiv(iert)
activity Tätigkeit, Aktivität
actor Schauspieler
actress Schauspielerin
add zusammenzählen, hinzufügen
address Adresse; adressieren
advert(isement) Werbung, Anzeige
afraid, I'm ~ leider
after nach
afternoon Nachmittag
again wieder
age Alter
agree zustimmen, vereinbaren, sich einigen
air Luft
airport Flughafen
all alle/r/s, ganze/r/s
allow erlauben, gestatten, (zu)lassen
almost fast, beinahe
alone allein/e
along entlang
already schon, bereits
also auch, außerdem
although obwohl
altogether insgesamt
always immer
a.m. vormittags, morgens (vor 12 Uhr)
among zwischen, unter
amount Menge, Betrag
angry wütend, verärgert
another noch eine/r/s
answer Antwort, Lösung; (be)antworten
anybody/anyone jemand, jede/r
anything etwas, alles
anyway jedenfalls, sowieso
anywhere irgendwo(hin)
apart from abgesehen von, außer
area Gebiet, Bereich
arrange arrangieren, vereinbaren, ausmachen
arrive ankommen
ask fragen, bitten
away weg, entfernt

B

back Rückseite, Rücken; zurück
bad schlecht, schlimm
bag Tasche, Tüte, Beutel
basic grundsätzlich, einfach
basically grundsätzlich, im Grunde
because weil
become werden
before vor(her)
begin anfangen, beginnen
beginning Anfang
behind hinter, hinten
believe glauben
belong gehören
below unter, unten (stehend)
best beste/r/s, am besten
better besser
between zwischen
big groß
biscuit Keks, Plätzchen
board Brett, Tafel
body Körper
book Buch; buchen, reservieren
bored gelangweilt
boring langweilig
born geboren
both beide
bottle Flasche
bottom Unterseite, Unterteil, Boden, Ende
box Kasten, Kästchen, Schachtel, Kiste
boy Junge
bracket Klammer
break Pause; (zer)brechen, kaputt machen
breakfast Frühstück
bring bringen, holen
broken kaputt
brother Bruder
build bauen, aufbauen, erbauen
building Gebäude
busy beschäftigt, besetzt
buy kaufen
bye tschüs

C

call Anruf; (an)rufen, nennen
caller Anrufer/in
camera Fotoapparat, Kamera
car Auto
care, take ~ of sich kümmern um
careful(ly) vorsichtig, sorgfältig
case Fall
cash Bargeld
certain(ly) sicher(lich), gewiss, bestimmt
chair Stuhl, Sessel

(continued)

change Änderung, Veränderung; (aus)wechseln, (sich) ändern
cheap billig, günstig
check überprüfen, kontrollieren
cheque Scheck
child Kind
choice Wahl, Auswahl
choose (aus)wählen
cinema Kino
city (Groß-)Stadt
class Klasse
classmate Klassenkamerad/in
clean sauber; reinigen, säubern
clear klar, deutlich
clever klug, intelligent
clock Uhr
close schließen, zumachen
close (to) nahe (bei)
clothes Kleidung, Kleider
clue Hinweis, Tipp
coffee Kaffee
colour Farbe
come kommen, geliefert werden
complete vollständig; vervollständigen
completely völlig
contact Kontakt, Verbindung
control Kontrolle; kontrollieren, regeln, steuern, überwachen
conversation Gespräch, Unterhaltung
copy Exemplar, Kopie; abschreiben, kopieren
corner Ecke
correct richtig, genau; korrigieren
cost Kosten; kosten
count zählen
country Land, Staat
couple Paar
course Kurs, Studiengang
create (er)schaffen, erstellen, gestalten
creative kreativ, schöpferisch
cross (an)kreuzen
culture Kultur
cup Tasse

D

damage Schaden, Beschädigung; beschädigen
danger Gefahr
dangerous gefährlich
dark Dunkelheit; dunkel
data Daten
date Datum, Termin
date of birth Geburtsdatum
day Tag
dear liebe/r/s
decide entscheiden, beschließen

133

Basic word list

definite(ly) (ganz) sicher, bestimmt, eindeutig
describe beschreiben
description Beschreibung, Schilderung
desk (Schreib-)Tisch, Schalter, Arbeitsplatz
details Einzelheiten, Angaben
dialogue Gespräch, Dialog
dictionary Wörterbuch
die sterben
difference Unterschied
different unterschiedlich, verschieden
difficult schwer, schwierig
dinner (Abend-)Essen
direct direkt, gerade
dirty schmutzig
dislike nicht mögen
door Tür
drink Getränk; trinken
drive fahren
during während

E
each jede/r/s
early früh
east (nach) Osten, Ost-
easy, easily leicht, einfach
education Erziehung, (Aus-, Schul-)Bildung
effective effektiv
either entweder
empty leer
end Ende, Schluss; (be)enden
ending Ende
energy Energie
enjoy genießen, gefallen, gern tun
enough ausreichend, genug
enter eintreten, betreten, eingeben
entrance Eingang, Einfahrt
especially besonders
even sogar (noch)
evening Abend
ever je(mals)
every jede/r/s
everybody jeder(mann), alle
everyone jeder(mann), alle
everything alles
exactly exakt, genau
example Beispiel
excellent hervorragend, ausgezeichnet
excited aufgeregt, begeistert
exciting aufregend, spannend
excuse Ausrede, Entschuldigung; entschuldigen
exercise Übung
exercise book (Schul-)Heft
expect erwarten, annehmen
expensive teuer

experience Erfahrung; erfahren, erleben
expert Fachmann/frau
extra zusätzlich
extreme äußerst
eye Auge

F
fact Tatsache
factory Fabrik
false falsch
family Familie
far weit (entfernt)
fast schnell
feel (sich) fühlen, meinen, glauben
feeling Gefühl, Meinung, Ansicht
(a) few ein paar, wenig/e
fight Kampf; (be)kämpfen
final letzte/r/s, endgültig
finally schließlich, endlich
financial finanziell
find finden, suchen
find out herausfinden
fine gut, schön, in Ordnung
finish (be)enden, abschließen, fertig werden
firm Firma
first erste/r/s; zuerst
flight Flug
floor Etage, Stockwerk; (Fuß-)Boden
fly fliegen
follow (be)folgen
(the) following der/die/das Folgende
food Essen, Nahrung
foreign ausländisch, Auslands-, fremd
forget vergessen
form Form, Formular; bilden, formen
forward nach vorne
free frei; gratis, kostenlos
friend Freund/in
friendly freund(schaft)lich
friendship Freundschaft
front Vorderseite
front, in ~ of vor
full voll
fully völlig
funny komisch, merkwürdig
further weitere/r/s, weiter
future Zukunft; (zu)künftig

G
gap Lücke
general allgemein, generell, normal
generally im Allgemeinen, normalerweise
get holen, bekommen, werden, gelangen

girl Mädchen
give geben
go gehen, fahren
go on weitermachen, fortfahren
go out ausgehen
good gut
goodbye auf Wiedersehen
great groß(artig)
greatly in hohem Maße
greet (be)grüßen
greeting Gruß(formel), Begrüßung
ground Boden, Grund
group Gruppe; gruppieren
grow wachsen, zunehmen
guess Annahme; raten, schätzen
guest Gast

H
half Hälfte; halb
hall Diele, Flur, Saal, Halle
handle umgehen mit, bearbeiten, erledigen, fertigwerden mit
happen passieren, geschehen
happy glücklich, zufrieden
health Gesundheit
hear hören
heart Herz
heavy schwer
height Höhe, Größe
help Hilfe; helfen
helpful hilfreich, nützlich
here hier
high; highly hoch; äußerst
history Geschichte
holiday Ferien, Urlaub, Feiertag
home Zuhause, Heim; nach Hause
hope Hoffnung; hoffen
horrible furchtbar, schrecklich
hot heiß, scharf
hour Stunde
house Haus
how wie
however doch, jedoch, allerdings
huge riesig
human menschlich
husband (Ehe-)Mann

I
idea Vorstellung, Idee
if wenn, falls, ob
ill krank
illness Krankheit
image Bild, Abbild
important wichtig
impossible unmöglich
individual Einzelperson; einzeln, individuell
industry Branche, Industrie
inform informieren, unterrichten

134

Basic word list

information Auskunft, Information(en), Angaben
inside innerhalb, innen, drinnen
instead stattdessen
instead of statt
interest Interesse; interessieren
interested interessiert
interesting interessant

J
job Arbeit(sstelle), Aufgabe
join beitreten, verbinden
just einfach, nur, genau

K
keep (be)halten, weiterhin tun
key Schlüssel, Taste, Haupt-
kind Art, Sorte; freundlich
kitchen Küche
knife Messer
know kennen, wissen

L
language Sprache
large groß
last dauern; letzte/r/s
late spät
later später
latest neueste/r/s
lead führen
learn lernen, erfahren
least, at ~ wenigstens
leave lassen, verlassen, hinterlassen, ab-/wegfahren
left links, übrig
length Länge
less weniger, abzüglich
let erlauben, (zu)lassen
letter Buchstabe, Brief
level Ebene, Niveau
lie Lüge; (be)lügen
life Leben
lift Fahrstuhl, Aufzug
light Licht, Leuchte; hell, leicht
like mögen, (ähnlich) wie
line Linie, Leitung, Zeile
list Liste; auflisten, notieren
listen zuhören
little klein, wenig
live wohnen, leben
local örtlich, lokal
log in/on einloggen
log off/out ausloggen
long lang
look Blick, Aussehen; (aus)sehen, blicken
look after sich kümmern um
look for suchen nach
look forward to sich freuen auf
lose verlieren
lots of/a lot of viel
love Liebe; lieben, sehr gern mögen

lovely schön, hübsch, reizend
low niedrig
lunch Mittagessen

M
machine Gerät, Maschine
magazine Zeitschrift
main Haupt-, wichtigste/r/s
make machen
manage leiten, verwalten, regeln, (es) schaffen
many viele
market Markt
match zuordnen, passen (zu)
maximum Maximum; maximal
may dürfen, können, mögen
maybe vielleicht
meal Essen, Mahlzeit
mean bedeuten, meinen, heißen
medium Medium, Mittel; mittlere/r/s
meet (zusammen)treffen, begegnen, sich (mit jdm) treffen
meeting Sitzung, Besprechung, Treffen
memory Gedächtnis, Erinnerung, Speicher
message Meldung, Nachricht, Mitteilung, Botschaft
metal Metall
middle Mitte
might könnte/n (vielleicht)
milk Milch
minimum Minimum; minimal
miss verpassen, vermissen
missing fehlende/r/s
mistake Fehler, Irrtum
mobile (phone) Mobiltelefon, Handy
money Geld
month Monat
more mehr
morning Morgen
most die meisten, am meisten
mountain Berg
mouse Maus
move (sich) bewegen, umziehen
movement Bewegung
much viel

N
name Name; nennen, benennen
national national, staatlich
near in der Nähe von
nearly beinahe, fast
necessary nötig, notwendig, erforderlich
need Bedarf, Bedürfnis; brauchen, benötigen
negative verneinend, negativ
neither … nor weder … noch
never nie(mals)
new neu

news Neuigkeit(en), Nachricht(en)
next nächste/r/s; danach
night Nacht
normal(ly) normal(erweise)
north (nach) Norden, Nord-
note Notiz, Anmerkung; beachten, notieren, bemerken, feststellen
nothing nichts
now nun, jetzt
nowadays heutzutage
number Nummer, Zahl, Anzahl

O
object Gegenstand
of course natürlich, selbstverständlich
offer Angebot; anbieten, bieten
office Büro
often oft, häufig
oil Öl
old alt
once einmal, einst, sobald
only nur, einzig
open öffnen, eröffnen; offen, geöffnet
opposite Gegenteil; gegensätzlich, gegenüber
option Möglichkeit, Option
or oder
order Bestellung, Auftrag, Reihenfolge; bestellen, ordnen
organisation Organisation
organise organisieren
original Original; original, ursprünglich
other andere/r/s
ought to sollen
outside außerhalb (von)
own eigen, besitzen

P
page Seite
pain Schmerz
pair Paar
paper Papier, Zeitung
part Teil, Bauteil
pay Lohn, Bezahlung; zahlen, bezahlen
per cent Prozent
perfect vollkommen, perfekt
perfectly völlig
perhaps vielleicht, eventuell
period Zeit(raum)
personal persönlich
phone Telefon; anrufen
photo(graphy) Foto(grafie)
phrase Redewendung, Satz(teil)
picture Bild
piece Stück, Teil
place Stelle, Platz; setzen, stellen
plan Plan; planen
plane Flugzeug

135

Basic word list

plastic Plastik, Kunststoff
plenty viel, reichlich
p.m. nachmittags, abends (nach 12 Uhr)
point Punkt
poor arm, schlecht, mangelhaft
popular beliebt, populär
position Stellung, Lage, Position
positive positiv, bejahend
possibility Möglichkeit
possible möglich
possibly möglicherweise
power Kraft, Strom; antreiben
powerful mächtig, stark
practical praktisch
practice Praxis, Training
practise (ein)üben, trainieren
prefer vorziehen, bevorzugen, lieber mögen
prepare (sich) vorbereiten, zubereiten, erstellen
present Gegenwart; Geschenk; aktuell, gegenwärtig; vorstellen, präsentieren
press drücken
price Preis
print Druck; drucken, ausdrucken
printer Drucker
private privat, persönlich
probably wahrscheinlich
produce produzieren, herstellen
product Produkt, Erzeugnis
program(me) Programm, Sendung
promise Versprechen; versprechen
provide liefern, (an)bieten, zur Verfügung stellen
public Öffentlichkeit; öffentlich
push schieben, drücken
put setzen, stellen, legen

Q

quality Eigenschaft, Qualität
(a) quarter past/to Viertel nach/vor
question Frage
quick(ly) schnell
quiet ruhig
quite ziemlich, ganz

R

rather ziemlich, lieber
reach erreichen, greifen
read lesen
reader Leser/in, Lektüre
ready bereit, fertig
real echt, wirklich
really wirklich, eigentlich, tatsächlich
reason Vernunft, Grund
receive erhalten, empfangen, bekommen

recent aktuell, neu, jüngst
recently neulich, vor kurzem, in letzter Zeit
recommend empfehlen
regular(ly) regelmäßig
relative Verwandte/r; relativ
remain (ver)bleiben
remember sich erinnern, daran denken
repeat wiederholen
report Bericht; berichten
reservation Reservierung, Buchung
reserve reservieren
respect Respekt, Achtung; (be)achten, respektieren
result Resultat, Ergebnis; folgen, resultieren
return zurückkehren, zurückgeben
rich reich
right rechts, richtig
risk Risiko; riskieren
road (Land-)Straße
role-play Rollenspiel
room Zimmer, Raum
round Runde; rund
rule Regel, Vorschrift
run laufen (lassen), betreiben, leiten

S

sad traurig
safe(ly) sicher
same der/die/das Gleiche, der-, die-, dasselbe
save retten, sparen
say sagen
school Schule
score Ergebnis, (Punkte-)Stand
screen Bildschirm, Leinwand
search Suche; (durch)suchen
second Sekunde; zweite/r/s
secretary Sekretär/in
see sehen, besuchen, verstehen
seem (er)scheinen
sell (sich) verkaufen
send senden, schicken
sentence Satz
serious ernst, ernsthaft
service Dienst, Dienstleistung, Service
set setzen, stellen
several etliche, einige, mehrere
shall sollen, werden
shelf Regal
shop Laden, Geschäft; einkaufen
short kurz, klein, knapp
should solle/n, sollte/n
shoulder Schulter
show zeigen
shut schließen
side Seite

sightseeing Besichtigen von Sehenswürdigkeiten
sign Zeichen, Anzeichen, Schild
simple einfach
since da, weil, seit
single einzig, einzeln
sit sitzen, sich hinsetzen
site Website
size Größe
slow langsam
small klein
smile Lächeln; lächeln
smoke Rauch; rauchen
someone jemand
something etwas
sometimes manchmal
somewhere irgendwo(hin)
soon bald
sorry Verzeihung; traurig
sound Klang, Geräusch; klingen, sich anhören
south (nach) Süden, Süd-
space Raum, Platz, Abstand
speak sprechen, reden
special besondere/r/s
specially speziell, extra, besonders
speed Geschwindigkeit
spell buchstabieren, schreiben
spelling Rechtschreibung, Schreibweise
spend (Geld) ausgeben, (Zeit) verbringen
stand stehen, aushalten
start Beginn; anfangen, starten
statement Aussage, Feststellung, Erklärung
stay Aufenthalt; bleiben
step Schritt, Stufe
still still, trotzdem, (immer) noch
stop (an)halten, aufhören (mit)
street Straße
strong stark, heftig
student Student/in, Lernende/r
study lernen, studieren, untersuchen, betrachten
stuff Material, Stoff, Zeug
subject (Schul-)Fach, Thema
success Erfolg
successful erfolgreich
sugar Zucker
suggest vorschlagen, andeuten
suggestion Vorschlag
suitcase Koffer
sun Sonne
sure sicher
surname Nach-/Familienname
surprise Überraschung; überraschen

T

table Tisch, Tabelle
take nehmen, bringen, dauern

136

Basic word list

take off   ausziehen, abnehmen, abheben
take part   teilnehmen, mitmachen
talk   Gespräch, Vortrag; sprechen, reden
tall   groß, hoch
task   Aufgabe
tea   Tee
teach   unterrichten, lehren
teacher   Lehrer/in
team   Mannschaft
technology   Technik, Technologie
telephone (call)   Telefon(anruf)
television   Fernsehen, Fernseher
tell   sagen, erzählen
test   untersuchen, prüfen
than   als
thank   danken
thank you   danke
thanks   Dank; danke
then   dann
thin   dünn
thing   Sache, Ding, Gegenstand
think   denken, meinen, finden, glauben
though   obwohl, allerdings, aber
through   durch
throw   werfen
tick (off)   mit einem Häkchen versehen, abhaken
ticket   Karte, Fahrschein
time   Zeit, Mal
tip   Hinweis, Tipp
today   heute
together   zusammen
tomorrow   morgen
tonight   heute Abend/Nacht
too   zu, auch
top   Spitze, Gipfel, Oberteil; Spitzen-
topic   Thema
total   (Gesamt-)Summe; Gesamt-
touch   anfassen, berühren
town   Stadt
traffic   Verkehr
train   Zug
translate   übersetzen
translation   Übersetzung

travel   Reisen; reisen, fahren
trip   Ausflug, Reise, Besuch
trouble   Mühe, Umstände, Problem(e), Ärger
true   wahr, richtig
try   versuchen, probieren
turn   (sich) drehen, wenden, werden
twice   zweimal
type   Art, Sorte, Typ; tippen, Schreibmaschine schreiben
typical   typisch

U
unable   unfähig, nicht in der Lage
under   unter
understand   verstehen, begreifen
university   Universität
unless   es sei denn, außer wenn
unlike   anders als, im Gegensatz zu
until   bis
use   Gebrauch, Nutzen; gebrauchen, benutzen, verwenden
useful   nützlich
user   Anwender/in, Benutzer/in
usual   gewöhnlich, normal, üblich
usually   gewöhnlich, normalerweise, meistens

V
verb   Verb
visit   Besuch; besuchen, besichtigen
visitor   Besucher/in, Gast

W
wait   warten
wall   Wand, Mauer
want   wollen
wash   waschen
watch   Armbanduhr
water   Wasser
way   Weg, Methode, Art (und Weise)
weather   Wetter
week   Woche
weekend   Wochenende

weekly   wöchentlich
welcome   Willkommen; willkommen heißen
well   gesund, gut, also
west   (nach) Westen, West-
whatever   was auch immer
when   wenn, als, wann
whenever   immer wenn, wann immer
where   wo(hin)
whether   ob
which   welche/r/s
while   während
whole   ganz
why   warum
wide   breit, weit
wife   (Ehe-)Frau
will   Wille; werde/n, wollen
window   Fenster
wine   Wein
wish   Wunsch; wünschen
with   mit, bei
within   innerhalb (von), in
without   ohne
woman   Frau
wonderful   wunderbar
wood   Holz
word   Wort
work   Arbeit; funktionieren, arbeiten
worker   Arbeiter/in
world   Welt
worldwide   weltweit
worried   besorgt, beunruhigt
worse   schlechter, schlimmer
worst   schlechteste/r/s, schlimmste/r/s, am schlechtesten, am schlimmsten
would   würde/n
write   schreiben
wrong   falsch

Y
year   Jahr
yesterday   gestern
young   jung

Chronological word list

Dieses Wörterverzeichnis enthält alle neuen Wörter aus *Business Matters* in der Reihenfolge ihres Erscheinens. Nicht angeführt sind die Wörter aus dem Grundwortschatz (vgl. *Basic word list*). Wörter aus den Hörverständnisübungen sind mit einem T *(Transkript)* gekennzeichnet. Die Zahl am linken Rand gibt die Seitenzahl an.

Abkürzungen	*etw* = etwas	*jds* = jemandes	*sth* = something
	jdm = jemandem	*pl* = plural noun	
	jdn = jemanden	*sb* = somebody	

UNIT 1

6	to **get to know** sb/sth [ˌget tə ˈnəʊ]	jdn/etw kennenlernen
	company [ˈkʌmpəni]	Unternehmen, Firma, Gesellschaft
	Pleased to meet you. [ˌpliːzd tə ˈmiːt ju]	Nett, Sie kennenzulernen.
	in person [ˌɪn ˈpɜːsn]	persönlich
	at last [ət ˈlɑːst]	endlich
	How do you do? [ˌhaʊ dju ˈduː]	Guten Tag.
7	**receptionist** [rɪˈsepʃənɪst]	Rezeptionist/in
	traineeship [treɪˈniːʃɪp]	Ausbildung, Lehre
	appointment [əˈpɔɪntmənt]	Termin, Verabredung
	to **let sb know** [ˌlet ˈnəʊ]	jdm Bescheid sagen
	reception [rɪˈsepʃn]	Empfang, Rezeption
	to **apologise** [əˈpɒlədʒaɪz]	sich entschuldigen, um Entschuldigung bitten
	Human Resources (HR) [ˌhjuːmən rɪˈsɔːsɪz]	Personalabteilung
	Assistant Human Resources Manager [əˌsɪstənt ˌhjuːmən rɪˈsɔːsɪz mænɪdʒə]	stellvertretende/r Personalleiter/in
	responsible [rɪˈspɒnsəbl]	zuständig, verantwortlich
	trainee [treɪˈniː]	Auszubildende/r
	to **introduce sb to sb** [ˌɪntrəˈdjuːs]	jdn mit jdm bekannt machen, jdn jdm vorstellen
	Human Resources Manager [ˌhjuːmən rɪˈsɔːsɪz mænɪdʒə]	Personalleiter/in
	introduction [ˌɪntrəˈdʌkʃn]	Einführung, Vorstellung
	background [ˈbækɡraʊnd]	Hintergrund
	to **show sb around** [ˌʃəʊ əˈraʊnd]	jdn herumführen, mit jdm einen Rundgang machen
	to **explain** [ɪkˈspleɪn]	erklären, erläutern
	department [dɪˈpɑːtmənt]	Abteilung
	Sales *(pl.)* [seɪlz]	Vertrieb, Verkauf

	Sales Manager [ˈseɪlz mænɪdʒə]	Verkaufsleiter/in
	proper(ly) [ˈprɒpə]	richtig
	to **highlight** [ˈhaɪlaɪt]	hervorheben
	to **consist of sth** [kənˈsɪst əv]	aus etw bestehen
8	**job interview** [ˈdʒɒb ɪntəvjuː]	Vorstellungs-/Bewerbungsgespräch
	training [ˈtreɪnɪŋ]	Ausbildung
	customer [ˈkʌstəmə]	Kunde/Kundin
	colleague [ˈkɒliːɡ]	Kollege/Kollegin
	Resources Manager [rɪˈsɔːsɪz mænɪdʒə]	Personalleiter/in
9	**structure** [ˈstrʌktʃə]	Struktur
	to **found** [faʊnd]	gründen
	employee [ɪmˈplɔɪiː]	Angestellte/r, Beschäftigte/r
	base [beɪs]	(Firmen-)Sitz
	situated [ˈsɪtʃueɪtɪd]	gelegen
	client [ˈklaɪənt]	Kunde/Kundin
	to **hire sb** [ˈhaɪə]	jdn einstellen
	to **establish** [ɪˈstæblɪʃ]	gründen
	runner [ˈrʌnə]	Läufer/in
	to **employ sb** [ɪmˈplɔɪ]	jdn beschäftigen
	staff [stɑːf]	Mitarbeiter, Personal
	annual [ˈænjuəl]	jährlich, Jahres-
	turnover [ˈtɜːnəʊvə]	Umsatz
	headquarters *(pl.)* [ˌhedˈkwɔːtəz]	Zentrale, Firmensitz
	production facilities *(pl.)* [prəˈdʌkʃn fəsɪlətiz]	Produktionsanlage(n), Werk(e)
	nearby [nɪəˈbaɪ]	nahegelegen
	distribution centre [ˌdɪstrɪˈbjuːʃn sentə]	Versandzentrum
	to **be located in** [bi ləʊˈkeɪtɪd ɪn]	sich befinden in
	incredibly [ɪnˈkredəbli]	unglaublich
	member [ˈmembə]	Mitglied
	to **maintain** [meɪnˈteɪn]	aufrechterhalten
	relation [rɪˈleɪʃn]	Beziehung
	function [ˈfʌŋkʃn]	Funktion, Aufgabe
	functional [ˈfʌŋkʃənl]	zweckmäßig, funktionell
	sort [sɔːt]	Art
	advertising [ˈædvətaɪzɪŋ]	Werbung

138

Chronological word list

	to **make sure** [ˌmeɪk 'ʃʊə]	sicherstellen, gewährleisten, sich vergewissern
	to **recruit sb** [rɪ'kruːt]	jdn einstellen, jdn anwerben
	to **brainstorm** ['breɪnstɔːm]	Ideen sammeln
	Production [prə'dʌkʃn]	Produktion, Herstellung, Fertigung
	Administration [ədˌmɪnɪ'streɪʃn]	Verwaltung
	Accounting [ə'kaʊntɪŋ]	Buchhaltung
	Distribution [ˌdɪstrɪ'bjuːʃn]	Versand, Auslieferung
10	**relationship** [rɪ'leɪʃnʃɪp]	Verhältnis, Beziehung
	alongside [ə'lɒŋsaɪd]	neben, mit
	in charge of [ɪn 'tʃɑːdʒ əv]	zuständig für, verantwortlich für
	to **head sth** [hed]	etw leiten
	to **report to sb** [rɪ'pɔːt tə]	jdm unterstehen
	responsibility [rɪˌspɒnsə'bɪləti]	Verantwortlichkeit, Aufgabenbereich, Zuständigkeit
	to **train sb** [treɪn]	jdn ausbilden, jdn schulen
	Managing Director [ˌmænɪdʒɪŋ də'rektə]	Geschäftsführer/in
	Operations Director [ˌɒpə'reɪʃnz dərektə]	Betriebs-/Produktionsleiter/in
	Production Manager [prə'dʌkʃn mænɪdʒə]	Produktionsleiter/in
	Logistics Manager [lə'dʒɪstɪks mænɪdʒə]	Leiter/in Logistik
	Production Assistant [prə'dʌkʃn əsɪstənt]	Produktionsassistent/in
	Logistics Assistant [lə'dʒɪstɪks əsɪstənt]	Logistikassistent/in
	Marketing Manager ['mɑːkɪtɪŋ mænɪdʒə]	Marketingleiter/in
	Marketing Assistant ['mɑːkɪtɪŋ əsɪstənt]	Marketingassistent/in
	Finance Director ['faɪnæns dərektə]	Leiter/in Finanzen
	Finance and Accounting Manager [ˌfaɪnæns ənd ə'kaʊntɪŋ mænɪdʒə]	Leiter/in Finanz- und Rechnungswesen
	Accounts Assistant [ə'kaʊnts əsɪstənt]	Buchhaltungsassistent/in
11	**tour** [tʊə]	Rundgang, Führung
	to **draw** [drɔː]	zeichnen
	photocopier ['fəʊtəʊkɒpiə]	Fotokopierer
T	**corridor** ['kɒrɪdɔː]	Flur, Korridor
	straight ahead [ˌstreɪt ə'hed]	geradeaus
	staff café [ˌstɑːf 'kæfeɪ]	Cafeteria

	to **ask for directions** [ɑːsk fə də'rekʃnz]	nach dem Weg fragen
	to **give sb directions** [gɪv də'rekʃnz]	jdm den Weg erklären
	directions [də'rekʃnz]	Wegbeschreibung
	to **take a turn(ing)** [ˌteɪk ə 'tɜːn]	abbiegen
	instruction [ɪn'strʌkʃn]	Anweisung, Anleitung
12 T	**office supplies** (pl.) ['ɒfɪs səplaɪz]	Büromaterial, Bürobedarf
	pen [pen]	Stift
	to **collect sth** [kə'lekt]	etw abholen; etw sammeln, zusammentragen
	to **fetch sth** [fetʃ]	etw holen
13 T	**sweet** [swiːt]	Süßigkeit, Bonbon; süß
	chocolate ['tʃɒklət]	Schokolade, Praline
	manufacturer [ˌmænju'fæktʃərə]	Hersteller, Produzent
	to **be based in …** [bi 'beɪst ɪn]	in … ansässig sein, seinen/ihren Sitz in … haben
	to **announce** [ə'naʊns]	ankündigen
	to **keep up with sb/ sth** [ˌkiːp 'ʌp wɪð]	mit jdm/etw Schritt halten
	demand [dɪ'mɑːnd]	Nachfrage
	brand [brænd]	Marke
	abroad [ə'brɔːd]	im/ins Ausland
	workshop ['wɜːkʃɒp]	Werkstatt
	to **package** ['pækɪdʒ]	verpacken
	to **distribute** [dɪ'strɪbjuːt]	vertreiben, verschicken
	owner ['əʊnə]	Besitzer/in, Inhaber/in
	sharp [ʃɑːp]	scharf
	among [ə'mʌŋ]	bei, unter
	to **manage** ['mænɪdʒ]	es schaffen, gelingen
	steadily ['stedɪli]	stetig, kontinuierlich
	to **continue to do sth** [kən'tɪnjuː]	etw weiterhin tun
	growth [grəʊθ]	Zunahme, Wachstum
	sales (pl.) [seɪlz]	Absatz, Umsatz
	to **increase sth** ['ɪŋkriːs]	etw erhöhen, aufstocken
	fizzy drink ['fɪzi drɪŋk]	Erfrischungsgetränk (mit Kohlensäure)
	juice [dʒuːs]	Saft
14	**brief** [briːf]	kurz, knapp
	guide [gaɪd]	Führer/in
	sole trader [ˌsəʊl 'treɪdə]	Einzelunternehmer, Einzelunternehmen
	sole proprietorship [ˌsəʊl prə'praɪətəʃɪp]	Einzelunternehmen
	company form ['kʌmpəni fɔːm]	Unternehmensform Gesellschaftsform
	profit ['prɒfɪt]	Gewinn
	debts (pl.) [dets]	Verbindlichkeiten, Schulden

139

Chronological word list

to **run sth up** [ˌrʌn ˈʌp]	etw anhäufen, (Schulden) machen	
loss [lɒs]	Verlust	
limited partnership [ˌlɪmɪtɪd ˈpɑːtnəʃɪp]	Kommanditgesell-schaft (KG)	
general partnership [ˌdʒenrəl ˈpɑːtnəʃɪp]	offene Handels-geselslchaft (OHG)	
liable [ˈlaɪəbl]	haftbar	
to **be liable for sth** [bi ˈlaɪəbl fə]	für etw haften	
to **divide** [dɪˈvaɪd]	teilen, aufteilen	
private limited company (Ltd) [ˌpraɪvət ˌlɪmɪtɪd ˈkʌmpəni]	Gesellschaft mit be-schränkter Haftung (GmbH)	
unlimited [ˌʌnˈlɪmɪtɪd]	unbegrenzt, unbeschränkt	
liability [ˌlaɪəˈbɪləti]	Haftung	
to **restrict** [rɪˈstrɪkt]	beschränken	
to **invest** [ɪnˈvest]	investieren	
contribution [ˌkɒntrɪˈbjuːʃn]	Beitrag	
complicated [ˈkɒmplɪkeɪtɪd]	kompliziert	
joint stock [ˌdʒɔɪnt ˈstɒk]	Gesellschaftskapital, Grundkapital	
to **fund** [fʌnd]	finanzieren	
various [ˈveəriəs]	verschieden	
source [sɔːs]	Quelle	
shareholder [ˈʃeəhəʊldə]	Teilhaber/in, Gesell-schafter/in	
share [ʃeə]	Anteil	
proportion [prəˈpɔːʃn]	Verhältnis	
to **back sth** [bæk]	etw unterstützen, *hier:* in etw investieren	
to **trade** [treɪd]	handeln	
stock exchange [ˈstɒk ɪkstʃeɪndʒ]	Börse	
public limited company (plc) [ˌpʌblɪk ˌlɪmɪtɪd ˈkʌmpəni]	Aktiengesellschaft (AG)	
to **set up (a business)** [ˌset ˈʌp]	(ein Unternehmen) gründen	
major [ˈmeɪdʒə]	größte/r/s, Haupt-, bedeutendste/r/s	
share [ʃeə]	Aktie	
the public [ðə ˈpʌblɪk]	die Öffentlichkeit	
stock market [ˈstɒk mɑːkɪt]	Aktienmarkt	
in contrast to [ɪn ˈkɒntrɑːst tə]	im Gegensatz zu	
public [ˈpʌblɪk]	öffentlich	
publicly owned [ˌpʌblɪki ˈəʊnd]	börsennotiert	
advantage [ədˈvɑːntɪdʒ]	Vorteil	
disadvantage [ˌdɪsədˈvɑːntɪdʒ]	Nachteil	

to **carry sth out** [ˌkæri ˈaʊt]	etw ausführen, etw durchführen	
to **extend sth** [ɪkˈstend]	etw erweitern	

UNIT 2

15	to **take turns** [ˌteɪk ˈtɜːnz]	sich abwechseln	
16	**boss** [bɒs]	Chef/in	
	potential [pəˈtenʃl]	potenziell	
	chain [tʃeɪn]	Kette	
	inbox [ˈɪnbɒks]	Posteingang	
	clothing [ˈkləʊðɪŋ]	Bekleidung, Kleidung	
	current [ˈkʌrənt]	aktuell	
	to **attach** [əˈtætʃ]	beifügen, anhängen	
	to **reply to sb** [rɪˈplaɪ tə]	jdm antworten	
	cap [kæp]	Mütze, Kappe	
	file [faɪl]	Akte	
	filing cabinet [ˈfaɪlɪŋ kæbɪnət]	Aktenschrank	
	to **include** [ɪnˈkluːd]	beinhalten, ein-schließen	
	quote [kwəʊt]	Angebot	
	to **be based on sth** [bi ˈbeɪst ɒn]	auf etw basieren	
	to **print sth out** [ˌprɪnt ˈaʊt]	etw ausdrucken	
	to **sign** [saɪn]	unterschreiben	
	refreshment [rɪˈfreʃmənt]	Erfrischung *(Tee, Saft, Wasser usw.)*	
	garage [ˈgærɑːʒ]	Autowerkstatt	
	check [tʃek]	*(Auto:)* Inspektion	
	to **contact sb** [ˈkɒntækt]	sich mit jdm in Verbindung setzen	
	to **suit** [suːt]	passen	
	stationery [ˈsteɪʃənri]	Büromaterial, Büro-bedarf	
	marker pen [ˈmɑːkə pen]	Textmarker	
17	**item** [ˈaɪtəm]	Artikel	
18	**calculator** [ˈkælkjuleɪtə]	Taschenrechner	
	staple [steɪpl]	Heftklammer	
	note pad [ˈnəʊt pad]	Notizblock	
	paper clip [ˈpeɪpə klɪp]	Büroklammer	
	cartridge [ˈkɑːtrɪdʒ]	Druckerpatrone	
	highlighter [ˈhaɪlaɪtə]	Textmarker	
	hole punch [ˈhəʊl pʌntʃ]	Locher	
	envelop [ɪnˈveləp]	Briefumschlag	
19	**importance** [ɪmˈpɔːtns]	Wichtigkeit, Bedeutung	
T	to **fill sth in** [ˌfɪl ˈɪn]	etw ausfüllen	
	account [əˈkaʊnt]	Konto	
	account number [əˈkaʊnt nʌmbə]	Kostenstelle	
	to **confirm** [kənˈfɜːm]	bestätigen	

Chronological word list

to **pick sb/sth up** [ˌpɪk 'ʌp]	jdn/etw abholen	
relevant ['reləvənt]	ensprechend	
straight away [ˌstreɪt ə'weɪ]	sofort, gleich	
term [tɜːm]	Begriff	
stage [steɪdʒ]	Phase, Etappe	
purpose ['pɜːpəs]	Zweck	
20 **step** [step]	Schritt	
button ['bʌtn]	Knopf, Taste	
to **mark** [mɑːk]	kennzeichnen	
eject [ɪ'dʒekt]	Auswurf	
to **seal** [siːl]	(luftdicht) verschließen	
to **dispose of sth** [dɪ'spəʊz əv]	etw entsorgen	
to **remove** [rɪ'muːv]	entfernen	
packaging ['pækɪdʒɪŋ]	Verpackung	
lock [lɒk]	Verschluss	
ink [ɪŋk]	Tinte	
21 to **take sb on** [ˌteɪk 'ɒn]	jdn einstellen	
feature ['fiːtʃə]	Merkmal, Eigenschaft	
to **unscramble** [ˌʌn'skræmbl]	entwirren	
to **guarantee** [ˌɡærən'tiː]	garantieren	
specific [spə'sɪfɪk]	bestimmt, speziell	
warranty ['wɒrənti]	Garantie, Gewähr-leistung	
shelf life ['ʃelf laɪf]	Haltbarkeit	
rating ['reɪtɪŋ]	Bewertung	
22 to **rent** [rent]	mieten	
premises *(pl.)* ['premɪsɪz]	Räumlichkeiten, (Betriebs-)Gelände	
to **operate** ['ɒpəreɪt]	(geschäftlich) tätig sein, operieren	
to **exist** [ɪɡ'zɪst]	existieren	
commercial space [kəˌmɜːʃl 'speɪs]	Gewerberaum, -räume	
to **furnish** ['fɜːnɪʃ]	ausstatten, einrichten	
equipment [ɪ'kwɪpmənt]	Ausstattung, Ausrüstung	
rental ['rentl]	Vermietung, Miete	
to **equip** [ɪ'kwɪp]	ausstatten, ausrüsten	
rental agreement ['rentl əɡriːmənt]	Mietvertrag	
to **require** [rɪ'kwaɪə]	benötigen, wünschen	
real estate ['rɪəl ɪsteɪt]	Immobilien	
to **specialise in sth** ['speʃəlaɪz ɪn]	sich auf etw speziali-sieren	
accommodation [əˌkɒmə'deɪʃn]	Unterbringung, Unterkunft	
freelancer ['friːlɑːnsə]	Selbständige/r, Freiberufler/in	
fully-fitted [ˌfʊli 'fɪtɪd]	voll ausgestattet	
broadband ['brɔːdbænd]	Breitband-	

connection [kə'nekʃn]	Verbindung	
potted plant [ˌpɒtɪd 'plɑːnt]	Topfpflanze	
refrigerator [rɪ'frɪdʒəreɪtə]	Kühlschrank	
microwave ['maɪkrəweɪv]	Mikrowelle	
obviously ['ɒbviəsli]	natürlich, selbst-verständlich	
facilities *(pl.)* [fə'sɪlətiz]	Einrichtungen	
rent [rent]	Miete	
convenient [kən'viːniənt]	praktisch, zweckmäßig	
convenience [kən'viːniəns]	Zweckmäßigkeit	
in particular [ɪn pə'tɪkjələ]	besonders	
operation [ˌɒpə'reɪʃn]	Betrieb	
core [kɔː]	Haupt-, Kern-	
to **waste** [weɪst]	verschwenden, vergeuden	
to **fit sth out** [ˌfɪt 'aʊt]	etw ausstatten	
appeal [ə'piːl]	Reiz	
to **run sth** [rʌn]	etw führen, leiten	
to **set sth up** [ˌset 'ʌp]	etw aufbauen, einrichten	
to **hold sth** [həʊld]	etw abhalten	
suite [swiːt]	Büroräume, Büroetage	
to **impress** [ɪm'pres]	beeindrucken	
effort ['efət]	Mühe, Anstrengungen	
furniture ['fɜːnɪtʃə]	Möbel	
deal [diːl]	Geschäft, Verein-barung	
suitable ['suːtəbl]	geeignet	
flexible ['fleksəbl]	flexibel	
to **get on with sth** [ˌget 'ɒn wɪð]	(mit etw) weitermachen	
23 **aim** [eɪm]	Ziel	
brief [briːf]	Auftrag	
to **investigate sb/sth** [ɪn'vestɪgeɪt]	Erkundigungen über jdn/etw einholen, Nachforschungen über jdn/etw anstellen	
alternative [ɔːl'tɜːnətɪv]	andere/r/s, alternativ	
summary ['sʌməri]	Zusammenfassung	
recommendation [ˌrekəmen'deɪʃn]	Empfehlung	
method ['meθəd]	Art, Methode	
rather ['rɑːðə]	vielmehr	
depending on [dɪ'pendɪŋ ɒn]	abhängig von	
currently ['kʌrəntli]	momentan, im Moment, aktuell	
to **work closely with sb** [ˌwɜːk 'kləʊsli]	mit jdm eng zu-sammenarbeiten	
portable ['pɔːtəbl]	tragbar, mobil	

141

Chronological word list

network ['netwɜːk]	Netzwerk	
access ['ækses]	Zugang, Zugriff	
device [dɪ'vaɪs]	Gerät	
available [ə'veɪləbl]	verfügbar	
to **be made available** [bi ˌmeɪd ə'veɪləbl]	zur Verfügung stellen	
to **pass sth on** [ˌpɑːs 'ɒn]	etw weitergeben, -reichen, -leiten	
on a day-to-day basis [ɒn ə ˌdeɪ tə deɪ 'beɪsɪs]	täglich, jeden Tag	
homeworking ['həʊmwɜːkɪŋ]	Heimarbeit	
to **reduce** [rɪ'djuːs]	reduzieren, senken	
need [niːd]	Bedarf	
additionally [ə'dɪʃənəli]	außerdem	
to **adopt** [ə'dɒpt]	annehmen, übernehmen	
combination [ˌkɒmbɪ'neɪʃn]	Verbindung	
scheme [skiːm]	Programm, Plan	
to **cut costs** [kʌt 'kɒsts]	Kosten senken	
investment [ɪn'vestmənt]	Investition(en)	
saving ['seɪvɪŋ]	Einsparung, Ersparnis	
24	to **summarise** ['sʌməraɪz]	zusammenfassen
petrol ['petrəl]	Benzin	
pressure ['preʃə]	Druck	
chance ['tʃɑːns]	Möglichkeit, Gelegenheit	
author ['ɔːθə]	Autor/in	
to **mention** ['menʃn]	erwähnen, nennen	
canteen [kæn'tiːn]	Kantine	

SITUATION 1

25	to **expand** [ɪk'spænd]	ausdehnen
head [hed]	Leiter/in, Chef/in	
reputation [ˌrepju'teɪʃn]	Ruf, Ansehen	
link [lɪŋk]	Verbindung, Kontakt	
to **invite** [ɪn'vaɪt]	einladen	
to **react to sth** [rɪ'ækt]	auf etw reagieren	
response [rɪ'spɒns]	Antwort, Reaktion	
comfortable ['kʌmftəbl]	bequem, angenehm, komfortabel	
pleasant ['pleznt]	angenehm	
smooth [smuːð]	glatt, reibungslos	
business card ['bɪznəs kɑːd]	Visitenkarte	
26	**male** [meɪl]	männlich, hier: Herren-
female ['fiːmeɪl]	weiblich, hier: Damen-	
raincoat ['reɪnkəʊt]	Regenmantel	
figure ['fɪgə]	Zahl	
worker ['wɜːkə]	Arbeiter/in	
wages (pl.) ['weɪdʒɪz]	Lohn, Gehalt	

to **taste** ['teɪst]	etw probieren, etw kosten	
production line [prə'dʌkʃn laɪn]	Fertigungsstraße, Produktionsverfahen	

UNIT 3

27	to **draw sth up** [ˌdrɔː 'ʌp]	etw erstellen
market research [ˌmɑːkɪt rɪ'sɜːtʃ]	Marktforschung	
to **promote sth** [prə'məʊt]	etw bewerben, für etw Werbung machen	
advertising space ['ædvətaɪzɪŋ speɪs]	Werbefläche(n), Werbezeit(en), Anzeigenraum	
to **design** [dɪ'zaɪn]	gestalten, entwerfen	
to **place** [pleɪs]	platzieren	
process ['prəʊses]	Verfahren, Ablauf, Prozess	
digital projector [ˌdɪdʒɪtl prə'dʒektə]	Beamer	
to **develop** [dɪ'veləp]	entwickeln	
to **base sth around sth** ['beɪs]	etw auf etw gründen, etw nach etw ausrichten	
strategy ['strætədʒi]	Strategie	
promotion [prə'məʊʃn]	Werbung	
campaign [kæm'peɪn]	Kampagne	
to **contain** [kən'teɪn]	enthalten, beinhalten	
to **examine** [ɪg'zæmɪn]	untersuchen, genau anschauen	
competitor [kəm'petɪtə]	Konkurrent/in, Konkurrenz	
to **evaluate** [ɪ'væljueɪt]	einschätzen, auswerten	
28	**questionnaire** [ˌkwestʃə'neə]	Fragebogen
focus group ['fəʊkəs gruːp]	Fokusgruppe	
lightweight ['laɪtweɪt]	leicht	
affinity [ə'fɪnəti]	Verwandtschaft, Affinität	
affinity marketing [ə'fɪnəti mɑːkɪtɪŋ]	Affinity-Marketing	
to **appeal to sb** [ə'piːl tə]	jdn ansprechen, jdm gefallen	
similar ['sɪmələ]	ähnlich	
to **tie** [taɪ]	schnüren, binden	
fresh [freʃ]	neu, frisch	
advertising agency ['ædvətaɪzɪŋ eɪdʒənsi]	Werbeagentur	
media buying agency ['miːdiə baɪɪŋ eɪdʒənsi]	Agentur für Medienplanung/-einkauf	
a good deal of [ə ˌgʊd 'diːl əvň]	eine Menge	
concept ['kɒnsept]	Begriff, Konzept	
expression [ɪk'spreʃn]	Ausdruck	
to **lay sth out** [ˌlaɪ 'aʊt]	etw darlegen	

Chronological word list

	to **identify** [aɪˈdentɪfaɪ]	identifizieren
	attitude [ˈætɪtjuːd]	Haltung, Einstellung
29	to **assess** [əˈses]	einschätzen, bewerten, beurteilen
	to **ignore** [ɪgˈnɔː]	ignorieren, nicht beachten
	functionality [ˌfʌŋkʃəˈnæləti]	Funktionen, Funktionalität
	to **advertise** sth [ˈædvətaɪz]	etw bewerben, für etw Werbung machen
	stylish [ˈstaɪlɪʃ]	elegant, schick, stilvoll
	entertaining [ˌentəˈteɪnɪŋ]	unterhaltsam
	to **express** [ɪkˈspres]	ausdrücken, zum Ausdruck bringen
	to **react to** sth [riˈækt]	auf etw reagieren
30	**impact** [ˈɪmpækt]	Einfluss, Auswirkungen
	unimpressive [ˌʌnɪmˈpresɪv]	wenig beeindruckend
	to **appear** [əˈpɪə]	erscheinen
	target market [ˈtɑːgɪt mɑːkɪt]	Zielgruppe, Zielmarkt
	national [ˈnæʃnəl]	(Zeitung:) überregional
	to **split** [splɪt]	teilen, aufteilen
	equally [ˈiːkwəli]	zu gleichen Teilen, gleich
	proportion [prəˈpɔːʃn]	Anteil, Teil
	daily newspaper [ˌdeɪli ˈnjuːzpeɪpə]	Tageszeitung
31	**versus (vs.)** ¢ [ˈvɜːsəs]	gegenüber, im Gegensatz zu
	jumbled up [ˌdʒʌmbld ˈʌp]	durcheinandergeworfen
	paragraph [ˈpærəgrɑːf]	(Text:) Absatz
	logical [ˈlɒdʒɪkl]	logisch
	popularity [ˌpɒpjuˈlærəti]	Beliebtheit
	to **measure** [ˈmeʒə]	messen
	accurate(ly) [ˈækjərət]	genau
	theoretical(ly) [ˌθɪəˈretɪkl]	theoretisch
	audience [ˈɔːdiəns]	Publikum, Zuhörer(-schaft), Zuschauer
	to **turn the page** [ˌtɜːn ðə ˈpeɪdʒ]	umblättern
	attraction [əˈtrækʃn]	Reiz, Anziehungskraft
	to **be fashionable** [bi ˈfæʃnəbl]	im Trend liegen
	computer-savvy [kəmˈpjuːtə sævi]	geübt/gewieft im Umgang mit Computern
	to **attract** [əˈtrækt]	anziehen
	to **become aware of** sth [bɪˌkʌm əˈweər əv]	sich einer Sache bewusst werden, etw bemerken
	eye-catching [ˈaɪ kætʃɪŋ]	ansprechend, auffallend
	to **feature** sth [ˈfiːtʃə]	etw aufweisen

	to **circulate** [ˈsɜːkjəleɪt]	sich verbreiten, kursieren
	means [miːnz]	Mittel
	to **spread** [spred]	verbreiten
	to **trace** [treɪs]	nachverfolgen, verfolgen
32	**vice versa** [ˌvaɪs ˈvɜːsə]	umgekehrt
	advertising campaign [ˈædvətaɪzɪŋ kæmpeɪn]	Werbekampagne
	print media [ˈprɪnt miːdiə]	Presse, Printmedien
	broadcast media [ˈbrɔːdkɑːst miːdiə]	Rundfunk
T	**glad** [glæd]	froh
	budget [ˈbʌdʒɪt]	Budget, Haushalt, Etat
	remaining [rɪˈmeɪnɪŋ]	übrige/r/s, restliche/r/s
	to **advise** [ədˈvaɪz]	(jdm, zu etw) raten
	opinion [əˈpɪniən]	Meinung
	to **perform well** [pəˌfɔːm ˈwel]	gute Ergebnisse liefern
	to **propose** [prəˈpəʊz]	vorschlagen
33	**internal** [ɪnˈtɜːnl]	Innen-
	pocket [ˈpɒkɪt]	Tasche
	to **come (in/with)** [kʌm]	(Produkt:) erhältlich sein (in/mit)
	range [reɪndʒ]	Auswahl, Palette
	briefcase [ˈbriːfkeɪs]	Aktentasche
	leather [ˈleðə]	Leder
34	**strapline** [ˈstræplaɪn]	(Werbe-)Slogan
	subheadline [ˈsʌb hedlaɪn]	Zwischenüberschrift, Dachzeile
	headline [ˈhedlaɪn]	Überschrift
T	**chat** [tʃæt]	Unterhaltung, Gespräch
	to **expand on** sth [ɪkˈspænd ɒn]	etw weiter ausführen
	to **draw** [drɔː]	ziehen
	conversational tone [kɒnvəˌseɪʃənl ˈtəʊn]	lockerer Plauderton
	formal [ˈfɔːml]	förmlich, formell
	call to action [ˌkɔːl tu ˈækʃn]	Handlungsaufforderung, Aufruf
	to **tie back to** sth [ˌtaɪ ˈbæk tə]	etwa: zu etw passen, etw aufnehmen
	to **overload** [ˌəʊvəˈləʊd]	überfrachten
	tone [təʊn]	Ton
	to **link** [lɪŋk]	verbinden
	strength [streŋθ]	Stärke
	weakness [ˈwiːknəs]	Schwäche
	to **improve** [ɪmˈpruːv]	verbessern
35	**executive** [ɪgˈzekjətɪv]	Manager/in
	to **fit** [fɪt]	passen
	to **fit neatly** [ˌfɪt ˈniːtli]	genau passen
	bright [braɪt]	(Farbe:) hell, leuchtend
	projection [prəˈdʒekʃn]	Projektion
	reliable [rɪˈlaɪəbl]	zuverlässig

143

Chronological word list

battery ['bætəri]	Akku, Batterie	
available [ə'veɪləbl]	verfügbar, erhältlich	
power supply ['paʊə səplaɪ]	Stromversorgung, -anschluss	
tough [tʌf]	solide, widerstands- fähig	
casing ['keɪsɪŋ]	Gehäuse	
colouring ['kʌlərɪŋ]	Farbe, Farbgebung	
amazed [ə'meɪzd]	verblüfft, erstaunt	
to **introduce** [ˌɪntrə'dju:s]	vorstellen, einführen	
to **weigh** [weɪ]	wiegen	
to **slip** [slɪp]	stecken, schieben	
advice [əd'vaɪs]	Rat, Ratschlag, Tipp	
36 **sunburn** ['sʌnbɜ:n]	Sonnenbrand	
irresponsible [ˌɪrɪ'spɒnsəbl]	unverantwortlich	
standard ['stændəd]	Norm, Maßstab, Standard	
authority [ɔ:'θɒrəti]	Behörde	
competition [ˌkɒmpə'tɪʃn]	Wettbewerb	
to **ban** [bæn]	verbieten	
comparison [kəm'pærɪsn]	Vergleich	
lobster ['lɒbstə]	Hummer	
prize [praɪz]	Preis, Gewinn	
winner ['wɪnə]	Gewinner/in	
sunscreen ['sʌnskri:n]	Sonnenschutz, -creme	
runner-up [ˌrʌnər 'ʌp]	Zweitplatzierte/r	
complaint [kəm'pleɪnt]	Beschwerde	
to **encourage** [ɪn'kʌrɪdʒ]	ermutigen, motivieren	
entrant ['entrənt]	Teilnehmer/in (an einem Wettbewerb)	
to **earn** [ɜ:n]	verdienen	
burn [bɜ:n]	Verbrennung	
to **get sunburnt** [ˌget 'sʌnbɜ:nt]	sich einen Sonnen- brand zuziehen	
parent company [ˌpeərənt 'kʌmpəni]	Muttergesellschaft	
to **argue** ['ɑ:gju:]	argumentieren	
aim [eɪm]	Ziel	
safety ['seɪfti]	Sicherheit, Schutz	
to **condone sth** [kən'dəʊn]	etw billigen	
explicit(ly) [ɪk'splɪsɪt]	ausdrücklich	
string [strɪŋ]	Reihe, Folge	
emphasis ['emfəsɪs]	Schwerpunkt	
overexposure [ˌəʊvərɪk'spəʊʒə]	hier: zu langes Sonnenbaden	
to **refer to sth** [rɪ'fɜ: tə]	sich auf etw beziehen, etw erwähnen	
tanning ['tænɪŋ]	Bräunung	
disaster [dɪ'zɑ:stə]	Katastrophe	
nightmare ['naɪtmeə]	Albtraum	

numerous ['nju:mərəs]	zahlreich	
specifically [spə'sɪfɪkli]	eigens, speziell	
watchdog ['wɒtʃdɒg]	Aufsichtsbehörde	
to **criticise** ['krɪtɪsaɪz]	kritisieren	
entry ['entri]	Teilnahme (an einem Wettbewerb)	
to **rule** [ru:l]	entscheiden, erklären	
to **trivialise** ['trɪviəlaɪz]	bagatellisieren	
37 **straightforward** [ˌstreɪt'fɔ:wəd]	einfach, unkompliziert	
to **target sb** ['tɑ:gɪt]	jdn (als Zielgruppe) ansprechen, jdn als Zielgruppe haben	
to **aim sth at sb/sth** ['eɪm ət]	etw auf jdn/etw abzielen, etw an jdn/ etw richten	
to **hire sb** ['haɪə]	jdn beauftragen	
to **sit back** [ˌsɪt 'bæk]	sich zurücklehnen	
to **communicate** [kə'mju:nɪkeɪt]	kommunizieren	
approach [ə'prəʊtʃ]	Vorgehen(sweise), Ansatz, Heran- gehensweise	
innovative ['ɪnəveɪtɪv]	innovativ	
increasingly [ɪn'kri:sɪŋli]	zunehmend, immer (+Komparativ)	
to **get up to speed** [get ˌʌp tə 'spi:d]	sich auf den neuesten Stand bringen	
factor ['fæktə]	Faktor	
to **involve** [ɪn'vɒlv]	beinhalten, mit sich bringen	
arrival [ə'raɪvl]	Einführung	
marketeer [ˌmɑ:kɪ'tɪə]	Vermarkter/in, (im Plu- ral:) Marketingleute	
to **discover** [dɪ'skʌvə]	entdecken	
willingness ['wɪlɪŋnəs]	Bereitschaft	
providing [prə'vaɪdɪŋ]	vorausgesetzt	
entertainment [ˌentə'teɪnmənt]	Unterhaltung	
value ['vælju:]	Wert	
surprised [sə'praɪzd]	erstaunt, überrascht	
nevertheless [ˌnevəðə'les]	trotzdem, dennoch, nichtsdestotrotz	
technique [tek'ni:k]	Methode, Technik	
buzz [bʌz]	Aufmerksamkeit (durch Mundpropaganda)	
conventional [kən'venʃnəl]	herkömmlich, konventionell	
to **aim at sth** ['eɪm ət]	auf etw abzielen	
crude(ly) [kru:d]	primitiv, simpel	
sticker ['stɪkə]	Aufkleber	
scene [si:n]	Szene	
in public [ɪn 'pʌblɪk]	öffentlich, in der Öffentlichkeit	
to **convey** [kən'veɪ]	vermitteln	
unconventional [ˌʌnkən'venʃənl]	unkonventionell	

144

Chronological word list

significant [sɪgˈnɪfɪkənt]	erheblich, bedeutend	

UNIT 4

38	**nervous** [ˈnɜːvəs]	nervös
	to **be available** [bi əˈveɪləbl]	(Telefon:) zu sprechen sein
	Speaking. [ˈspiːkɪŋ]	Am Apparat.
	to **hold on** [ˌhəʊld ˈɒn]	warten
	That's a pity. [ˌdæts ə ˈpɪti]	Schade.
	to **catch sb/sth** [kætʃ]	jdn/etw erreichen, jdn/etw erwischen, jdn/etw bekommen
39	to **take a message** [ˌteɪk ə ˈmesɪdʒ]	(Telefon:) etw ausrichten
	to **leave a message** [liːv ə ˈmesɪdʒ]	eine Nachricht hinterlassen
	to **catch sth** [kætʃ]	etw verstehen
	scooter [ˈskuːtə]	Roller
	to **ring sb back** [ˌrɪŋ ˈbæk]	jdn zurückrufen
	anytime [ˌeniˈtaɪm]	jederzeit
	native speaker [ˌneɪtɪv ˈspiːkə]	Muttersprachler/in
	to **be afraid** [bi əˈfreɪd]	Angst haben
	after all [ˌɑːftər ˈɔːl]	schließlich
40 T	to **return a call** [rɪˌtɜːn ə ˈkɔːl]	jdn zurückrufen
	guided tour [ˌgaɪdɪd ˈtʊə]	Führung, Rundfahrt
	wheel [wiːl]	Rad
	sporty [ˈspɔːti]	sportlich
	Go ahead. [ˌgəʊ əˈhed]	Nur zu. / Bitte sehr.
	to **reckon** [ˈrekən]	glauben, annehmen
	to **turn out** [ˌtɜːn ˈaʊt]	sich herausstellen
	including [ɪnˈkluːdɪŋ]	einschließlich
	VAT (value added tax) [ˌviː eɪ ˈtiː/ˌvæljuː ˈædɪd tæks]	Mehrwertsteuer (MwSt)
	delivery [dɪˈlɪvəri]	Lieferung, Zustellung
41	**scale** [skeɪl]	Größenordnung
	to **consider sb/sth** [kənˈsɪdə]	jdn/etw in Betracht/Erwägung ziehen
	assistance [əˈsɪstəns]	Hilfe, Unterstützung
42	**confirmation** [ˌkɒnfəˈmeɪʃn]	Bestätigung
	to **place an order** [ˌpleɪs ən ˈɔːdə]	einen Auftrag erteilen, eine Bestellung aufgeben
	to **dispatch** [dɪˈspætʃ]	verschicken, absenden
	additional [əˈdɪʃənəl]	zusätzlich, Zusatz-
	to **get in touch with sb** [ˌget ɪn ˈtʌtʃ wɪð]	sich bei jdm melden
	to **do business** [du ˈbɪznəs]	Geschäfte machen

	to **come across sth** [ˌkʌm əˈkrɒs]	von etw hören, einer Sache begegnen
	speech bubble [ˈspiːtʃ bʌbl]	Sprechblase
	discount [ˈdɪskaʊnt]	Rabatt
	worth [wɜːθ]	wert
	guy [gaɪ]	Typ, Kerl
43	**re** [riː]	Betreff, betreffs
	to **represent** [ˌreprɪˈzent]	darstellen, repräsentieren
	gratitude [ˈgrætɪtjuːd]	Anerkennung, Dankbarkeit
	continued [kənˈtɪnjuːd]	fortgesetzt, anhaltend
	custom [ˈkʌstəm]	Kundentreue
	payment [ˈpeɪmənt]	Zahlung
	due [djuː]	fällig
	receipt [rɪˈsiːt]	Erhalt, Eingang
	invoice [ˈɪnvɔɪs]	Rechnung
	by means of [baɪ ˈmiːnz əv]	mittels, per
	mark [mɑːk]	Zeichen
	appreciation [əˌpriːʃiˈeɪʃn]	Wertschätzung
	ongoing [ˈɒngəʊɪŋ]	fortdauernd
	charge [tʃɑːdʒ]	Gebühr
	to **hesitate** [ˈhezɪteɪt]	zögern
	Yours sincerely [jɔːz sɪnˈsɪəli]	Mit freundlichen Grüßen
44	**immediately** [ɪˈmiːdiətli]	unverzüglich, sofort
	leader [ˈliːdə]	Führer/in
45	**single speed (bicycle)** [ˈsɪŋgl spiːd]	Eingangrad
46	**inexpensive** [ˌɪnɪkˈspensɪv]	preiswert
	pointer [ˈpɔɪntə]	Hinweis
	informal [ɪnˈfɔːml]	informell, zwanglos, locker
	to **take place** [teɪk ˈpleɪs]	stattfinden
	to **consider sth** [kənˈsɪdə]	etw berücksichtigen, etw betrachten, über etw nachdenken
	issue [ˈɪʃuː]	Frage, Thema
	to **come along** [ˌkʌm əˈlɒŋ]	kommen, aufkommen
	previously [ˈpriːviəsli]	zuvor, vorher
	stiff [stɪf]	steif
	to **sign sth off** [ˌsaɪn ˈɒf]	(Brief etc.:) (be)enden, schließen, unterschreiben
	cheers [tʃɪəz]	tschüs, danke
	informality [ˌɪnfɔːˈmæləti]	Zwanglosigkeit
	to **stick to sth** [ˈstɪk tə]	bei etw bleiben
	old-fashioned [ˌəʊldˈfæʃənd]	altmodisch

145

Chronological word list

style [staɪl] — Stil

to **pay attention to sth** [ˌpeɪ əˈtenʃn tə] — auf etw achten

comma [ˈkɒmə] — Komma

full stop [ˌfʊl ˈstɒp] — Punkt (am Satzende)

to **arrange sth** [əˈreɪndʒ] — etw anordnen, etw aufbauen

neat(ly) [niːt] — ordentlich, sauber

unfortunately [ʌnˈfɔːtʃənətli] — leider, unglücklicherweise

error [ˈerə] — Fehler

punctuation [ˌpʌŋktʃuˈeɪʃn] — Zeichensetzung, Interpunktion

embarrassing [ɪmˈbærəsɪŋ] — peinlich

impression [ɪmˈpreʃn] — Eindruck

professionalism [prəˈfeʃnlɪzm] — Professionalität

in general [ɪn ˈdʒenrəl] — im Allgemeinen

to **claim** [kleɪm] — behaupten

SITUATION 2

47 cheese [tʃiːz] — Käse

to **chair** [tʃeə] — (Sitzung etc.) leiten

to **point out** [ˌpɔɪnt ˈaʊt] — darauf hinweisen

competition [ˌkɒmpəˈtɪʃn] — Konkurrenz

to **be enthusiastic about sth** [bi ɪnˌθjuːziˈæztɪk əbaʊt] — sich für etw begeistern

view [vjuː] — Ansicht, Meinung

cautious [ˈkɔːʃəs] — vorsichtig

outlet [ˈaʊtlət] — Verkaufsstelle, Absatzmöglichkeit

unknown [ˌʌnˈnəʊn] — unbekannt

48 to **launch sth** [lɔːntʃ] — etw starten

bullet point [ˈbʊlɪt pɔɪnt] — Stichpunkt

aspect [ˈæspekt] — Aspekt

signposting [ˈsaɪnpəʊstɪŋ] — richtungweised

on the contrary [ɒn ðə ˈkɒntrəri] — (ganz) im Gegenteil

present [ˈpreznt] — anwesend

introduction [ˌɪntrəˈdʌkʃn] — Einleitung

opportunity [ˌɒpəˈtjuːnəti] — Möglichkeit, Gelegenheit, Chance

conclusion [kənˈkluːʒn] — Fazit, Schluss

overall view [ˌəʊvərˌɔːl ˈvjuː] — Überblick, (Gesamt-)Übersicht

to **sort sth into sth** [sɔːt] — etw nach etw ordnen

category [ˈkætəgəri] — Kategorie

unimportant [ˌʌnɪmˈpɔːtnt] — unwichtig

urgent [ˈɜːdʒənt] — dringend, eilig

T figure [ˈfɪgə] — Zahl

sheet [ʃiːt] — Blatt

to **pop in** [ˌpɒp ˈɪn] — vorbeischauen

diary [ˈdaɪəri] — Terminkalender

to **cancel** [ˈkænsl] — streichen

first thing [ˈfɜːst θɪŋ] — gleich morgens, als Erstes

UNIT 5

49 trade fair [ˈtreɪd feə] — Handelsmesse, Fachmesse

T brochure [ˈbrəʊʃə] — Prospekt, Werbebroschüre

trade [ˈtreɪd] — Handel

in the meantime [ɪn ðə ˈmiːntaɪm] — in der Zwischenzeit

seat [siːt] — Platz, Sitz

promotional [prəˈməʊʃənl] — Werbe-

gift [gɪft] — Geschenk

50 to **rearrange** [ˌriːəˈreɪndʒ] — umstellen

51 possibly [ˈpɒsəbli] — möglicherweise, vielleicht

supplier [səˈplaɪə] — Lieferant/in, Zulieferer

as yet [əz ˈjet] — bis jetzt

splendid [ˈsplendɪd] — großartig

52 diary [ˈdaɪəri] — Terminkalender

hospital [ˈhɒspɪtl] — Krankenhaus

dentist [ˈdentɪst] — Zahnarzt/-ärztin

transportation [ˌtrænspɔːˈteɪʃn] — Beförderung, Transport

to **get down to business** [ˌget ˈdaʊn tə ˈbɪznəs] — zur Sache kommen

53 That depends. [ðət dɪˈpendz] — Kommt drauf an.

wholesale [ˈhəʊlseɪl] — Großhandel

shipping [ˈʃɪpɪŋ] — Versand

shipment [ˈʃɪpmənt] — Versand, Transport

option [ˈɒpʃn] — Möglichkeit, Option

freight [freɪt] — Fracht

sea freight [ˈsiː freɪt] — Seefracht

relevant [ˈreləvənt] — relevant

road haulage [ˈrəʊd hɔːlɪdʒ] — Straßentransport

to **ship** [ʃɪp] — verschicken

rail [reɪl] — Schiene, Bahn

air freight [ˈeə freɪt] — Luftfracht

significance [sɪgˈnɪfɪkəns] — Bedeutung

54 to **discount** [dɪsˈkaʊnt] — (Preis) nachlassen, einen Rabatt gewähren

to **run the risk** [ˌrʌn ðə ˈrɪsk] — riskieren

Chronological word list

at the latest [ət ðə ˈleɪtɪst]	spätestens	
to be due to sth [bi ˈdjuː tə]	an etw liegen	
delayed [dɪˈleɪd]	verspätet	
55	unlikely [ʌnˈlaɪkli]	unwahrscheinlich T
recipient [rɪˈsɪpiənt]	Empfänger/in	
ID number [ˌaɪ ˈdiː nʌmbə]	Identifikationsnummer	
subtotal [ˈsʌbtəʊtl]	Zwischensumme	
carriage [ˈkærɪdʒ]	Transport	
transfer [ˈtrænsfɜː]	Überweisung	
sorting code [ˈsɔːtɪŋ kəʊd]	Bankleitzahl	
56	reminder [rɪˈmaɪndə]	Mahnung
grateful [ˈɡreɪtfl]	dankbar	
to overlook [ˌəʊvəˈlʊk]	übersehen	
to clear an account [ˌklɪər ən əˈkaʊnt]	ein Konto ausgleichen, eine offene Rechnung begleichen	
to remit [rɪˈmɪt]	überweisen, bezahlen	
reference [ˈrefərəns]	Bezug	
to settle [ˈsetl]	begleichen, bezahlen	
extract [ˈekstrækt]	Auszug	
despite [dɪˈspaɪt]	trotz	
to force [fɔːs]	zwingen	
to take legal steps [teɪk ˌliːɡl ˈsteps]	rechtliche Schritte unternehmen	
straightaway [ˌstreɪt əˈweɪ]	sofort, umgehend	
to press sb [pres]	jdn nachdrücklich auffordern	
matter [ˈmætə]	Angelegenheit, Sache	
solicitor [səˈlɪsɪtə]	Anwalt/Anwältin (für Zivilrecht)	
to insist [ɪnˈsɪst]	darauf bestehen	
concerned [kənˈsɜːnd]	besorgt, beunruhigt	
regarding [rɪˈɡɑːdɪŋ]	betreffend, bezüglich	
57	a shame [ə ˈʃeɪm]	schade
T	to cancel [ˈkænsl]	absagen, stornieren
to reschedule [ˌriːˈʃedjuːl]	verlegen	
range [reɪndʒ]	Sortiment, (Kleidung:) Kollektion	
point of view [ˌpɔɪnt əv ˈvjuː]	Standpunkt	
review [rɪˈvjuː]	Bewertung	
58	to update [ˌʌpˈdeɪt]	aktualisieren, auf den neusten Stand bringen
border [ˈbɔːdə]	Grenze	
to cover [ˈkʌvə]	(Kosten) decken, aufkommen für	
involved [ɪnˈvɒlvd]	(Kosten:) entstehend, anfallend	
seller [ˈselə]	Verkäufer	
goods (pl.) [ɡʊdz]	Ware(n)	

ship [ʃɪp]	Schiff
insurance [ɪnˈʃʊərəns]	Versicherung
port of destination [ˌpɔːt əv destɪˈneɪʃn]	Bestimmungshafen
to clear for export [ˌklɪə fər ˈekspɔːt]	Ausfuhrformalitäten erledigen, zur Ausfuhr abfertigen lassen
forwarding agent [ˈfɔːwədɪŋ eɪdʒənt]	Spediteur, Spedition
carrier [ˈkæriə]	Frachtführer
destination [ˌdestɪˈneɪʃn]	Bestimmungsort
buyer [ˈbaɪə]	Käufer
customs duty [ˌkʌstəmz ˈdjuːti]	Zollgebühr(en)
loading [ˈləʊdɪŋ]	Verladen, Verladung
contract [ˈkɒntrækt]	Vertrag
contract of carriage [ˌkɒntrækt əv ˈkærɪdʒ]	Beförderungsvertrag
export clearance [ˈekspɔːt klɪərəns]	(Erledigung der) Ausfuhrformalitäten
terminal [ˈtɜːmɪnl]	Entladestation, -stelle, Terminal
port of shipment [ˌpɔːt əv ˈʃɪpmənt]	Verladehafen
import clearance [ˈɪmpɔːt klɪərəns]	(Erledigung der) Einfuhrformalitäten
unloading [ˌʌnˈləʊdɪŋ]	Entladen, Entladung
pre-carriage [ˌpriː ˈkærɪdʒ]	Vorlauf
main carriage [ˌmeɪn ˈkærɪdʒ]	Hauptlauf
post-carriage [ˌpəʊst ˈkærɪdʒ]	Nachlauf
CIF (Cost, Insurance and Freight) [ˌsiː aɪ ˈef/ˌkɒst ɪnˈʃʊərəns ənd ˈfreɪt]	Kosten, Versicherung, Fracht
FCA (Free Carrier) [ˌef siː ˈeɪ/ˌfriː ˈkæriə]	frei Frachtführer
CPT (Carriage Paid to) [ˌsiː piː ˈtiː/ˌkærɪdʒ ˈpeɪd tə]	frachtfrei
DDP (Delivery Duty Paid) [ˌdiː diː ˈpiː/dɪˌlɪvəri ˌdjuːti ˈpeɪd]	geliefert verzollt
FOB (Free On Board) [ˌef əʊ ˈbiː/ˌfriː ɒn ˈbɔːd]	frei an Bord
CIP (Carriage and Insurance Paid to) [ˌsiː aɪ ˈpiː/ˈkærɪdʒ ənd ɪnˈʃʊərəns ˈpeɪd tə]	frachtfrei versichert bis

UNIT 6

59	customer care [ˈkʌstəmə keə]	Kundenbetreuung
	to complain [kəmˈpleɪn]	sich beschweren

147

Chronological word list

	to **be about to do sth** [bɪ əˈbaʊt tə duː]	im Begriff sein, etw zu tun; gerade etw tun wollen
	lunch break [ˈlʌntʃ breɪk]	Mittagspause
60	to **say hello to sb** [ˌseɪ həˈləʊ tə]	jdn begrüßen
	firm [fɜːm]	fest, hart, unnachgiebig
	polite [pəˈlaɪt]	höflich
	guideline [ˈgaɪdlaɪn]	Richtlinie
	incoming [ˈɪnkʌmɪŋ]	eingehend
	satisfied [ˈsætɪsfaɪd]	zufrieden
	package [ˈpækɪdʒ]	Paket
	to **meet sb's needs** [ˌmiːt ˈniːdz]	jds Bedürfnissen entsprechen
	to **maximise** [ˈmæksɪmaɪz]	maximieren
	revenue [ˈrevənjuː]	Einkünfte
	to **avoid** [əˈvɔɪd]	vermeiden, verhindern
	to **ring** [rɪŋ]	klingeln
	ring [rɪŋ]	Klingeln
	alternative [ɔːlˈtɜːnətɪv]	Alternative
	voucher [ˈvaʊtʃə]	Gutschein
	to **hurry** [ˈhʌri]	eilen, sich beeilen
	customer satisfaction [ˌkʌstəmə sætɪsˈfækʃn]	Kundenzufriedenheit
	stupid [ˈstjuːpɪd]	dumm
	likely [ˈlaɪkli]	wahrscheinlich
	to **cancel a contract** [ˌkænsl ə ˈkɒntrækt]	einen Vertrag auflösen
	at all cost [ət ˌɔːl ˈkɒst]	um jeden Preis
	to **solve** [sɒlv]	lösen
	customer retention [ˈkʌstəmə rɪtenʃn]	Kundenbindung
	valuable [ˈvæljuəbl]	wertvoll
61	to **ensure** [ɪnˈʃʊə]	sicherstellen, gewährleisten
	common [ˈkɒmən]	gemeinsam
	priority [praɪˈɒrəti]	Priorität
62	**cartoon** [kɑːˈtuːn]	Karikatur, Comiczeichnung
T	**pub** [pʌb]	Kneipe
	It's just not on. [ɪts ˌdʒʌst nɒt ˈɒn]	Das geht doch einfach nicht!
	to **wonder** [ˈwʌndə]	sich fragen
	to **attend to sb** [əˈtend tə]	sich um jdn kümmern, jdn bedienen
	to **deal with sb** [ˈdiːl wɪð]	sich um jdn kümmern, mit jdm zu tun haben
	face-to-face [ˌfeɪs tə ˈfeɪs]	persönlich
	immediate [ɪˈmiːdiət]	unverzüglich, unmittelbar
	attention [əˈtenʃn]	Aufmerksamkeit
	for instance [fəˈrɪnstəns]	zum Beispiel

	to **mind** [maɪnd]	etw dagegen haben
	shortly [ˈʃɔːtli]	in Kürze
	to **emphasise sth** [ˈemfəsaɪz]	etw betonen, den Schwerpunkt auf etw legen
	benefit [ˈbenɪfɪt]	Vorteil, Nutzen
63	to **irritate** [ˈɪrɪteɪt]	verärgern, belästigen
	policy [ˈpɒləsi]	Politik, Vorgehensweise, Regeln
	rude [ruːd]	unhöflich, unverschämt
	to **post** [pəʊst]	(Brief) einwerfen, zur Post bringen
	to **annoy sb** [əˈnɔɪ]	jdm lästig werden, jdm auf die Nerven gehen
64	**sales assistant** [ˈseɪlz əsɪstənt]	Verkäufer/in
	to **switch sth off** [ˌswɪtʃ ˈɒf]	etw ausschalten
	text message [ˈtekst mesɪdʒ]	SMS
	annoying [əˈnɔɪɪŋ]	ärgerlich
	receipt [rɪˈsiːt]	Quittung, Beleg
	to **not be supposed to do sth** [ˌnɒt bi səˈpəʊzd tə duː]	etw nicht tun dürfen
	obvious [ˈɒbviəs]	offensichtlich
	refund [ˈriːfʌnd]	Erstattung, Rückerstattung
	faulty [ˈfɔːlti]	defekt, mangelhaft
	repair [rɪˈpeə]	Reparatur
	to **be supposed to do sth** [bɪ səˈpəʊzd tə duː]	etw tun sollen
	acceptable [əkˈseptəbl]	akzeptabel
65	**useless** [ˈjuːsləs]	nutzlos, unfähig
	to **take sb for a ride** [ˌteɪk fər ə ˈraɪd]	jdn übers Ohr hauen, jdn reinlegen
	supposedly [səˈpəʊzɪdli]	angeblich
	to **sort sth out** [ˌsɔːt ˈaʊt]	etw klären, etw in Ordnung bringen
	upset [ˌʌpˈset]	verärgert
	to **shout** [ʃaʊt]	schreien
	to **calm down** [ˌkɑːm ˈdaʊn]	sich beruhigen
	replacement [rɪˈpleɪsmənt]	Ersatz
	to **repair** [rɪˈpeə]	reparieren
	I suppose [ˌaɪ səˈpəʊz]	immerhin, nun ja
	to **turn sth off** [ˌtɜːn ˈɒf]	etw ausschalten
	to **replace** [rɪˈpleɪs]	ersetzen
66	**performance** [pəˈfɔːməns]	Leistung
	flowchart [ˈfləʊtʃɑːt]	Flussdiagramm
	to **assist sb** [əˈsɪst]	jdm helfen, jdn unterstützen
	complaint [kəmˈpleɪnt]	Reklamation
	to **report sth** [rɪˈpɔːt]	etw melden

Chronological word list

fault [fɔːlt]	Defekt, Schaden
to process ['prəʊses]	bearbeiten
fault report ['fɔːlt rɪpɔːt]	Schadensmeldung
to fix [fɪks]	(Problem) beheben, (Schaden) reparieren
to return [rɪ'tɜːn]	zurückschicken
67 support [sə'pɔːt]	Unterstützung, Kundendienst
to assure [ə'ʃʊə]	versichern, zusichern
to state [steɪt]	sagen, erklären
to deal with sth ['diːl wɪð]	etw bearbeiten, etw erledigen
to fulfil [fʊl'fɪl]	erfüllen
terms [tɜːmz]	Konditionen, Bedingungen
to continue [kən'tɪnjuː]	anhalten, andauern
68 customer acquistion ['kʌstəmər ækwɪzɪʃn]	Kundenwerbung
to regard sth as sth [rɪ'gɑːd əz]	etw für etw halten
to acquire [ə'kwaɪə]	gewinnen, erwerben
in the first place [ɪn ðə 'fɜːst pleɪs]	zunächst einmal, überhaupt erst
profitable ['prɒfɪtəbl]	rentabel, gewinn-bringend
competition [ˌkɒmpə'tɪʃn]	Konkurrenz
to take action [teɪk 'ækʃn]	Maßnahmen ergreifen
to hold onto sb [ˌhəʊld 'ɒntə]	jdn festhalten
retail ['riːteɪl]	Einzelhandel
frequently ['friːkwəntli]	häufig
loyalty card ['lɔɪəlti kɑːd]	Kundenkarte
enormous [ɪ'nɔːməs]	gewaltig, enorm
to prevent [prɪ'vent]	verhindern
tariff ['tærɪf]	Tarif
retailer ['riːteɪlə]	Einzelhändler
to involve sb in sth [ɪn'vɒlv ɪn]	jdn an etw beteiligen
to evaluate [ɪ'væljueɪt]	bewerten, beurteilen
review [rɪ'vjuː]	Besprechung, Rezension, Kritik
comment ['kɒment]	Kommentar
in theory [ɪn 'θɪəri]	theoretisch
to retain [rɪ'teɪn]	(be)halten

SITUATION 3

69 to indicate ['ɪndɪkeɪt]	angeben
quantity ['kwɒntəti]	Menge
racquet ['rækɪt]	Tennisschläger
net [net]	Netz
hopper ['hɒpə]	Behälter, Magazin
umpire ['ʌmpaɪə]	Schiedsrichter/in
70 to compare [kəm'peə]	vergleichen

shipment ['ʃɪpmənt]	Sendung, Lieferung
unsent [ˌʌn'sent]	nicht gesendet
to specify ['spesɪfaɪ]	(genau) angeben
humorous(ly) ['hjuːmərəs]	humorvoll

UNIT 7

72 to depart [dɪ'pɑːt]	abfliegen
tax [tæks]	Steuer
to suppose [sə'pəʊz]	annehmen, glauben
passport ['pɑːspɔːt]	Reisepass
on time [ɒn 'taɪm]	pünktlich
boarding card ['bɔːdɪŋ kɑːd]	Bordkarte
alcohol ['ælkəhɒl]	Alkohol
73 arrival [ə'raɪvl]	Ankunft
departure [dɪ'pɑːtʃə]	Abreise, Abfahrt, Abflug
security check [sɪ'kjʊərəti tʃek]	Sicherheitskontrolle
immigration [ˌɪmɪ'greɪʃn]	Passkontrolle
customs ['kʌstəmz]	Zoll
gate [geɪt]	Flugsteig
baggage ['bægɪdʒ]	Gepäck
baggage reclaim ['bægɪdʒ riːkleɪm]	Gepäckausgabe
past sth [pɑːst]	an etw vorbei
beside [bɪ'saɪd]	neben
announcement [ə'naʊnsmənt]	Durchsage
T to proceed [prə'siːd]	sich begeben
to board ['bɔːd]	an Bord gehen, einsteigen
row [rəʊ]	Reihe
call [kɔːl]	Aufruf
luggage ['lʌgɪdʒ]	Gepäck
unattended [ˌʌnə'tendɪd]	unbeaufsichtigt
to destroy [dɪ'strɔɪ]	zerstören
74 single room [ˌsɪŋgl 'ruːm]	Einzelzimmer
business centre ['bɪznəs sentə]	Business-Center
conference room ['kɒnfərəns ruːm]	Tagungsraum, Konferenzzimmer
gym [dʒɪm]	Fitnessstudio
exercise ['eksəsaɪz]	Bewegung
sauna ['sɔːnə]	Sauna
to hire sth ['haɪə]	etw mieten
car park ['kɑː pɑːk]	Parkplatz, Parkhaus, Tiefgarage
to comprise [kəm'praɪz]	umfassen, bestehen aus
suite [swiːt]	Suite

Chronological word list

double room [ˌdʌbl ˈruːm]	Doppelzimmer	
fully-equipped [ˌfʊli ɪˈkwɪpt]	voll ausgestattet	
satellite [ˈsætəlaɪt]	Satellit	
en-suite bathroom [ɒ ˌswiːt ˈbɑːθruːm]	eigenes Badezimmer	
to **accommodate** [əˈkɒmədeɪt]	unterbringen, Platz bieten für	
participant [pɑːˈtɪsɪpənt]	Teilnehmer/in	
meeting room [ˈmiːtɪŋ ruːm]	Besprechungszimmer	
latest [ˈleɪtɪst]	neueste/r/s	
cordless [ˈkɔːdləs]	schnurlos	
microphone [ˈmaɪkrəfəʊn]	Mikrofon	
to **complement** [ˈkɒmplɪmənt]	ergänzen	
to **photocopy** [ˈfəʊtəʊkɒpi]	fotokopieren	
secure [sɪˈkjʊə]	sicher	
leisure [ˈleʒə]	Freizeit	
to **unwind** [ˌʌnˈwaɪnd]	sich entspannen, abschalten	
to **dine** [daɪn]	speisen	
to **be spoilt for choice** [bi ˌspɔɪlt fə ˈtʃɔɪs]	die Qual der Wahl haben	
eatery [ˈiːtəri]	Restaurant, Speiselokal	
snack [snæk]	Imbiss	
course [kɔːs]	*(Menü:)* Gang	

76	**conference** [ˈkɒnfərəns]	Konferenz
	scheduled [ˈʃedjuːld]	planmäßig
	entry [ˈentri]	Eintrag
	opening [ˈəʊpənɪŋ]	Eröffnung
	agenda [əˈdʒendə]	Tagesordnung
T	**dessert** [dɪˈzɜːt]	Nachspeise, Dessert
	speciality [ˈspeʃəlti]	Spezialität
	delicious [dɪˈlɪʃəs]	köstlich
	boring [ˈbɔːrɪŋ]	langweilig
	spare time [ˌspeə ˈtaɪm]	Freizeit
	sailing [ˈseɪlɪŋ]	Segeln
	boat [bəʊt]	Boot
	lake [leɪk]	See
	to **sail** [seɪl]	segeln
	race [reɪs]	Regatta
	pressure [ˈpreʃə]	Druck
	to **defend** [dɪˈfend]	verteidigen
	opportunity [ˌɒpəˈtjuːnəti]	Möglichkeit, Gelegenheit, Chance
	to **support** [səˈpɔːt]	unterstützen, *hier:* Fan sein von
	waiter [ˈweɪtə]	Kellner
	bill [bɪl]	Rechnung

	to **head for sth** [ˈhed fə]	zu etw gehen/fahren
77	**salad** [ˈsæləd]	Salat
	credit card [ˈkredɪt kɑːd]	Kreditkarte
	wine list [ˈwaɪn lɪst]	Weinkarte
	safe [seɪf]	sicher
	pastime [ˈpɑːstaɪm]	Freizeitbeschäftigung
	politics [ˈpɒlətɪks]	Politik
	in advance of [ɪn ədˈvɑːns əv]	vor
	business contact [ˈbɪznəs kɒntækt]	Geschäftspartner/in
	to **compare** [kəmˈpeə]	vergleichen
	to **imagine sth** [ɪˈmædʒɪn]	sich etw vorstellen
78	**intercultural** [ˌɪntəˈkʌltʃərəl]	kulturübergreifend, interkulturell
	awareness [əˈweənəs]	Wissen, Bewusstsein
	neighbouring [ˈneɪbərɪŋ]	benachbart, Nachbar-
	understanding [ˌʌndəˈstændɪŋ]	Verständnis
	to **tend to do sth** [ˈtend tə duː]	dazu neigen, etw zu tun
	far flung [ˌfɑː ˈflʌŋ]	weit vom Schuss
	consultancy [kənˈsʌltənsi]	Beratung, Beratungsfirma
	to **realise sth** [ˈrɪəlaɪz]	etw erkennen
	due to [ˈdjuː tə]	aufgrund von
	to **arise** [əˈraɪz]	auftreten, entstehen
	misunderstanding [ˌmɪsʌndəˈstændɪŋ]	Missverständnis
	direction [dəˈrekʃn]	Ausrichtung
	business card [ˈbɪznəs kɑːd]	Visitenkarte
	negotiating partner [nɪˈɡəʊʃieɪtɪŋ pɑːtnə]	Verhandlungspartner/in
	to **be regarded as sth** [bi rɪˈɡɑːdɪd əz]	als etw gelten
	shallow [ˈʃæləʊ]	oberflächlich
	to **stereotype sb** [ˈsteriətaɪp]	jdn in ein Klischee zwängen
	insight [ˈɪnsaɪt]	Einblick
	thanks to [ˈθæŋks tə]	dank
	to **assume** [əˈsjuːm]	annehmen, davon ausgehen
	to **suffer** [ˈsʌfə]	leiden
79	to **gain** [ɡeɪn]	gewinnen, erwerben
	status [ˈsteɪtəs]	Status, Ansehen
	to **afford sth** [əˈfɔːd]	sich etw leisten (können)
	manner [ˈmænə]	Art (und Weise)
	to **attempt** [əˈtemt]	versuchen
	initial [ɪˈnɪʃəl]	erste/r/s, anfänglich
	to **overcome sth** [ˌəʊvəˈkʌm]	etw überwinden

Chronological word list

in favour of sth [ɪn 'feɪvər əv]	für etw, zugunsten einer Sache	
occasion [ə'keɪʒn]	Anlass, Ereignis	
budget airline ['bʌdʒɪt eəlaɪn]	Billigflieger	
to **apply to sth** [ə'plaɪ tə]	für etw gelten	
prepared [prɪ'peəd]	bereit	
upmarket [,ʌp'mɑːkɪt]	schick, teuer	
glamour ['glæmə]	Glanz	
to **stretch one's legs** [,stretʃ wʌnz 'legz]	die Beine ausstrecken	
demand [dɪ'mɑːnd]	Bedarf	

UNIT 8

80	**audio-visual** [,ɔːdiəʊ'vɪʒuəl]	audiovisuell
81	to **require** [rɪ'kwaɪə]	benötigen, wünschen
	loudspeaker ['laʊdspiːkə]	Lautsprecher
T	**OHP** [,əʊ eɪtʃ 'piː]	Overheadprojektor
82	to **bore sb** [bɔː]	jdn langweilen
	unprepared [,ʌnprɪ'peəd]	unvorbereitet
	disorganised [dɪs'ɔːgənaɪzd]	chaotisch, desorganisiert
	to **reveal** [rɪ'viːl]	verraten, offenbaren
	nervousness ['nɜːvəsnəs]	Nervosität
	content [kən'tent]	Inhalt
	to **appreciate** [ə'priːʃieɪt]	schätzen, zu schätzen wissen
T	**tasty** ['teɪsti]	lecker
	healthy ['helθi]	gesund
	to **begin with** [tə bɪ'gɪn wɪð]	zunächst
	to **focus on sth** ['fəʊkəs ɒn]	sich auf etw konzentrieren
	dynamic [daɪ'næmɪk]	dynamisch
	impressed [ɪm'prest]	beeindruckt
	to **taste** ['teɪst]	etw probieren, etw kosten
	to **look closely at sth** [,lʊk 'kləʊsli ət]	sich etw genau ansehen
	time frame ['taɪm freɪm]	Zeitrahmen
83	**section** ['sekʃn]	Teil, Abschnitt
	outline ['aʊtlaɪn]	Überblick
84	to **gather** ['gæðə]	sammeln
	proposal [prə'pəʊzl]	Vorschlag, Angebot
85	**visuals** ['vɪʒuəlt]	visuelle Hilfsmittel
	low in sth ['ləʊ ɪn]	arm an etw
	fat [fæt]	Fett
	variety [və'raɪəti]	Sorte
	nut [nʌt]	Nuss
	raisin ['reɪzn]	Rosine

	banana [bə'nɑːnə]	Banane
	apple [æpl]	Apfel
	award [ə'wɔːd]	Preis, Auszeichnung
	solid ['sɒlɪd]	solide
	base [beɪs]	Basis
	logistics *(pl)* [lə'dʒɪstɪks]	Logistik
T	**pie chart** ['paɪ tʃɑːt]	Tortendiagramm
	fairly ['feəli]	ziemlich
	line graph ['laɪn grɑːf]	Liniendiagramm, Kurve
	to **demonstrate** ['demənstreɪt]	zeigen
	to **direct sth at sth** [də'rekt]	etw auf etw lenken
	event [ɪ'vent]	Ereignis
	to **prove sth** [pruːv]	sich als etw erweisen
	bar chart ['bɑː tʃɑːt]	Säulendiagramm
	to **depict** [dɪ'pɪkt]	darstellen
	to **detail** ['diːteɪl]	(im Einzelnen) aufführen, darstellen
	net [net]	netto
86	**introduction** [,ɪntrə'dʌkʃn]	Einleitung
	to **note** [nəʊt]	bemerken
	profile ['prəʊfaɪl]	Porträt, Profil
87	to **turn to sth** ['tɜːn tə]	sich einer Sache zuwenden
	loser ['luːzə]	Verlierer/in
	to **stand to do sth** ['stænd tə duː]	etw tun werden
	to **profit** ['prɒfɪt]	profitieren
	to **secure** [sɪ'kjuə]	sichern
	crucial ['kruːʃl]	entscheidend
	to **hit** [hɪt]	treffen, (Ziel) erreichen
	to **enable** [ɪ'neɪbl]	befähigen, (es) ermöglichen
	to **cement** [sɪ'ment]	festigen, stärken, zementieren
	partnership ['pɑːtnəʃɪp]	Zusammenarbeit, Partnerschaft
	to **admit** [əd'mɪt]	zugeben, gestehen, eingestehen
	to **strengthen** ['streŋθn]	stärken
	joint [dʒɔɪnt]	gemeinsam
	branding ['brændɪŋ]	Markenbildung, Markenentwicklung
	to **pour sth into sth** ['pɔːr ɪntə]	etw in etw fließen lassen
	cash flow ['kæʃ fləʊ]	Geldmittel
88	**body language** ['bɒdi læŋgwɪdʒ]	Körpersprache
	to **jump about** [,dʒʌmp ə'baʊt]	herumhüpfen
	to **succeed** [sək'siːd]	erfolgreich sein, Erfolg haben
	to **fail** [feɪl]	scheitern
	presenter [prɪ'zentə]	Redner/in

Chronological word list

to **behave** [bɪ'heɪv]	sich verhalten	
to **turn sth down** [ˌtɜːn 'daʊn]	(Blick) senken, nach unten richten	
as **though** [əz 'ðəʊ]	als ob	
eye contact ['aɪ kɒntækt]	Blickkontakt	
to **connect** [kə'nekt]	eine Verbindung herstellen	
to **trust** [trʌst]	vertrauen	
to **distract** [dɪ'strækt]	ablenken	
the **latter** [ðə 'lætə]	Letztere/r/s, der/die/das Letztgenannte	
chin [tʃɪn]	Kinn	
to **point to sth** ['pɔɪnt tə]	auf etw zeigen	
gesture ['dʒestʃə]	Geste	
to **lack in sth** ['læk ɪn]	zu wenig von etw haben	
lazy ['leɪzi]	faul, schlaff	
to **be committed to sth** [bi kə'mɪtɪd tə]	hinter einer Sache stehen	
frantically ['fræntɪkli]	wie verrückt	
spot [spɒt]	Fleck, Punkt	
pace [peɪs]	Schritt	
occasionally [ə'keɪʒənəli]	gelegentlich	
strange [streɪndʒ]	seltsam, merkwürdig	
facial gesture [ˌfeɪʃl 'dʒestʃə]	Miene, Grimasse	
to **bite sth** [baɪt]	auf etw beißen	
lip [lɪp]	Lippe	
to **suck sth in** [ˌsʌk 'ɪn]	etw einziehen	
cheek [tʃiːk]	Wange	
to **pucker sth** ['pʌkə]	etw verziehen	
to **be aware of sth** [bi ə'weər əv]	sich einer Sache bewusst sein, etw wissen	
impatient [ɪm'peɪʃnt]	ungeduldig, unduldsam	

SITUATION 4

89	**marriage** ['mærɪdʒ]	Ehe
	travel agent ['trævl eɪdʒənt]	Reisebüro
	requirement [rɪ'kwaɪəmənt]	Anforderung, Wunsch
	vegetarian [ˌvedʒə'teəriən]	vegetarisch
	close to ['kləʊs tə]	nahe bei, in der Nähe von
	location [ləʊ'keɪʃn]	Lage
	tiny ['taɪni]	winzig
90	**wedding** ['wedɪŋ]	Hochzeit
	champagne [ʃæm'peɪn]	Champagner
	civil ['sɪvl]	standesamtlich
	church [tʃɜːtʃ]	Kirche; kirchlich

charity shop ['tʃærəti ʃɒp]	Secondhandladen (für wohltätige Zwecke)	
invitation [ˌɪnvɪ'teɪʃn]	Einladung	
decoration [ˌdekə'reɪʃn]	Dekoration	
peak [piːk]	Höchststand, Spitzenwert	
high season [ˌhaɪ 'siːzn]	Hochsaison	

UNIT 9

91	**call-up** ['kɔːl ʌp]	Abruf
	to **request** [rɪ'kwest]	anfordern
	packing ['pækɪŋ]	Verpackung
	storage ['stɔːrɪdʒ]	Lagerung
	to **cover** ['kʌvə]	abdecken, bedecken
	protective [prə'tektɪv]	Schutz-
	to **store** [stɔː]	lagern
	warehouse ['weəhaʊs]	Lager, Lagerhalle
	procurement [prə'kjʊəmənt]	Beschaffung
	inspection [ɪn'spekʃn]	Kontrolle, Überprüfung
	to **assemble** [ə'sembl]	montieren, zusammenbauen
	to **call sth up** [ˌkɔːl 'ʌp]	etw abrufen
92	**work experience placement** ['wɜːk ɪkspɪəriəns pleɪsmənt]	Praktikum
	to **be made up of sth** [bi ˌmeɪd 'ʌp əv]	aus etw bestehen, sich aus etw zusammensetzen
	to **be delighted** [bi dɪ'laɪtɪd]	sich freuen
	to **be involved in sth** [bi ɪn'vɒlvd ɪn]	an etw beteiligt sein, bei etw mitmachen
	management ['mænɪdʒmənt]	Steuerung, Kontrolle, Verwaltung
	related to [rɪ'leɪtɪd tə]	bezüglich
	raw material [ˌrɔː mə'tɪəriəl]	Rohstoff, Rohmaterial
	component [kəm'pəʊnənt]	Bauteil, Teil, Komponente
	production line [prə'dʌkʃn laɪn]	Fertigungsstraße
	to **negotiate** [nɪ'gəʊʃieɪt]	verhandeln, aushandeln
	delivery terms [dɪ'lɪvəri tɜːmz]	Lieferbedingungen
	enterprise ['entəpraɪz]	Unternehmen
	resource [rɪ'sɔːs]	Rohstoff, Ressource
	to **co-ordinate** [kəʊ'ɔːdɪneɪt]	koordinieren
	to **monitor** ['mɒnɪtə]	überwachen
	to **be out and about** [bi ˌaʊt ənd ə'baʊt]	unterwegs sein
93	**protective gloves** (pl.) [prə'tektɪv glʌvz]	Schutzhandschuhe
	hard hat [ˌhɑːd 'hæt]	Schutzhelm
	boot [buːt]	Stiefel

Chronological word list

	harness ['hɑːnɪs]	(Sicherheits-)Gurt
T	warehouse manager ['weəhaʊs mænɪdʒə]	Leiter/in des Waren-lagers, Lagerleiter/in
	to fill sb in [ˌfɪl 'ɪn]	jdn informieren, jdn ins Bild setzen
	regulations (pl.) [ˌregjuˈleɪʃnz]	Bestimmungen, Vorschriften
	to sign in [ˌsaɪn 'ɪn]	sich eintragen
	measure ['meʒə]	Maßnahme
	storage rack ['stɔːrɪdʒ ræk]	Lagergestell
	to lift sth [lɪft]	etw hochheben, etw anheben
	flammable ['flæməbl]	brennbar, leicht entzündbar
	high voltage [ˌhaɪ 'vəʊltɪdʒ]	Hochspannung
	electricity [ɪˌlek'trɪsəti]	Elektrizität, Strom
	delivery bay [dɪ'lɪvəri beɪ]	Ladebucht
	forklift truck ['fɔːklɪft trʌk]	Gabelstapler
	in operation [ˌɪn ɒpə'reɪʃn]	in Betrieb
	naked flame [ˌneɪkɪd 'fleɪm]	offene Flamme, offenes Feuer
	to put sth out [ˌpʊt 'aʊt]	etw löschen
94	accident ['æksɪdənt]	Unfall
	injured ['ɪndʒəd]	verletzt
	first aid [ˌfɜːst 'eɪd]	erste Hilfe
	first-aid kit [ˌfɜːst 'eɪd kɪt]	Verbandskasten
	medical ['medɪkl]	medizinisch
	comfortable ['kʌmftəbl]	bequem, angenehm
	neck [nek]	Hals
	injury ['ɪndʒəri]	Verletzung
	ambulance ['æmbjələns]	Krankenwagen
	in the event of [ɪn ði ɪ'vent əv]	im Fall eine/r/s
	to injure ['ɪndʒə]	verletzen
	to raise alarm [ˌreɪz ə'lɑːm]	Alarm schlagen
	to reassure [ˌriːə'ʃʊə]	beruhigen
	to suffer sth ['sʌfə]	etw erleiden
95	hub [hʌb]	Nabel, Drehkreuz
	supply chain [sə'plaɪ tʃeɪn]	Versorgungskette, Lieferkette
	to unload [ˌʌn'ləʊd]	entladen
	paperwork ['peɪpəwɜːk]	Unterlagen
	delivery note [dɪ'lɪvəri nəʊt]	Lieferschein
	to file [faɪl]	ablegen, zu den Akten legen
	record ['rekɔːd]	Nachweis

	stocktaking ['stɒkteɪkɪŋ]	Inventur, Bestands-aufnahme
	delay [dɪ'leɪ]	Verzögerung
	to pack [pæk]	packen, verpacken
	manually ['mænjuəli]	von Hand
	to pick sth out [ˌpɪk 'aʊt]	etw heraussuchen
	to make sense [meɪk 'sens]	sinnvoll sein
	route [ruːt]	Weg
96	series ['sɪəriːz]	Reihe
	assembly [ə'sembli]	Montage
	floor space ['flɔː speɪs]	Nutzfläche
	at all times [ət ˌɔːl 'taɪmz]	jederzeit
97	robot ['rəʊbɒt]	Roboter
T	to tool sth up [ˌtuːl 'ʌp]	etw maschinell ausrüsten
	manual ['mænjuəl]	Hand-
	to stamp [stæmp]	stempeln
	automated ['ɔːtəmeɪtɪd]	automatisch, auto-matisiert
	brake [breɪk]	Bremse
	gear [gɪə]	Gangschaltung
	to mount [maʊnt]	montieren
	quantity ['kwɒntəti]	Menge
	to determine [dɪ'tɜːmɪn]	bestimmen
	supplies (pl.) [sə'plaɪz]	Ware(n), Vorräte
	to forecast ['fɔːkɑːst]	voraussagen
	unneeded [ˌʌn'niːdɪd]	nicht benötigt, unnötig
	to roll off [ˌrəʊl 'ɒf]	vom Band rollen
	quality control ['kwɒləti kəntrəʊl]	Qualitätskontrolle
	to inspect [ɪn'spekt]	untersuchen, über-prüfen
	to fit sth [fɪt]	etw einbauen, etw montieren
	to wrap sth up [ˌræp 'ʌp]	etw verpacken, etw einwickeln
	condition [kən'dɪʃn]	Zustand
	passageway ['pæsɪdʒweɪ]	Gang, Durchgang
	shipping bay ['ʃɪpɪŋ beɪ]	Ladebucht
	haulage contractor ['hɔːlɪdʒ kəntræktə]	Spediteur
	in a nutshell [ɪn ə 'nʌtʃel]	in aller Kürze
	to nip along [ˌnɪp ə'lɒŋ]	(kurz) mitkommen
98	downhill [ˌdaʊn'hɪl]	bergab, Abfahrts-
	race [reɪs]	Rennen
	smooth [smuːð]	eben
	signature ['sɪgnətʃə]	Unterschrift
99	gripper ['grɪpə]	Greifer
	brake block ['breɪk blɒk]	Bremsklotz, Brems-belag

153

Chronological word list

brake lever ['breɪk liːvə]	Bremsgriff	
gear changer ['gɪə tʃeɪndʒə]	Gangschaltung, Schalthebel	
chainset ['tʃeɪnset]	Kurbelgarnitur	
100 **consultant** [kən'sʌltənt]	Berater/in	
to **protect** [prə'tekt]	schützen	
reputation [ˌrepjuˈteɪʃn]	(guter) Ruf	
quality assurance ['kwɒləti əʃʊərəns]	Qualitätssicherung	
machinery [məˈʃiːnəri]	Maschinen	
to **set sth up** [ˌset ˈʌp]	etw einrichten, etw einstellen	
to **be up to standard** [bi ˌʌp tə ˈstændəd]	den Vorgaben entsprechen	
to **differ** ['dɪfə]	sich unterscheiden	
depending on [dɪˈpendɪŋ ɒn]	je nachdem	
to **mass produce** ['mæs prədjuːs]	in Massen herstellen	
sample ['sɑːmpl]	Stichprobe	
batch production ['bætʃ prədʌkʃn]	Kleinserienfertigung	
to **contribute** [kən'trɪbjuːt]	beitragen	
finishing ['fɪnɪʃɪŋ]	Endfertigung	

UNIT 10

101 **career** [kə'rɪə]	Karriere, Beruf, Laufbahn	
to **apply for a job** [əˌplaɪ fər ə ˈdʒɒb]	sich um/auf eine Stelle bewerben	
102 **skill** [skɪl]	Fähigkeit, Fertigkeit	
to **rate** [reɪt]	bewerten	
scale [skeɪl]	Skala	
honest ['ɒnɪst]	ehrlich	
hard-working [ˌhɑːd ˈwɜːkɪŋ]	fleißig	
ambitious [əm'bɪʃəs]	ehrgeizig	
a good communicator [ˌgʊd kəˈmjuːnɪkeɪtə]	ein kommunikativer Mensch	
to **be self-motivated** [bi ˌself ˈməʊtɪveɪtɪd]	motiviert sein, Eigeninitiative zeigen	
to **be numerate** [bi ˈnjuːmərət]	gut mit Zahlen umgehen können	
job advertisment ['dʒɒb ədvɜːtɪsmənt]	Stellenanzeige	
to **have good arithmetic** [həv ˌgʊd əˈrɪθmətɪk]	gut rechnen können	
103 **Administrative Support Assistant** [ədˌmɪnɪstrətɪv səˈpɔːt əsɪstənt]	Verwaltungsmitarbeiter/in	
salary ['sæləri]	Lohn, Gehalt	
benefits (pl.) ['benɪfɪt]	Sozialleistungen, Zulagen	

according to [əˈkɔːdɪŋ tə]	je nach, entsprechend	
motivated ['məʊtɪveɪtɪd]	motiviert	
background ['bækgraʊnd]	Hintergrund, Erfahrung, Herkunft	
candidate ['kændɪdət]	Kandidat/in, Bewerber/in	
on one's own [ˌɒn wʌnz ˈəʊn]	allein, selbstständig	
schedule ['ʃedjuːl]	Plan, Programm	
to **compile** [kəm'paɪl]	erstellen, zusammenstellen	
to **maintain** [meɪn'teɪn]	instandhalten, (Datenbank) pflegen	
database ['deɪtəbeɪs]	Datenbank	
proven ['pruːvn]	nachweislich, erwiesen	
requirement [rɪˈkwaɪəmənt]	Anforderung	
qualification [ˌkwɒlɪfɪˈkeɪʃn]	Abschluss, Qualifikation	
business administration ['bɪznəs ədmɪnɪstreɪʃn]	Betriebswirtschaft	
driving licence ['draɪvɪŋ laɪsns]	Führerschein	
fluency ['fluːənsi]	(fließende) Beherrschung (einer Sprache)	
closing date ['kləʊzɪŋ deɪt]	Einsendeschluss	
application [ˌæplɪˈkeɪʃn]	Bewerbung	
curriculum vitae (CV) [kəˌrɪkjələm ˈviːtaɪ/ ˌsiː ˈviː]	Lebenslauf	
covering letter ['kʌvərɪŋ letə]	Anschreiben, Begleitschreiben	
referee [refə'riː]	Referenzgeber	
agent ['eɪdʒənt]	Angestellte/r	
rapid(ly) ['ræpɪd]	rasch, schnell	
to **expand** [ɪk'spænd]	expandieren	
24/7 [twenti ˌfɔː ˈsevn]	rund um die Uhr	
patience ['peɪʃns]	Geduld	
humour ['hjuːmə]	Humor	
to **persuade** [pə'sweɪd]	überzeugen, überreden	
to **convince** [kən'vɪns]	überzeugen	
to **value** ['væljuː]	wertschätzen	
to **get out of one's way** [get ˌaʊt əv wʌnz ˈweɪ]	alle Hebel in Bewegung setzen	
century ['sentʃəri]	Jahrhundert	
to **back sth up** [ˌbæk ˈʌp]	etw absichern, etw unterstützen	
bonus ['bəʊnəs]	Zulage	
organic [ɔː'gænɪk]	Bio-	
figure ['fɪgə]	Zahl	

Chronological word list

	creativity [ˌkriːeɪˈtɪvəti]	Kreativität
	ability [əˈbɪləti]	Fähigkeit
	senior management [ˌsiːniə ˈmænɪdʒmənt]	leitende Angestellte, Unternehmensführung
	handy [ˈhændi]	nützlich, praktisch
	independent(ly) [ˌɪndɪˈpendənt]	unabhängig
	workload [ˈwɜːkləʊd]	Arbeitspensum
104	to motivate [ˈməʊtɪveɪt]	motivieren
	maths [mæθs]	Mathe
105	to advertise [ˈædvətaɪz]	(Stelle) ausschreiben
	whilst [waɪlst]	während
106	nationality [ˌnæʃəˈnæləti]	Staatsangehörigkeit
	backwards [ˈbækwədz]	rückwärts
	to list [lɪst]	auflisten
	competence [ˈkɒmpɪtəns]	Kompetenz
	to take up space [teɪk ˌʌp ˈspeɪs]	Platz einnehmen
	employer [ɪmˈplɔɪə]	Arbeitgeber
	professional [prəˈfeʃənl]	Berufstätige/r
	certificate [səˈtɪfɪkət]	Zeugnis
107	youth [juːθ]	Jugend
	life guard [ˈlaɪf gɑːd]	Rettungsschwimmer/in
	certificate [səˈtɪfɪkət]	Zertifikat, Diplom
	carnival [ˈkɑːnɪvl]	Karneval
	template [ˈtempleɪt]	Vorlage
108	book shop [ˈbʊk ʃɒp]	Buchhandlung
	geography [dʒiˈɒgrəfi]	Erdkunde, Geographie
	chemistry [ˈkemɪstri]	Chemie
	part-time [ˌpɑːt ˈtaɪm]	Teilzeit
T	direction [dəˈrekʃn]	Richtung
	to concentrate [ˈkɒnsəntreɪt]	sich konzentrieren
	satisfaction [ˌsætɪsˈfækʃn]	Zufriedenheit, Befriedigung
	excellent [ˈeksələnt]	ausgezeichnet, hervorragend
	to let go of sth [ˌlet ˈgəʊ əv]	etw loslassen
109	to take sth on [ˌteɪk ˈɒn]	etw übernehmen
	beforehand [bɪˈfɔːhænd]	vorher, zuvor
	in advance [ɪn ədˈvɑːns]	im Voraus
	pay [peɪ]	Bezahlung, Lohn, Gehalt
110	to hate [heɪt]	hassen, nicht mögen
T	to select [sɪˈlekt]	auswählen
	to take sth into account [ˌteɪk ɪntu əˈkaʊnt]	etw berücksichtigen
	to rely on sth [rɪˈlaɪ ɒn]	sich auf etw verlassen, sich auf etw stützen

	to invite [ɪnˈvaɪt]	einladen
	to conduct sth [kənˈdʌkt]	etw durchführen
	unexpected(ly) [ˌʌnɪkˈspektɪd]	unerwartet
	to interview sb [ˈɪntəvjuː]	mit jdm ein Bewerbungsgespräch führen
	on the spot [ɒn ðə ˈspɒt]	gleich, auf der Stelle
	to be designed to do sth [bi dɪˈzaɪnd tə]	dazu gedacht sein, etw zu tun
	to cope with sth [kəʊp]	mit etw zurechtkommen
	to invite sb to do sth [ɪnˈvaɪt]	jdn dazu auffordern, etw zu tun
	to check sb/sth out [ˌtʃek ˈaʊt]	sich jdn/etw ansehen
	to do the rounds [ˌduː ðə ˈraʊndz]	die Runde machen
	elevator [ˈelɪveɪtə]	Aufzug
	pitch [pɪtʃ]	Präsentation
	logic [ˈlɒdʒɪk]	Logik
	to ride [raɪd]	fahren
	predictable [prɪˈdɪktəbl]	vorraussagbar, vorhersehbar
111	assessment [əˈsesmənt]	Einschätzung, Beurteilung
	time-consuming [ˈtaɪm kənsjuːmɪŋ]	zeitraubend
	to talk sth up [ˌtɔːk ˈʌp]	etw schönreden
	to be closely related to sth [bi ˌkləʊsli rɪˈleɪtɪd tə]	engen Bezug zu etw haben
	to perform sth [pəˈfɔːm]	etw durchführen, etw ausführen
	to respond to sth [rɪˈspɒnd tə]	auf etw reagieren, auf etw antworten
	in writing [ɪn ˈraɪtɪŋ]	schriftlich
	initiative [ɪˈnɪʃətɪv]	Initiative
	to be on the look out for sb [bi ɒn ðə ˈlʊk aʊt fə]	jdn suchen, nach jdm Ausschau halten
	setting [ˈsetɪŋ]	Umgebung, Rahmen
	to display sth [dɪsˈpleɪ]	etw zur Schau stellen
	leadership qualities (pl.) [ˈliːdəʃɪp kwɒlətiz]	Führungsqualitäten
	social event [ˌsəʊʃl ɪˈvent]	geselliger/gesellschaftlicher Anlass
	to relate to sb [rɪˈleɪt tə]	eine Beziehung zu jdm herstellen
	working environment [ˌwɜːkɪŋ ɪnˈvaɪrənmənt]	Arbeitsumfeld
	according to [əˈkɔːdɪŋ tə]	laut, nach, gemäß
	to panic [ˈpænɪk]	in Panik geraten
	to relax [rɪˈlæks]	sich lockern, sich entspannen

155

Chronological word list

confident ['kɒnfɪdənt]   selbstsicher, selbstbewusst

SITUATION 5

112	short-term [,ʃɔːt 'tɜːm]	befristet, kurzfristig
	to liaise with sb [li'eɪz wɪð]	mit jdm zusammen-arbeiten
	to be familiar with sth [fə'mɪliə wɪð]	mit etw vertraut sein, mit etw umgehen können
	patient ['peɪʃnt]	geduldig
	diplomatic [,dɪplə'mætɪk]	diplomatisch
	to graduate ['grædʒueɪt]	einen Abschluss machen
	boy scout ['bɔɪ skaʊt]	Pfadfinder
	accountant [ə'kaʊntənt]	Buchhalter/in
	care [keə]	Sorgfalt
113	drawer [drɔː]	Schublade
T	Personnel Manager [,pɜːsə'nel mænɪdʒə]	Personalleiter/in
	Health & Safety officer [,helθ ənd 'seɪfti ɒfɪsə]	Beauftragte/r für Arbeitsschutz
	investigator [ɪn'vestɪgeɪtə]	Ermittler/in, Untersuchende/r
	treatment ['triːtmənt]	Behandlung
	cause [kɔːz]	Ursache
	involvement [ɪn'vɒlvmənt]	Beteiligung
	witness ['wɪtnəs]	Zeuge/Zeugin
	present ['preznt]	anwesend
	to hurt [hɜːt]	verletzen, wehtun
	mild [maɪld]	leicht
	to trip [trɪp]	stolpern
	wiring ['waɪərɪŋ]	Verkabelung
	wire [waɪə]	Kabel

MOCK EXAM

114	mock exam [,mɒk ɪg'zæm]	Musterprüfung
T	business community ['bɪznəs kəmjuːnəti]	Geschäftswelt
	advance [əd'vɑːns]	Fortschritt
	solution [sə'luːʃn]	Lösung
	chamber of commerce [,tʃeɪmbər əv 'kɒmɜːs]	Handelskammer
	luck [lʌk]	Glück
	engineering [,endʒɪ'nɪərɪŋ]	Maschinenbau
	medium-sized ['miːdiəm saɪzd]	mittelständisch
	recession [rɪ'seʃn]	Rezession, Konjunktur-rückgang

	to hit [hɪt]	zuschlagen, sich voll auswirken
	to close down [,kləʊz 'daʊn]	schließen
	to downsize [,daʊn'saɪz]	Personal abbauen
	to expand [ɪk'spænd]	steigern
	principally ['prɪnsəpli]	hauptsächlich
	lighting ['laɪtɪŋ]	Licht, Beleuchtung
	sculpture ['skʌlptʃə]	Skulptur
	built to order [,bɪlt tu 'ɔːdə]	auf Bestellung angefertigt
	to compromise sth ['kɒmprəmaɪz]	gefährden, aufs Spiel setzen
	overseas [,əʊvə'siːz]	aus dem Ausland
	on your doorstep [ɒn jɔː 'dɔːstep]	vor der eigenen Tür
115	to shape [ʃeɪp]	formen
	to stick to the rules [,stɪk tə ðə 'ruːlz]	sich an die Regeln halten
	punctuality [,pʌŋktʃu'æləti]	Pünktlichkeit
	waste of time [,weɪst əf 'taɪm]	Zeitverschwendung
	insult ['ɪnsʌlt]	Beleidigung
	drive [draɪv]	Fahrt
	to shake hands [,ʃeɪk 'hændz]	die Hand geben, die Hände schütteln
	nod [nɒd]	Kopfnicken
	bow [baʊ]	Verbeugung
	to initiate sth [ɪ'nɪʃieɪt]	mit etw beginnen
	to be familiar with sth [fə'mɪliə wɪð]	mit etw vertraut sein, etw kennen
	casually ['kæʒuəli]	beiläufig, nebenbei
	decade ['dekeɪd]	Jahrzehnt
	uncommon [,ʌn'kɒmən]	unüblich
	seating arrangement ['siːtɪŋ əreɪndʒmənt]	Sitzordnung
	relaxed [rɪ'lækst]	locker
	to host [həʊst]	(Sitzung etc.) leiten
	facing sth ['feɪsɪŋ]	gegenüber von etw
	senior ['siːniə]	hoch-/höherrangig
	to seat [siːt]	sich setzen, sich platzieren
	descending [dɪ'sendɪŋ]	absteigend
	status ['steɪtəs]	Rang
116	mobility [məʊ'bɪləti]	Mobilität
	country of origin [,kʌntri əv 'ɒrɪdʒɪn]	Herkunftsland
	host [həʊst]	Gastgeber/in
	host country ['həʊst kʌntri]	Gast(geber)land
	duration [dju'reɪʃn]	Dauer
	to be intended for sb [bi ɪn'tendɪd fə]	für jdn gedacht sein, sich an jdn richten
	to undergo [,ʌndə'gəʊ]	erleben, mitmachen bei

Chronological word list

	to concern [kən'sɜːn]	betreffen
	to obtain [əb'teɪn]	erhalten, bekommen
118	apprentice [ə'prentɪs]	Auszubildende/r
	to benefit ['benɪfɪt]	profitieren
	internship ['ɪntɜːnʃɪp]	Praktikum

INCOTERMS

119	obligation [ˌɒblɪ'geɪʃn]	Pflicht
	EXW (Ex Works) [ˌeks 'wɜːks]	ab Werk
	DAP (Delivered At Place) [ˌdiː eɪ 'piː/ dɪˌlɪvəd ət 'pleɪs]	geliefert benannter Ort
	DAT (Delivered At Terminal) [ˌdiː eɪ 'tiː/ dɪˌlɪvəd ət 'tɜːmɪnl]	geliefert an Terminal
	inland ['ɪnlænd]	Binnen-
	waterway ['wɔːtəweɪ]	Wasserstraße
	FAS (Free Alongside Ship) [ˌef eɪ 'es/ ˌfriː əlɒŋˌsaɪd 'ʃɪp]	frei Längsseite Schiff
	CFR (Cost and Freight) [ˌsiː ef 'ɑː/ ˌkɒst ənd 'freɪt]	Kosten und Fracht
120	mode of transport [ˌməʊd əv 'trænspɔːt]	Transportart
	customary ['kʌstəməri]	handelsüblich
	at sb's expense [ət ˌsʌmbədiz ɪk'spens]	auf jds Kosten
	multimodal transport [mʌltiˌməʊdl 'trænspɔːt]	kombinierte Beförderung, multimodaler Transport
	to nominate ['nɒmɪneɪt]	benennen
	commercial invoice [kəˌmɜːʃl 'ɪnvɔɪs]	Handelsrechnung
	certificate of origin [səˌtɪfɪkət əv 'ɒrɪdʒɪn]	Ursprungszeugnis
	to bear [beə]	tragen
	custody ['kʌstədi]	Obhut
	excluding [ɪk'skluːdɪŋ]	ausgenommen
	to insure [ɪn'ʃʊə]	versichern
121	vessel ['vesl]	Schiff
	thereafter [ˌðeər'ɑːftə]	danach

157

Alphabetical word list

Dieses Wörterverzeichnis enthält alle neuen Wörter aus *Business Matters* in alphabetischer Reihenfolge. Nicht angeführt sind Wörter, die zum Grundwortschatz (*Basic word list*) gehören. Die Zahl nach dem Stichwort bezieht sich auf die Seite, auf der das Wort zum ersten Mal erscheint. Wörter aus den Hörverständnisübungen sind zusätzlich mit einem **T** (Transkript) gekennzeichnet.

A

ability *103* Fähigkeit

about, to be ~ to do sth *59* im Begriff sein, etw zu tun; gerade etw tun wollen; **to be out and ~** *92* unterwegs sein

abroad *13T* im/ins Ausland

acceptable *64* akzeptabel

access *23* Zugang, Zugriff

accident *94* Unfall

to **accommodate** *74* unterbringen, Platz bieten für

accommodation *22* Unterbringung, Unterkunft

according to *103* je nach, entsprechend; *111* laut, nach, gemäß

account *19T* Konto; to **clear an ~** *56* ein Konto ausgleichen, eine offene Rechnung begleichen; to **take sth into ~** *110T* etw berücksichtigen

account number *19T* Kostenstelle

accountant *112* Buchhalter/in

Accounting *9* Buchhaltung

Accounts Assistant *10* Buchhaltungsassistent/in

to **acquire** *68* gewinnen, erwerben

action, call to ~ *34T* Handlungsaufforderung, Aufruf; to **take ~** *68* Maßnahmen ergreifen

accurate(ly) *31* genau

additional *42* zusätzlich, Zusatz-

additionally *23* außerdem

Administration *9* Verwaltung

Administrative Support Assistant *103* Verwaltungsmitarbeiter/in

to **admit** *87* zugeben, gestehen, eingestehen

to **adopt** *23* annehmen, übernehmen

advance *114T* Fortschritt; **in ~** *109* im Voraus; **in ~ of** *77* vor

advantage *14* Vorteil

to **advertise** *105* (Stelle:) ausschreiben; **~ sth** *29* etw bewerben, für etw Werbung machen

advertising *9* Werbung

advertising agency *28* Werbeagentur

advertising campaign *32* Werbekampagne

advertising space *27* Werbefläche(n), Werbezeit(en), Anzeigenraum

advice *35* Rat, Ratschlag, Tipp

to **advise** *32T* (jdm, zu etw) raten

affinity *28* Verwandtschaft, Affinität

affinity marketing *28* Affinity-Marketing

to **afford sth** *79* sich etw leisten (können)

afraid, to be ~ *39* Angst haben

after all *39* schließlich

agenda *76* Tagesordnung

agent *103* Angestellte/r

agreement, rental ~ *22* Mietvertrag

aim *23* Ziel

to **aim sth at sb/sth** *37* etw auf jdn/etw abzielen, etw an jdn/etw richten

air freight *53* Luftfracht

alcohol *72* Alkohol

alongside *10* neben, mit

alternative *23* andere/r/s, alternativ; *60* Alternative

amazed *35* verblüfft, erstaunt

ambitious *102* ehrgeizig

ambulance *94* Krankenwagen

among *13T* bei, unter

to **announce** *13T* ankündigen

announcement *73* Durchsage

to **annoy sb** *63* jdm lästig werden, jdm auf die Nerven gehen

annoying *64* ärgerlich

annual *9* jährlich, Jahres-

anytime *39* jederzeit

to **apologise** *7* sich entschuldigen, um Entschuldigung bitten

appeal *22* Reiz

to **appeal to sb** *28* jdn ansprechen, jdm gefallen

to **appear** *30* erscheinen

apple *85* Apfel

application *103* Bewerbung

to **apply to sth** *79* für etw gelten

to **apply for a job** *101* sich um/ auf eine Stelle bewerben

appointment *7* Termin, Verabredung

to **appreciate** *82* schätzen, zu schätzen wissen

appreciation *43* Wertschätzung

apprentice *118* Auszubildende/r

approach *37* Vorgehen(sweise), Ansatz, Herangehensweise

to **argue** *36* argumentieren

to **arise** *78* auftreten, enstehen

arithmetic, to have good ~ *102* gut rechnen können

to **arrange sth** *46* etw anordnen, etw aufbauen

arrival *37* Einführung; *73* Ankunft

as though *88* als ob

as yet *51T* bis jetzt

to **ask for directions** *11* nach dem Weg fragen

aspect *48* Aspekt

to **assemble** *91* montieren, zusammenbauen

assembly *96* Montage

to **assess** *29* einschätzen, bewerten, beurteilen

assessment *111* Einschätzung, Beurteilung

to **assist sb** *66* jdm helfen, jdn unterstützen

assistance *41* Hilfe, Unterstützung

Assistant Human Resources Manager *7* stellvertretende/r Personalleiter/in

to **assume** *78* annehmen, davon ausgehen

to **assure** *67* versichern, zusichern

at last *6* endlich

to **attach** *16* beifügen, anhängen

to **attempt** *79* versuchen

to **attend to sb** *62* sich um jdn kümmern, jdn bedienen

attention *62* Aufmerksamkeit; to **pay ~ to sth** *46* auf etw achten

attitude *28* Haltung, Einstellung

to **attract** *31* anziehen

attraction *31* Reiz, Anziehungskraft

audience *31* Publikum, Zuhörer(schaft), Zuschauer

audio-visual *80* audiovisuell

author *24* Autor/in

authority *36* Behörde

automated *97T* automatisch, automatisiert

available *23* verfügbar; erhältlich; **to be ~** *38* (Telefon:) zu sprechen sein; to **be made ~** *23* zur Verfügung stellen

Alphabetical word list

to **avoid** *60* vermeiden, verhindern
award *85* Preis, Auszeichnung
aware, to **be ~ of sth** *88* sich einer Sache bewusst sein, etw wissen; to **become ~ of sth** *31* sich einer Sache bewusst werden, etw bemerken
awareness *78* Wissen, Bewusst-sein

B

to **back sth** *14* etw unterstützen, *hier:* in etw investieren
to **back sth up** *103* etw absichern, etw unterstützen
background *7* Hintergrund; *103* Erfahrung, Herkunft
backwards *106* rückwärts
baggage *73* Gepäck
baggage reclaim *73* Gepäck-ausgabe
to **ban** *36* verbieten
banana *85* Banane
bar chart *85T* Säulendiagramm
base *9* (Firmen-)Sitz; *85* Basis
to **base sth around sth** *27* etw auf etw gründen, etw nach etw ausrichten
based, to **be ~ in** *13T* in … an-sässig sein, seinen/ihren Sitz in … haben; to be **~ on sth** *16* auf etw basieren
batch production *100* Klein-serienfertigung
battery *35* Akku, Batterie
to **bear** *120* tragen
beforehand *109* vorher, zuvor
begin, to **~ with** *82T* zunächst
to **behave** *88* sich verhalten
benefit *62* Vorteil, Nutzen
to **benefit** *118* profitieren
benefits *(pl.)* *103* Sozial-leistungen, Zulagen
beside *73* neben
bill *76T* Rechnung
to **bite sth** *88* auf etw beißen
to **board** *73T* an Bord gehen, einsteigen
boarding card *72* Bordkarte
boat *76T* Boot
body language *88* Körpersprache
bonus *103* Zulage
book shop *108* Buchhandlung
boot *93* Stiefel
border *58* Grenze
to **bore sb** *82* jdn langweilen
boring *76T* langweilig
boss *16* Chef/in
bow *115* Verbeugung
boy scout *112* Pfadfinder
to **brainstorm** *9* Ideen sammeln
brake *97T* Bremse

brake block *99* Bremsklotz, Bremsbelag
brake lever *99* Bremsgriff
brand *13T* Marke
branding *87* Markenbildung, Markenentwicklung
brief *14* kurz, knapp
brief *23* Auftrag
briefcase *33* Aktentasche
bright *35* (Farbe:) hell, leuchtend
broadband *22* Breitband-
broadcast media *32* Rundfunk
brochure *49T* Prospekt, Werbe-broschüre
budget *32T* Budget, Haushalt, Etat
budget airline *79* Billigflieger
built to order *114T* auf Bestellung angefertigt
bullet point *48* Stichpunkt
burn *36* Verbrennung
business, to **do ~** *42* Geschäfte machen; to **get down to ~** *52* zur Sache kommen
business administration *103* Betriebswirtschaft
business card *25* Visitenkarte
business centre *74T* Business-Center
business community *114T* Geschäftswelt
business contact *77* Geschäfts-partner/in
button *20* Knopf, Taste
buyer *58* Käufer
buzz *37* Aufmerksamkeit (durch Mundpropaganda)

C

cabinet, filing ~ *16* Aktenschrank
calculator *18* Taschenrechner
call *73T* Aufruf; **~ to action** *34T* Handlungsaufforderung, Aufruf
call-up *91* Abruf
to **call sth up** *91* etw abrufen
to **calm down** *65* sich beruhigen
campaign *27* Kampagne
to **cancel** *48T* streichen; *57T* ab-sagen, stornieren; **~ a contract** *60* einen Vertrag auflösen
candidate *103* Kandidat/in, Bewerber/in
canteen *24* Kantine
cap *16* Mütze, Kappe
car park *74T* Parkplatz, Park-haus, Tiefgarage
care *112* Sorgfalt
career *101* Karriere, Beruf, Lauf-bahn
carnival *107* Karneval
carriage *55* Transport; **contract of ~** *58* Beförderungsvertrag;

main ~ *58* Hauptlauf; **post-~** *58* Nachlauf; **pre-~** *58* Vorlauf
carrier *58* Frachtführer
to **carry sth out** *14* etw aus-führen, etw durchführen
cartoon *62* Karikatur, Comic-zeichnung
cartridge *18* Druckerpatrone
cash flow *87* Geldmittel
casing *35* Gehäuse
casually *115* beiläufig, nebenbei
to **catch sb/sth** *38* jdn/etw er-reichen, jdn/etw erwischen, jdn/etw bekommen; **~ sth** *39* etw verstehen
category *48* Kategorie
cause *113* Ursache
cautious *47* vorsichtig
to **cement** *87* festigen, stärken, zementieren
century *103* Jahrhundert
certificate *106* Zeugnis; *107* Zertifikat, Diplom
certificate of origin *120* Ursprungszeugnis
CFR (Cost and Freight) *119* Kosten und Fracht
chain *16* Kette
chainset *99* Kurbelgarnitur
to **chair** *47* (Sitzung etc.:) leiter
chamber of commerce *114T* Handelskammer
champagne *90* Champagner
chance *24* Möglichkeit, Gelegen-heit
charge *43* Gebühr
charge, in ~ of *10* zuständig für, verantwortlich für
charity shop *90* Secondhand-laden (für wohltätige Zwecke)
chart, bar ~ *85T* Säulen-diagramm; **pie ~** *85T* Torten-diagramm
chat *34T* Unterhaltung, Gespräch
check *16* (Auto:) Inspektion
to **check sb/sth out** *110T* sich jdn/etw ansehen
cheek *88* Wange
cheers *46* tschüs, danke
cheese *47* Käse
chemistry *108* Chemie
chin *88* Kinn
chocolate *13T* Schokolade, Praline
church *90* Kirche; kirchlich
CIF (Cost, Insurance and Freight) *58* Kosten, Versicherung, Fracht
CIP (Carriage and Insurance Paid to) *58* frachtfrei versich-tert bis
to **circulate** *31* sich verbreiten kursieren

159

Alphabetical word list

civil *90* standesamtlich

to claim *46* behaupten

to clear, ~ an account *56* ein Konto ausgleichen, eine offene Rechnung begleichen; **~ for export** *58* Ausfuhrformalitäten erledigen, zur Ausfuhr abfertigen lassen

clearance, export ~ *58* (Erledigung der) Ausfuhrformalitäten; **import ~** *58* (Erledigung der) Einfuhrformalitäten

client *9* Kunde/Kundin

close to *89* nahe bei, in der Nähe von

to close down *114T* schließen

closely, to look ~ at sth *82T* sich etw genau ansehen; **to be ~ related to sth** *111* engen Bezug zu etw haben; **to work ~ with sb** *23* mit jdm eng zusammenarbeiten

closing date *103* Einsendeschluss

clothing *16* Bekleidung, Kleidung

colleague *8* Kollege/Kollegin

to collect sth *12T* etw abholen; etw sammeln, zusammentragen

colouring *35* Farbe, Farbgebung

combination *23* Verbindung

to come (in/with) *33* (Produkt:) erhältlich sein (in/mit); **~ across sth** *42* von etw hören, einer Sache begegnen; **~ along** *46* kommen, aufkommen

comfortable *25* bequem, angenehm, komfortabel

comma *46* Komma

comment *68* Kommentar

commerce, chamber of ~ *114T* Handelskammer

commercial invoice *120* Handelsrechnung

commercial space *22* Gewerberaum, -räume

committed, to be ~ to sth *88* hinter einer Sache stehen

common *61* gemeinsam

to communicate *37* kommunizieren

communicator, a good ~ *102* ein kommunikativer Mensch

company *6* Unternehmen, Firma, Gesellschaft; **parent ~** *36* Muttergesellschaft; **private limited ~ (Ltd)** *14* Gesellschaft mit beschränkter Haftung (GmbH); **public limited ~ (plc)** *14* Aktiengesellschaft (AG)

company form *14* Unternehmensform, Gesellschaftsform

to compare *70* vergleichen

comparison *36* Vergleich

competence *106* Kompetenz

competition *36* Wettbewerb; *47* Konkurrenz

competitor *27* Konkurrent/in, Konkurrenz

to compile *103* erstellen, zusammenstellen

to complain *59* sich beschweren

complaint *36* Beschwerde; *66* Reklamation

to complement *74* ergänzen

complicated *14* kompliziert

component *92* Bauteil, Teil, Komponente

to comprise *74* umfassen, bestehen aus

to compromise sth *114T* gefährden, aufs Spiel setzen

computer-savvy *31* geübt/gewieft im Umgang mit Computern

to concentrate *108T* sich konzentrieren

concept *28* Begriff, Konzept

to concern *116* betreffen

concerned *56* besorgt, beunruhigt

conclusion *48* Fazit, Schluss

condition *97T* Zustand

to condone sth *36* etw billigen

to conduct sth *110T* etw durchführen

conference *76* Konferenz

conference room *74T* Tagungsraum, Konferenzzimmer

confident *111* selbstsicher, selbstbewusst

to confirm *19T* bestätigen

confirmation *42* Bestätigung

to connect *88* eine Verbindung herstellen

connection *22* Verbindung

to consider sb/sth *41* jdn/etw in Betracht/Erwägung ziehen; **~ sth** *46* etw berücksichtigen, etw betrachten, über etw nachdenken

to consist of sth *7* aus etw bestehen

consultancy *78* Beratung, Beratungsfirma

consultant *100* Berater/in

to contact sb *16* sich mit jdm in Verbindung setzen

to contain *27* enthalten, beinhalten

content *82* Inhalt

to continue *67* anhalten, andauern; **~ to do sth** *13T* etw weiterhin tun

continued *43* fortgesetzt, anhaltend

contract *58* Vertrag; **to cancel a ~** *60* einen Vertrag auflösen

contract of carriage *58* Beförderungsvertrag

contrary, on the ~ *48* (ganz) im Gegenteil

contrast, in ~ to *14* im Gegensatz zu

to contribute *100* beitragen

contribution *14* Beitrag

convenience *22* Zweckmäßigkeit

convenient *22* praktisch, zweckmäßig

conventional *37* herkömmlich, konventionell

conversational tone *34T* lockerer Plauderton

to convey *37* vermitteln

to convince *103* überzeugen

to co-ordinate *92* koordinieren

to cope with sth *110T* mit etw zurechtkommen

cordless *74* schnurlos

core *22* Haupt-, Kern-

corridor *11T* Flur, Korridor

cost, at all ~ *60* um jeden Preis

country of origin *116* Herkunftsland

course *74* (Menü:) Gang

to cover *58* (Kosten:) decken, aufkommen für; *91* abdecken, bedecken

covering letter *103* Anschreiben, Begleitschreiben

CPT (Carriage Paid to) *58* frachtfrei

creativity *103* Kreativität

credit card *77* Kreditkarte

to criticise *36* kritisieren

crucial *87* entscheidend

crude(ly) *37* primitiv, simpel

current *16* aktuell

currently *23* momentan, im Moment, aktuell

curriculum vitae (CV) *103* Lebenslauf

custody *120* Obhut

custom *43* Kundentreue

customary *120* handelsüblich

customer *8* Kunde/Kundin

customer acquistion *68* Kundenwerbung

customer care *59* Kundenbetreuung

customer retention *60* Kundenbindung

customer satisfaction *60* Kundenzufriedenheit

customs *73* Zoll

customs duty *58* Zollgebühr(en)

to cut costs *23* Kosten senken

D

daily newspaper *30* Tageszeitung

Alphabetical word list

DAP (Delivered At Place) *119* geliefert benannter Ort

DAT (Delivered At Terminal) *119* geliefert an Terminal

database *103* Datenbank

day-to-day basis, on a ~ *23* täglich, jeden Tag

DDP (Delivery Duty Paid) *58* geliefert verzollt

deal *22* Geschäft, Vereinbarung; **a good ~ of** *28* eine Menge

to deal with sb *62* sich um jdn kümmern, mit jdm zu tun haben; **~ with sth** *67* etw bearbeiten, etw erledigen

debts *(pl.)* *14* Verbindlichkeiten, Schulden

decade *115* Jahrzehnt

decoration *90* Dekoration

to defend *76T* verteidigen

delay *95* Verzögerung

delayed *54* verspätet

delicious *76T* köstlich

delighted, to be ~ *92* sich freuen

delivery *40T* Lieferung, Zustellung

delivery bay *93T* Ladebucht

delivery note *95* Lieferschein

delivery terms *92* Lieferbedingungen

demand *13T* Nachfrage; *79* Bedarf

to demonstrate *85T* zeigen

dentist *52* Zahnarzt/-ärztin

to depart *72* abfliegen

department *7* Abteilung

departure *73* Abreise, Abfahrt, Abflug

depend, That ~s. *53* Kommt drauf an.

depending on *23* abhängig von; *100* je nachdem

to depict *85T* darstellen

descending *115* absteigend

to design *27* gestalten, entwerfen

designed, to be ~ to do sth *110T* dazu gedacht sein, etw zu tun

despite *56* trotz

dessert *76T* Nachspeise, Dessert

destination *58* Bestimmungsort; **port of ~** *58* Bestimmungshafen

to destroy *73T* zerstören

to detail *85T* (im Einzelnen) aufführen, darstellen

to determine *97T* bestimmen

to develop *27* entwickeln

device *23* Gerät

diary *48T* Terminkalender

to differ *100* sich unterscheiden

digital projector *27* Beamer

to dine *74* speisen

diplomatic *112* diplomatisch

to direct sth at sth *85T* etw auf etw lenken

direction *78* Ausrichtung; *108T* Richtung

directions *11* Wegbeschreibung; **to ask for ~** *11* nach dem Weg fragen; **to give sb ~** *11* jdm den Weg erklären

disadvantage *14* Nachteil

disaster *36* Katastrophe

discount *42* Rabatt

to discount *54* (Preis:) nachlassen, einen Rabatt gewähren

to discover *37* entdecken

disorganised *82* chaotisch, desorganisiert

to dispatch *42* verschicken, absenden

to display sth *111* etw zur Schau stellen

to dispose of sth *20* etw entsorgen

to distract *88* ablenken

to distribute *13T* vertreiben, verschicken

Distribution *9* Versand, Auslieferung

distribution centre *9* Versandzentrum

to divide *14* teilen, aufteilen

doorstep, on your ~ *114T* vor der eigenen Tür

double room *74* Doppelzimmer

downhill *98* bergab, Abfahrts-

to downsize *114T* Personal abbauen

to draw *11* zeichnen; *34T* ziehen; **~ sth up** *27* etw erstellen

drawer *113T* Schublade

drive *115* Fahrt

driving licence *103* Führerschein

due *43* fällig

due to *78* aufgrund von; **to be ~ sth** *54* an etw liegen

duration *116* Dauer

dynamic *82T* dynamisch

E

to earn *36* verdienen

eatery *74* Restaurant, Speiselokal

effort *22* Mühe, Anstrengungen

eject *20* Auswurf

electricity *93T* Elektrizität, Strom

elevator *110T* Aufzug

embarrassing *46* peinlich

emphasis *36* Schwerpunkt

to emphasise sth *62* etw betonen, den Schwerpunkt auf etw legen

to employ sb *9* jdn beschäftigen

employee *9* Angestellte/r, Beschäftigte/r

employer *106* Arbeitgeber

to enable *87* befähigen, (es) ermöglichen

to encourage *36* ermutigen, motivieren

engineering *114T* Maschinenbau

enormous *68* gewaltig, enorm

en-suite bathroom *74* eigenes Badezimmer

to ensure *61* sicherstellen, gewährleisten

enterprise *92* Unternehmen

entertaining *29* unterhaltsam

entertainment *37* Unterhaltung

enthusiastic, to be ~ about sth *47* sich für etw begeistern

entrant *36* Teilnehmer/in (an einem Wettbewerb)

entry *36* Teilnahme (an einem Wettbewerb); *76* Eintrag

envelop *18* Briefumschlag

equally *30* zu gleichen Teilen, gleich

to equip *22* ausstatten, ausrüsten

equipment *22* Ausstattung, Ausrüstung

error *46* Fehler

to establish *9* gründen

to evaluate *27* einschätzen, auswerten; *68* bewerten, beurteilen

event *85T* Ereignis; **in the ~ of** *94* im Fall eine/r/s; **social ~** *111* geselliger/gesellschaftlicher Anlass

to examine *27* untersuchen, genau anschauen

excellent *108T* ausgezeichnet, hervorragend

excluding *120* ausgenommen

executive *35* Manager/in

exercise *74T* Bewegung

to exist *22* existieren

to expand *25* ausdehnen; *103* expandieren; *114T* steigern; **~ on sth** *34T* etw weiter ausführen

expense, at sb's ~ *120* auf jds Kosten

to explain *7* erklären, erläutern

explicit(ly) *36* ausdrücklich

export clearance *58* (Erledigung der) Ausfuhrformalitäten

to express *29* ausdrücken, zum Ausdruck bringen

expression *28* Ausdruck

to extend sth *14* etw erweitern

extract *56* Auszug

EXW (Ex Works) *119* ab Werk

eye-catching *31* ansprechend, auffallend

eye contact *88* Blickkontakt

F

face-to-face *62* persönlich

facial gesture *88* Miene, Grimasse

facilities *(pl.)* *22* Einrichtungen

161

Alphabetical word list

facing sth *115* gegenüber von etw
factor *37* Faktor
to **fail** *88* scheitern
fairly *85T* ziemlich
familiar, to be ~ with sth *112* mit etw vertraut sein, mit etw umgehen können
far flung *78* weit vom Schuss
FAS (Free Alongside Ship) *119* frei Längsseite Schiff
fashionable, to be ~ *31* im Trend liegen
fat *85* Fett
fault *66* Defekt, Schaden
fault report *66* Schadensmeldung
faulty *64* defekt, mangelhaft
favour, in ~ of sth *79* für etw, zugunsten einer Sache
FCA (Free Carrier) *58* frei Frachtführer
feature *21* Merkmal, Eigenschaft
to **feature sth** *31* etw aufweisen
female *26* weiblich, *hier:* Damen-
to **fetch sth** *12* etw holen
figure *26* Zahl
file *16* Akte
to **file** *95* ablegen, zu den Akten legen
filing cabinet *16* Aktenschrank
to **fill sb in** *93T* jdn informieren, jdn ins Bild setzen; **~ sth in** *19T* etw ausfüllen
Finance and Accounting Manager *10* Leiter/in Finanz- und Rechnungswesen
Finance Director *10* Leiter/in Finanzen
finishing *100* Endfertigung
firm *60* fest, hart, unnachgiebig
first aid *94* erste Hilfe
first-aid kit *94* Verbandskasten
first place, in the ~ *68* zunächst einmal, überhaupt erst
first thing *48T* gleich morgens, als Erstes
to **fit** *35* passen; **~ sth** *97T* etw einbauen, etw montieren; **~ sth out** *22* etw ausstatten; **~ neatly** *35* genau passen
to **fix** *66* *(Problem:)* beheben, *(Schaden:)* reparieren
fizzy drink *13* Erfrischungsgetränk *(mit Kohlensäure)*
flame, naked ~ *93T* offene Flamme, offenes Feuer
flammable *93T* brennbar, leicht entzündbar
flexible *22* flexibel
floor space *96* Nutzfläche
flowchart *66* Flussdiagramm
fluency *103* (fließende) Beherrschung *(einer Sprache)*

FOB (Free On Board) *58* frei an Bord
to **focus on sth** *82T* sich auf etw konzentrieren
focus group *28* Fokusgruppe
to **force** *56* zwingen
to **forecast** *97T* voraussagen
forklift truck *93T* Gabelstapler
formal *34T* förmlich, formell
forwarding agent *58* Spediteur, Spedition
to **found** *9* gründen
frantically *88* wie verrückt
freelancer *22* Selbständige/r, Freiberufler/in
freight *53* Fracht; **air ~** *53* Luftfracht; **sea ~** *53* Seefracht
frequently *68* häufig
fresh *28* neu, frisch
to **fulfil** *67* erfüllen
full stop *46* Punkt *(am Satzende)*
fully-equipped *74* voll ausgestattet
fully-fitted *22* voll ausgestattet
function *9* Funktion, Aufgabe
functional *9* zweckmäßig, funktionell
functionality *29* Funktionen, Funktionalität
to **fund** *14* finanzieren
to **furnish** *22* ausstatten, einrichten
furniture *22* Möbel

G

to **gain** *79* gewinnen, erwerben
garage *16* Autowerkstatt
gate *73* Flugsteig
to **gather** *84* sammeln
gear *97T* Gangschaltung
gear changer *99* Gangschaltung, Schalthebel
general, in ~ *46* im Allgemeinen
general partnership *14* offene Handelsgeselslchaft (OHG)
geography *108* Erdkunde, Geographie
gesture *88* Geste
to **get on with sth** *22* (mit etw) weitermachen
gift *49T* Geschenk
to **give sb directions** *11* jdm den Weg erklären
glad *32T* froh
glamour *79* Glanz
Go ahead. *40T* Nur zu. / Bitte sehr.
goods *(pl.)* *58* Ware(n)
to **graduate** *112* einen Abschluss machen
graph, line ~ *85T* Liniendiagramm, Kurve
grateful *56* dankbar

gratitude *43* Anerkennung, Dankbarkeit
gripper *99* Greifer
growth *13T* Zunahme, Wachstum
to **guarantee** *21* garantieren
guide *14* Führer/in
guided tour *40T* Führung, Rundfahrt
guideline *60* Richtlinie
guy *42* Typ, Kerl
gym *74T* Fitnessstudio

H

handy *103* nützlich, praktisch
hard hat *93* Schutzhelm
hard-working *102* fleißig
harness *93* (Sicherheits-)Gurt
to **hate** *110T* hassen, nicht mögen
haulage, road ~ *53* Straßentransport
haulage contractor *97T* Spediteur
head *25* Leiter/in, Chef/in
to **head sth** *10* etw leiten; **~ for sth** *76T* zu etw gehen/fahren
headline *34* Überschrift
headquarters *(pl.)* *9* Zentrale, Firmensitz
Health & Safety officer *113* Beauftragte/r für Arbeitsschutz
healthy *82T* gesund
hello, to say ~ to sb *60* jdn begrüßen
to **hesitate** *43* zögern
high season *90* Hochsaison
high voltage *93T* Hochspannung
to **highlight** *7* hervorheben
highlighter *18* Textmarker
to **hire sb** *9* jdn einstellen; *37* jdn beauftragen; **~ sth** *74T* etw mieten
to **hit** *87* treffen, *(Ziel:)* erreichen; *114T* zuschlagen, sich voll auswirken
to **hold sth** *22* etw abhalten; **~ on** *38* warten; **~ onto sb** *68* jdn festhalten
hole punch *18* Locher
homeworking *23* Heimarbeit
honest *102* ehrlich
hopper *69* Behälter, Magazin
hospital *52* Krankenhaus
host *116* Gastgeber/in; **~ country** *116* Gast(geber)land
to **host** *115* *(Sitzung etc.:)* leiten
How do you do? *6* Guten Tag.
hub *95* Nabel, Drehkreuz
Human Resources (HR) *7* Personalabteilung
Human Resources Manager *7* Personalleiter/in
humour *103* Humor
humorous(ly) *70* humorvoll

Alphabetical word list

to **hurry** *60* eilen, sich beeilen
to **hurt** *113* verletzen, wehtun

I

ID number *55* Identifikations-
nummer
to **identify** *28* identifizieren
to **ignore** *29* ignorieren, nicht
beachten
to **imagine sth** *77* sich etw
vorstellen
immediate *62* unverzüglich,
unmittelbar
immediately *44* unverzüglich,
sofort
immigration *73* Passkontrolle
impact *30* Einfluss, Auswirkungen
impatient *88* ungeduldig,
unduldsam
import clearance *58* (Erledigung
der) Einfuhrformalitäten
importance *19* Wichtigkeit,
Bedeutung
to **impress** *22* beeindrucken
impressed *82T* beeindruckt
impression *46* Eindruck
to **improve** *34* verbessern
inbox *16* Posteingang
to **include** *16* beinhalten, ein-
schließen
including *40T* einschließlich
incoming *60* eingehend
to **increase sth** *13T* etw erhöhen,
aufstocken
increasingly *37* zunehmend,
immer (+Komparativ)
incredibly *9* unglaublich
independent(ly) *103* unabhängig
to **indicate** *69* angeben
inexpensive *46* preiswert
informal *46* informell, zwanglos,
locker
informality *46* Zwanglosigkeit
initial *79* erste/r/s, anfänglich
to **initiate sth** *115* mit etw
beginnen, etw einleiten
initiative *111* Initiative
to **injure** *94* verletzen
injured *94* verletzt
injury *94* Verletzung
ink *20* Tinte
inland *119* Binnen-
innovative *37* innovativ
insight *78* Einblick
to **insist** *56* darauf bestehen
to **inspect** *97T* untersuchen,
überprüfen
inspection *91* Kontrolle, Über-
prüfung
instance, for ~ *62* zum Beispiel
instruction *11* Anweisung,
Anleitung
insult *115* Beleidigung

insurance *58* Versicherung
to **insure** *120* versichern
intended for, to be ~ sb *116* für
jdn gedacht sein, sich an jdn
richten
intercultural *78* kulturüber-
greifend, interkulturell
internal *33* Innen-
internship *118* Praktikum
to **interview sb** *110T* mit jdm ein
Bewerbungsgespräch führen
to **introduce** *35* vorstellen,
einführen; **~ sb to sb** *7* jdn mit
jdm bekannt machen, jdm jdn
vorstellen
introduction *7* Einführung,
Vorstellung; *48* Einleitung
to **invest** *14* investieren
to **investigate sb/sth** *23* Erkun-
digungen über jdn/etw einholen,
Nachforschungen über jdn/etw
anstellen
investigator *113* Ermittler/in,
Untersuchende/r
investment *23* Investition(en)
invitation *90* Einladung
to **invite** *25* einladen; **~ sb to do
sth** *110T* jdn dazu auffordern,
etw zu tun
invoice *43* Rechnung
to **involve** *37* beinhalten, mit sich
bringen; **~ sb in sth** *68* jdn an
etw beteiligen
involved *58* (Kosten:) entstehend,
anfallend; **to be ~ in sth** *92* an
etw beteiligt sein, bei etw mitmachen
involvement *113* Beteiligung
irresponsible *36* unverantwortlich
to **irritate** *63* verärgern, belästigen
issue *46* Frage, Thema
item *17* Artikel

J

job advertisment *102* Stellenanzeige
job interview *8* Vorstellungs-/
Bewerbungsgespräch
joint *87* gemeinsam
joint stock *14* Gesellschafts-
kapital, Grundkapital
juice *13* Saft
jumbled up *31* durcheinander-
geworfen
to **jump about** *88* herumhüpfen

K

to **keep up with sb/sth** *13T* mit
jdm/etw Schritt halten
know, to get to ~ sb/sth *6* jdn/
etw kennenlernen; **to let sb ~**
7 jdm Bescheid sagen

L

to **lack in sth** *88* zu wenig von
etw haben
lake *76T* See
last, at ~ *6* endlich
latest *74* neueste/r/s; **at the ~** *54*
spätestens
the latter *88* Letztere/r/s, der/die/
das Letztgenannte
to **launch sth** *48* etw starten
to **lay sth out** *28* etw darlegen
lazy *88* faul, schlaff
leader *44* Führer/in
leadership qualities *(pl.)* *111*
Führungsqualitäten
leather *33* Leder
to **leave a message** *39* eine
Nachricht hinterlassen
legal, to take ~ steps *56* rechtliche Schritte unternehmen
leisure *74* Freizeit
to **let go of sth** *108T* etw loslassen
to **let sb know** *7* jdm Bescheid
sagen
liability *14* Haftung
liable *14* haftbar; **to be ~ for sth**
14 für etw haften
to **liaise with sb** *112* mit jdm
zusammenarbeiten
life guard *107* Rettungs-
schwimmer/in
to **lift sth** *93T* etw hochheben
etw anheben
lighting *114T* Licht, Beleuchtung
lightweight *28* leicht
likely *60* wahrscheinlich
limited partnership *14* Kommanditgesellschaft (KG)
line graph *85T* Liniendiagramm,
Kurve
link *25* Verbindung, Kontakt
to **link** *34* verbinden
lip *88* Lippe
to **list** *106* auflisten
loading *58* Verladen, Verladung
lobster *36* Hummer
located, to be ~ in *9* sich
befinden in
location *89* Lage
lock *20* Verschluss
logic *110T* Logik
logical *31* logisch
logistics *(pl)* *85* Logistik
Logistics Assistant *10* Logistik-
assistent/in
Logistics Manager *10* Leiter/in
Logistik
look out, to be on the ~ for sb
111 jdn suchen, nach jdm
Ausschau halten
to **look closely at sth** *82T* sich
etw genau ansehen

163

Alphabetical word list

loser *87* Verlierer/in
loss *14* Verlust
loudspeaker *81* Lautsprecher
low in sth *85* arm an etw
loyalty card *68* Kundenkarte
luck *114T* Glück
luggage *73T* Gepäck
lunch break *59* Mittagspause

M

machinery *100* Maschinen
made up, to be ~ of sth *92* aus
   etw bestehen, sich aus etw
   zusammensetzen
main carriage *58* Hauptlauf
to **maintain** *9* aufrechterhalten;
   103 instandhalten, *(Datenbank:)*
   pflegen
major *14* größte/r/s, Haupt-,
   bedeutendste/r/s
to **make sense** *95* sinnvoll sein
to **make sure** *9* sicherstellen,
   gewährleisten, sich vergewissern
male *26* mänlich, *hier:* Herren-
to **manage** *13T* es schaffen,
   gelingen
management *92* Steuerung,
   Kontrolle, Verwaltung
Managing Director *10*
   Geschäftsführer/in
manner *79* Art (und Weise)
manual *97T* Hand-
manually *95* von Hand
manufacturer *13T* Hersteller,
   Produzent
mark *43* Zeichen
to **mark** *20* kennzeichnen
marker pen *16* Textmarker
market research *27* Markt-
   forschung
marketeer *37* Vermarkter/in, *(im
   Plural:)* Marketingleute
Marketing Assistant *10*
   Marketingassistent/in
Marketing Manager *10*
   Marketingleiter/in
marriage *89* Ehe
to **mass produce** *100* in Massen
   herstellen
material, raw ~ *92* Rohstoff,
   Rohmaterial
maths *104* Mathe
matter *56* Angelegenheit, Sache
to **maximise** *60* maximieren
means *31* Mittel; **by ~ of** *43*
   mittels, per
meantime, in the ~ *49T* in der
   Zwischenzeit
measure *93T* Maßnahme
to **measure** *31* messen
media buying agency *28* Agentur
   für Medienplanung/-einkauf
medical *94* medizinisch

medium-sized *114T* mittel-
   ständisch
to **meet sb's needs** *60* jds
   Bedürfnissen entsprechen
meeting room *74* Besprechungs-
   zimmer
member *9* Mitglied
to **mention** *24* erwähnen, nennen
message, to leave a ~ *39* eine
   Nachricht hinterlassen; to **take a
   ~** *39* *(Telefon:)* etw ausrichten
method *23* Art, Methode
microphone *74* Mikrofon
microwave *22* Mikrowelle
mild *113* leicht
to **mind** *62* etw dagegen haben
misunderstanding *78* Miss-
   verständnis
mobility *116* Mobilität
mock exam *114* Musterprüfung
mode of transport *120*
   Transportart
to **monitor** *92* überwachen
to **motivate** *104* motivieren
motivated *103* motiviert
to **mount** *97T* montieren
multimodal transport *120*
   kombinierte Beförderung,
   multimodaler Transport

N

naked flame *93T* offene Flamme,
   offenes Feuer
national *30* *(Zeitung:)* über-
   regional
nationality *106* Staats-
   angehörigkeit
native speaker *39* Mutter-
   sprachler/in
nearby *9* nahegelegen
neat(ly) *46* ordentlich, sauber; to
   fit ~ *35* genau passen
neck *94* Hals
need *23* Bedarf
to **negotiate** *92* verhandeln, aus-
   handeln
negotiating partner *78* Verhand-
   lungspartner/in
neighbouring *78* benachbart,
   Nachbar-
nervous *38* nervös
nervousness *82* Nervosität
net *69* Netz; *85T* netto
network *23* Netzwerk
nevertheless *37* trotzdem,
   dennoch, nichtsdestotrotz
newspaper, daily ~ *30* Tageszeitung
nightmare *36* Albtraum
to **nip along** *97T* (kurz) mit-
   kommen
nod *115* Kopfnicken
to **nominate** *120* benennen

to **note** *86* bemerken
note pad *18* Notizblock
numerate, to be ~ *102* gut mit
   Zahlen umgehen können
numerous *36* zahlreich
nut *85* Nuss
nutshell, in a ~ *97T* in aller Kürze

O

obligation *119* Pflicht
to **obtain** *116* erhalten,
   bekommen
obvious *64* offensichtlich
obviously *22* natürlich, selbstverständlich
occasion *79* Anlass, Ereignis
occasionally *88* gelegentlich
office supplies *(pl.)* *12T* Büromaterial, Bürobedarf
OHP *81T* Overheadprojektor
old-fashioned *46* altmodisch
on, It's just not ~. *62T* Das geht
   doch einfach nicht!
ongoing *43* fortdauernd
opening *76* Eröffnung
to **operate** *22* (geschäftlich) tätig
   sein, operieren
operation *22* Betrieb; **in ~** *93T*
   in Betrieb
Operations Director *10*
   Betriebs-/Produktionsleiter/in
opinion *32T* Meinung
opportunity *48* Möglichkeit,
   Gelegenheit, Chance
option *53* Möglichkeit, Option
order, built to ~ *114T* auf Bestellung angefertigt; to **place an
   ~** *42* einen Auftrag erteilen, eine
   Bestellung aufgeben
organic *103* Bio-
origin, country of ~ *116*
   Herkunftsland
out and about, to be ~ *92* unterwegs sein
outlet *47* Verkaufsstelle, Absatzmöglichkeit
outline *83* Überblick
overall view *48* Überblick,
   (Gesamt-)Übersicht
to **overcome sth** *79* etw über-
   winden
overexposure *36* *hier:* zu langes
   Sonnenbaden
to **overload** *34T* überfrachten
to **overlook** *56* übersehen
overseas *114T* aus dem Ausland
own, on one's ~ *103* allein,
   selbstständig
owner *13T* Besitzer/in, Inhaber/in

P

pace *88* Schritt
to **pack** *95* packen, verpacken

Alphabetical word list

package *60* Paket
to package *13T* verpacken
packaging *20* Verpackung
packing *91* Verpackung
to panic *111* in Panik geraten
paper clip *18* Büroklammer
paperwork *95* Unterlagen
paragraph *31* *(Text:)* Absatz
parent company *36* Muttergesellschaft
participant *74* Teilnehmer/in
particular, in ~ *22* besonders
partnership *87* Zusammenarbeit, Partnerschaft; **general** ~ *14* offene Handelsgeselslchaft (OHG); **limited** ~ *14* Kommanditgesellschaft (KG)
part-time *108T* Teilzeit
to pass sth on *23* etw weitergeben, -reichen, -leiten
passageway *97T* Gang, Durchgang
passport *72* Reisepass
past sth *73* an etw vorbei
pastime *77* Freizeitbeschäftigung
patience *103* Geduld
patient *112* geduldig
pay *109* Bezahlung, Lohn, Gehalt
to pay attention to sth *46* auf etw achten
payment *43* Zahlung
peak *90* Höchststand, Spitzenwert
pen *12T* Stift
to perform sth *111* etw durchführen, etw ausführen; ~ **well** *32T* gute Ergebnisse liefern
performance *66* Leistung
person, in ~ *6* persönlich
Personnel Manager *113* Personalleiter/in
to persuade *103* überzeugen, überreden
petrol *24* Benzin
photocopier *11* Fotokopierer
to photocopy *74* fotokopieren
to pick sth out *95* etw heraussuchen; ~ **sb/sth up** *19T* jdn/ etw abholen
pie chart *85T* Tortendiagramm
pitch *110T* Präsentation
pity, That's a ~. *38* Schade.
place, to take ~ *46* stattfinden
to place *27* platzieren; ~ **an order** *42* einen Auftrag erteilen, eine Bestellung aufgeben
pleasant *25* angenehm
Pleased to meet you. *6* Nett, Sie kennenzulernen.
pocket *33* Tasche
point of view *57T* Standpunkt
to point to sth *88* auf etw zeigen; ~ **out** *47* darauf hinweisen

pointer *46* Hinweis
policy *63* Politik, Vorgehensweise, Regeln
polite *60* höflich
politics *77* Politik
to pop in *48T* vorbeischauen
popularity *31* Beliebtheit
port of destination *58* Bestimmungshafen
port of shipment *58* Verladehafen
portable *23* tragbar, mobil
possibly *51T* möglicherweise, vielleicht
to post *63* *(Brief)* einwerfen, zur Post bringen
post-carriage *58* Nachlauf
potential *16* potenziell
potted plant *22* Topfpflanze
to pour sth into sth *87* etw in etw fließen lassen
power supply *35* Stromversorgung, -anschluss
pre-carriage *58* Vorlauf
predictable *110T* vorraussagbar, vorhersehbar
premises *(pl.)* *22* Räumlichkeiten, (Betriebs-)Gelände
prepared *79* bereit
present *48* anwesend
presenter *88* Redner/in
to press sb *56* jdn nachdrücklich auffordern
pressure *24* Druck
to prevent *68* verhindern
previously *46* zuvor, vorher
principally *114T* hauptsächlich
to print sth out *16* etw ausdrucken
print media *32* Presse, Printmedien
priority *61* Priorität
private limited company (Ltd) *14* Gesellschaft mit beschränkter Haftung (GmbH)
prize *36* Preis, Gewinn
to proceed *73T* sich begeben
process *27* Verfahren, Ablauf, Prozess
to process *66* bearbeiten
procurement *91* Beschaffung
Production *9* Produktion, Herstellung, Fertigung
Production Assistant *10* Produktionsassistent/in
production facilities *(pl.)* *9* Produktionsanlage(n), Werk(e)
production line *26* Fertigungsstraße, Produktionsverfahen
Production Manager *10* Produktionsleiter/in
professional *106* Berufstätige/r
professionalism *46* Professionalität

profile *86* Porträt, Profil
profit *14* Gewinn
to profit *87* profitieren
profitable *68* rentabel, gewinnbringend
projection *35* Projektion
projector, digital ~ *27* Beamer
to promote sth *27* etw bewerben, für etw Werbung machen
promotion *27* Werbung
promotional *49T* Werbe-
proper(ly) *7* richtig
proportion *14* Verhältnis; *30* Anteil, Teil
proposal *84* Vorschlag, Angebot
to propose *32* vorschlagen
to protect *100* schützen
protective *91* Schutz-
protective gloves *(pl.)* *93* Schutzhandschuhe
to prove sth *85T* sich als etw erweisen
proven *103* nachweislich, erwiesen
providing *37* vorausgesetzt
pub *62T* Kneipe
public *14* öffentlich; **in** ~ *37* öffentlich, in der Öffentlichkeit
the ~ *14* die Öffentlichkeit
public limited company (plc) *14* Aktiengesellschaft (AG)
publicly owned *86* börsennotiert
to pucker sth *88* etw verziehen
punctuality *115* Pünktlichkeit
punctuation *46* Zeichensetzung, Interpunktion
purpose *19* Zweck
to put sth out *93T* etw löscher

Q

qualification *103* Abschluss, Qualifikation
quality assurance *100* Qualitätssicherung
quality control *97T* Qualitätskontrolle
quantity *69* Menge
questionnaire *28* Fragebogen
quote *16* Angebot

R

race *76T* Regatta; *98* Rennen
racquet *69* Tennisschläger
rail *53* Schiene, Bahn
raincoat *26* Regenmantel
to raise alarm *94* Alarm schlagen
raisin *85* Rosine
range *33* Auswahl, Palette; *57T* Sortiment, *(Kleidung:)* Kollektion
rapid(ly) *103* rasch, schnell
to rate *102* bewerten
rather *23* vielmehr
rating *21* Bewertung

Alphabetical word list

raw material *92* Rohstoff, Rohmaterial

re *43* Betreff, betreffs

to react to sth *25* auf etw reagieren

real estate *22* Immobilien

to realise sth *78* etw erkennen

to rearrange *50* umstellen

to reassure *94* beruhigen

receipt *43* Erhalt, Eingang; *64* Quittung, Beleg

reception *7* Empfang, Rezeption

receptionist *7* Rezeptionist/in

recession *114T* Rezession, Konjunkturrückgang

recipient *55* Empfänger/in

to reckon *40T* glauben, annehmen

recommendation *23* Empfehlung

record *95* Nachweis

to recruit sb *9* jdn einstellen, jdn anwerben

to reduce *23* reduzieren, senken

to refer to sth *36* sich auf etw beziehen, etw erwähnen

referee *103* Referenzgeber/in

reference *56* Bezug

refreshment *16* Erfrischung *(Tee, Saft, Wasser usw.)*

refrigerator *22* Kühlschrank

refund *64* Erstattung, Rückerstattung

to regard sth as sth *68* etw für etw halten

regarded, to be ~ as sth *78* als etw gelten

regarding *56* betreffend, bezüglich

regulations *(pl.)* *93T* Bestimmungen, Vorschriften

to relate to sb *111* eine Beziehung zu jdm herstellen

related to *92* bezüglich; **to be closely ~ sth** *111* engen Bezug zu etw haben

relation *9* Beziehung

relationship *10* Verhältnis, Beziehung

to relax *111* sich lockern, sich entspannen

relaxed *115* locker

relevant *19T* ensprechend; *53* relevant

reliable *35* zuverlässig

to rely on sth *110T* sich auf etw verlassen, sich auf etw stützen

remaining *32T* übrige/r/s, restliche/r/s

reminder *56* Mahnung

to remit *56* überweisen, bezahlen

to remove *20* entfernen

rent *22* Miete

to rent *22* mieten

rental *22* Vermietung, Miete

rental agreement *22* Mietvertrag

repair *64* Reparatur

to repair *65* reparieren

to replace *65* ersetzen

replacement *65* Ersatz

to reply to sb *16* jdm antworten

to report sth *66* etw melden; **~ to sb** *10* jdm unterstehen

to represent *43* darstellen, repräsentieren

reputation *25* (guter) Ruf, Ansehen

to request *91* anfordern

to require *22* benötigen, wünschen

requirement *89* Anforderung, Wunsch

to reschedule *57T* neu ansetzen, neu planen

resource *92* Rohstoff, Ressource

Resources Manager *8* Personalleiter/in

to respond to sth *111* auf etw reagieren, auf etw antworten

response *25* Antwort, Reaktion

responsibility *10* Verantwortlichkeit, Aufgabenbereich, Zuständigkeit

responsible *7* zuständig, verantwortlich

to restrict *14* beschränken

retail *68* Einzelhandel

retailer *68* Einzelhändler

to retain *68* (be)halten

to return *66* zurückschicken; **~ a call** *40T* jdn zurückrufen

to reveal *82* verraten, offenbaren

revenue *60* Einkünfte

review *57T* Bewertung; *68* Besprechung, Rezension, Kritik

ride, to take sb for a ~ *65* jdn übers Ohr hauen, jdn reinlegen

to ride *110T* fahren

ring *60* Klingeln

to ring *60* klingeln; **~ sb back** *39* jdn zurückrufen

road haulage *53* Straßentransport

robot *97T* Roboter

to roll off *97T* vom Band rollen

rounds, to do the ~ *110T* die Runde machen

route *95* Weg

row *73T* Reihe

rude *63* unhöflich, unverschämt

to rule *36* entscheiden, erklären

to run sth *22* etw führen, leiten; **~ sth up** *14* etw anhäufen, *(Schulden:)* machen; **~ the risk** *54* riskieren

runner *9* Läufer/in

runner-up *36* Zweitplatzierte/r

S

safe *77* sicher

safety *36* Sicherheit, Schutz

to sail *76T* segeln

sailing *76T* Segeln

salad *77* Salat

salary *103* Lohn, Gehalt

sales *(pl.)* *7* Vertrieb, Verkauf; *13T* Absatz, Umsatz

sales assistant *64* Verkäufer/in

Sales Manager *7* Verkaufsleiter/in

sample *100* Stichprobe

satellite *74* Satellit

satisfaction *108T* Zufriedenheit, Befriedigung

satisfied *60* zufrieden

sauna *74T* Sauna

saving *23* Einsparung, Ersparnis

savvy, computer-~ *31* geübt/gewieft im Umgang mit Computern

to say hello to sb *60* jdn begrüßen

scale *41* Größenordnung; *102* Skala

scene *37* Szene

schedule *103* Plan, Programm

scheduled *76* planmäßig

scheme *23* Programm, Plan

scientific(ally) *101* wissenschaftlich

scooter *39* Roller

scout, boy ~ *112* Pfadfinder

sculpture *114T* Skulptur

sea freight *53* Seefracht

to seal *20* (luftdicht) verschließen

season, high ~ *90* Hochsaison

seat *49T* Platz, Sitz

to seat *115* sich setzen, sich platzieren

seating arrangement *115* Sitzordnung

section *83* Teil, Abschnitt

secure *74* sicher

to secure *87* sichern

security check *73* Sicherheitskontrolle

to select *110T* auswählen

self-motivated, to be ~ *102* motiviert sein, Eigeninitiative zeigen

seller *58* Verkäufer

senior *115* hoch-/höherrangig

senior management *103* leitende Angestellte, Unternehmensführung

sense, to make ~ *95* sinnvoll sein

series *96* Reihe

to set sth up *22* etw aufbauen, einrichten; *100* etw einrichten, etw einstellen; **~ a business** *14* ein Unternehmen gründen

setting *111* Umgebung, Rahmen

to settle *56* begleichen, bezahlen

Alphabetical word list

to **shake hands** 115 die Hand geben, die Hände schütteln
shallow 78 oberflächlich
shame 57T schade
to **shape** 115 formen
share 14 Anteil; 14 Aktie
shareholder 14 Teilhaber/in, Gesellschafter/in
sharp 13T scharf
sheet 48T Blatt
shelf life 21 Haltbarkeit
ship 58 Schiff
to **ship** 53 verschicken
shipment 53 Versand, Transport; 70 Sendung, Lieferung; **port of ~** 58 Verladehafen
shipping 53 Versand
shipping bay 97T Ladebucht
shortly 62 in Kürze
short-term 112 befristet, kurzfristig
to **shout** 65 schreien
to **show sb around** 7 jdn herumführen, mit jdm einen Rundgang machen
to **sign** 16 unterschreiben; **~ in** 93T sich eintragen; **~ sth off** 46 (Brief etc.:) (be)enden, schließen, unterschreiben
signature 98 Unterschrift
significance 53 Bedeutung
significant 37 erheblich, bedeutend
signposting 48 richtungweisend
similar 28 ähnlich
single room 74T Einzelzimmer
single speed (bicycle) 45 Eingangrad
to **sit back** 37 sich zurücklehnen
situated 9 gelegen
skill 102 Fähigkeit, Fertigkeit
to **slip** 35 stecken, schieben
smooth 25 glatt, reibungslos; 98 eben
snack 74 Imbiss
social event 111 geselliger/ gesellschaftlicher Anlass
sole proprietorship 14 Einzelunternehmen
sole trader 14 Einzelunternehmer, Einzelunternehmen
solicitor 56 Anwalt/Anwältin (für Zivilrecht)
solid 85 solide
solution 114T Lösung
to **solve** 60 lösen
sort 9 Art
to **sort sth into sth** 48 etw nach etw ordnen; **~ sth out** 65 etw klären, etw in Ordnung bringen
sorting code 55 Bankleitzahl
source 14 Quelle
spare time 76T Freizeit

Speaking. 38 Am Apparat.
to **specialise in sth** 22 sich auf etw spezialisieren
speciality 76T Spezialität
specific 21 bestimmt, speziell
specifically 36 eigens, speziell
to **specify** 70 (genau) angeben
speech bubble 42 Sprechblase
speed, to get up to ~ 37 sich auf den neuesten Stand bringen
splendid 51T großartig
to **split** 30 teilen, aufteilen
spoilt for choice, to be ~ 74 die Qual der Wahl haben
sporty 40T sportlich
spot 88 Fleck, Punkt; **on the ~** 110T gleich, auf der Stelle
to **spread** 31 verbreiten
staff 9 Mitarbeiter, Personal
staff café 11T Cafeteria
stage 19 Phase, Etappe
to **stamp** 97T stempeln
to **stand to do sth** 87 etw tun werden
standard 36 Norm, Maßstab, Standard
staple 18 Heftklammer
to **state** 67 sagen, erklären
stationery 16 Büromaterial, Bürobedarf
status 79 Status, Ansehen; 115 Rang
steadily 13T stetig, kontinuierlich
step 20 Schritt
to **stereotype sb** 78 jdn in ein Klischee zwängen
to **stick to sth** 46 bei etw bleiben; **~ to the rules** 115 sich an die Regeln halten
sticker 37 Aufkleber
stiff 46 steif
stock exchange 14 Börse
stock market 14 Aktienmarkt
stocktaking 95 Inventur, Bestandsaufnahme
storage 91 Lagerung
storage rack 93T Lagergestell
to **store** 91 lagern
straight ahead 11T geradeaus
straight away 19T sofort, gleich, umgehend
straightforward 37 einfach, unkompliziert
strange 88 seltsam, merkwürdig
strapline 34 (Werbe-)Slogan
strategy 27 Strategie
strength 34 Stärke
to **strengthen** 87 stärken
to **stretch one's legs** 79 die Beine ausstrecken
string 36 Reihe, Folge
structure 9 Struktur
stupid 60 dumm

style 46 Stil
stylish 29 elegant, schick, stilvoll
subheadline 34 Zwischenüberschrift, Dachzeile
subtotal 55 Zwischensumme
to **succeed** 88 erfolgreich sein, Erfolg haben
to **suck sth in** 88 etw einziehen
to **suffer** 78 leiden; **~ sth** 94 etw erleiden
to **suit** 16 passen
suitable 22 geeignet
suite 22 Büroräume, Büroetage; 74 Suite
to **summarise** 24 zusammenfassen
summary 23 Zusammenfassung
sunburn 36 Sonnenbrand
sunburnt, to get ~ 36 sich einen Sonnenbrand zuziehen
sunscreen 36 Sonnenschutz, -creme
supplier 51T Lieferant/in, Zulieferer
supplies (pl.) 97T Ware(n), Vorräte
supply chain 95 Versorgungskette, Lieferkette
support 67 Unterstützung, Kundendienst
to **support** 76T unterstützen, hier: Fan sein von
to **suppose** 72 annehmen, glauben; **I ~** 65 immerhin, nun ja
supposed, to be ~ to do sth 64 etw tun sollen; **to not be ~ to do sth** 64 etw nicht tun dürfen
supposedly 65 angeblich
surprised 37 erstaunt, überrascht
sweet 13T süß; Süßigkeit, Bonbon
to **switch sth off** 64 etw ausschalten

T

to **take sb on** 21 jdn einstellen; **~ sth on** 109 etw übernehmen; **~ sth up** 111 etw schönreden; **~ action** 68 Maßnahmen ergreifen; **~ place** 46 stattfinden; **~ turns** 15 sich abwechseln; **~ sth into account** 110T etw berücksichtigen; **~ up space** 106 Platz einnehmen; **~ a message** 39 (Telefon:) etw ausrichten; **~ a turn(ing)** 11 abbiegen; **~ legal steps** 56 rechtliche Schritte unternehmen; **~ sb for a ride** 65 jdn übers Ohr hauen, jdn reinlegen
tanning 36 Bräunung
to **target sb** 37 jdn (als Zielgruppe) ansprechen, jdn als Zielgruppe haben

Alphabetical word list

target market *30* Zielgruppe, Zielmarkt
tariff *68* Tarif
to **taste** *26* etw probieren, etw kosten
tasty *82T* lecker
tax *72* Steuer
technique *37* Methode, Technik
template *107* Vorlage
to **tend to do sth** *78* dazu neigen, etw zu tun
term *19* Begriff
terminal *58* Entladestation, -stelle, Terminal
terms *67* Konditionen, Bedingungen; **delivery ~** *92* Lieferbedingungen
text message *64* SMS
thanks to *78* dank
theoretical(ly) *31* theoretisch
theory, in ~ *68* theoretisch
thereafter *121* danach
though, as ~ *88* als ob
to **tie** *28* schnüren, binden; **~ back to sth** *34T etwa:* zu etw passen, etw aufnehmen
time, at all ~s *96* jederzeit; **on ~** *72* pünktlich; **waste of ~** *115* Zeitverschwendung
time-consuming *111* zeitraubend
time frame *82T* Zeitrahmen
tiny *89* winzig
tone *34* Ton; **conversational ~** *34T* lockerer Plauderton
to **tool sth up** *97T* etw maschinell ausrüsten
touch, to get in ~ with sb *42* sich bei jdm melden
tough *35* solide, widerstandsfähig
tour *11* Rundgang, Führung; **guided ~** *40T* Führung, Rundfahrt
to **trace** *31* nachvervolgen, vervolgen
trade *49T* Handel
to **trade** *14* handeln
trade fair *49* Handelsmesse, Fachmesse
to **train sb** *10* jdn ausbilden, jdn schulen
trainee *7* Auszubildende/r
traineeship *7* Ausbildung, Lehre
training *8* Ausbildung
transfer *55* Überweisung
transport, mode of ~ *120* Transportart; **multimodal ~** *120* kombinierte Beförderung, multimodaler Transport
transportation *52* Beförderung, Transport
travel agent *89* Reisebüro
treatment *113* Behandlung
to **trip** *113* stolpern

to **trivialise** *36* bagatellisieren
to **trust** *88* vertrauen
to **turn sth down** *88* *(Blick:)* senken, nach unten richten; **~ sth off** *65* etw ausschalten; **~ out** *40T* sich herausstellen; **~ to sth** *87* sich einer Sache zuwenden; **~ the page** *31* umblättern
turn(ing), to take a ~ *11* abbiegen
turnover *9* Umsatz

U

umpire *69* Schiedsrichter/in
unattended *73T* unbeaufsichtigt
uncommon *115* unüblich
unconventional *37* unkonventionell
to **undergo** *116* erleben, mitmachen bei
understanding *78* Verständnis
unexpected(ly) *110T* unerwartet
unfortunately *46* leider, unglücklicherweise
unimportant *48* unwichtig
unimpressive *30* wenig beeindruckend
unknown *47* unbekannt
unlikely *55T* unwahrscheinlich
unlimited *14* unbegrenzt, unbeschränkt
to **unload** *95* entladen
unloading *58* Entladen, Entladung
unneeded *97T* nicht benötigt, unnötig
unprepared *82* unvorbereitet
to **unscramble** *21* entwirren
unsent *70* nicht gesendet
to **unwind** *74* sich entspannen, abschalten
up to speed, to get ~ *37* sich auf den neuesten Stand bringen
up to standard, to be ~ *100* den Vorgaben entsprechen
to **update** *58* aktualisieren, auf den neusten Stand bringen
upmarket *79* schick, teuer
upset *65* verärgert
urgent *48* dringend, eilig
useless *65* nutzlos, unfähig

V

to **validate** *101* prüfen
valuable *60* wertvoll
value *37* Wert
to **value** *103* wertschätzen
variety *85* Sorte
various *14* verschieden
VAT (value added tax) *40T* Mehrwertsteuer (MwSt)
vegetarian *89* vegetarisch
versus (vs.) *31* gegenüber, im Gegensatz zu
vessel *121* Schiff

vice versa *32* umgekehrt
view *47* Ansicht, Meinung; **overall ~** *48* Überblick, (Gesamt-)Übersicht
visuals *85* visuelle Hilfsmittel
voltage, high ~ *93T* Hochspannung
voucher *60* Gutschein

W

wages *(pl.)* *26* Lohn, Gehalt
waiter *76T* Kellner
warehouse *91* Lager, Lagerhalle
warehouse manager *93T* Leiter/in des Warenlagers, Lagerleiter/in
warranty *21* Garantie, Gewährleistung
to **waste** *22* verschwenden, vergeuden
waste of time *115* Zeitverschwendung
watchdog *36* Aufsichtsbehörde
waterway *119* Wasserstraße
way, to get out of one's ~ *103* alle Hebel in Bewegung setzen
weakness *34* Schwäche
wedding *90* Hochzeit
to **weigh** *35* wiegen
wheel *40T* Rad
whilst *105* während
wholesale *53* Großhandel
willingness *37* Bereitschaft
wine list *77* Weinkarte
winner *36* Gewinner/in
wire *113* Kabel
wiring *113* Verkabelung
witness *113* Zeuge/Zeugin
to **wonder** *62T* sich fragen
to **work closely with sb** *23* mit jdm eng zusammenarbeiten
work experience placement *92* Praktikum
worker *26* Arbeiter/in
working environment *111* Arbeitsumfeld
workload *103* Arbeitspensum
workshop *13T* Werkstatt
worth *42* wert
to **wrap sth up** *97T* etw verpacken, etw einwickeln
writing, in ~ *111* schriftlich

Y

yet, as ~ *51T* bis jetzt
Yours sincerely *43* Mit freundlichen Grüßen
youth *107* Jugend

0–9

24/7 *103* rund um die Uhr

Basic business vocabulary (German – English)

Firmenorganisation – Company organization

Aktie	share
Aktiengesellschaft (AG)	public limited company (plc) *BE*; (open) corporation *AE*
Aktionär/in, Teilhaber/in	shareholder
Einzelunternehmen	sole proprietorship, sole trader
Gesellschaft mit beschränkter Haftung (GmbH)	limited company (Ltd) *BE*; closed corporation *AE*
Kommanditgesellschaft (KG)	limited partnership
offene Handelsgesellschaft (OHG)	(general) partnership

Firmenabteilungen – Company departments

Buchhaltung	Accounting (Department)
Einkauf(sabteilung)	Purchasing (Department)
Forschung(s-) und Entwicklung (sabteilung)	Research and Development (Department, R&D)
Geschäftsführung, Vorstand	board (of directors)
Herstellung	Production (Department)
Lager(halle)	warehouse
Marktforschung (sabteilung)	Market Research (Department)
Personal(abteilung)	Human Resources (Department, HR)
Rechnungswesen	Finance (Department)
Rechtswesen	Legal Department
Rezeption, Empfang	Reception
Verkauf(sabteilung), Vertrieb	Sales (Department)
Vertrieb	Distribution (Department)
Vertrieb(sabteilung)	Marketing (Department)
Verwaltung	Administration
Zentrale	head office, headquarters

Mitarbeiter/innen – Members of staff

Abteilungsleiter/in	head of department
Arbeitgeber/in, Unternehmer/in	employer
Arbeitnehmer/in, Beschäftigte/r	employee
Arbeitsplatz	workplace
Ausbildung	training
Beförderung	promotion
Buchhalter/in	accountant
Bürokaufmann/-frau	Office Management Assistant
Gehalt	salary
Geschäftsführer/in	Managing Director (MD), Chief Executive Officer (CEO)
Handelsvertreter/in	sales representative
Herstellungsleiter/in	Production Manager
Kollege/Kollegin	colleague
Lehre	apprenticeship
Leiter/in der Finanzabteilung	Finance Director
Logistikleiter/in	Logistics Manager
Manager/in	manager
Personal	staff
Persönliche/r Assistent/in	Personal Assistant (PA)
Qualifikation, Abschluss	qualification
Sekretär/in	secretary
Technische/r Leiter/in	Operations Director
Vertriebsleiter/in	Marketing Manager

Büromaterial – Office supplies and equipment

Akte(nordner)	file
Aktenschrank	storage/filing cabinet
Beamer	projector
Bildschirm	screen
Briefumschlag	envelope
Büroklammer	paper clip
Drucker	printer
Druckerpatrone	printer cartridge
Etikette	label
Flipchart	flip chart
Fotokopierer	photocopier
Heftklammer	staple
Klammerhefter	stapler
Locher	hole punch
Marker	highlighter
Notizblock	note pad
Rechner	computer, PC
Schreibwaren, Briefpapier	stationery
Stift	pen
Taschenrechner	calculator

Bürotätigkeiten – office activities

die **Ablage** machen	to organize files, to do the filing
etw **ausrichten**	to take a message
Berichte schreiben	to write reports
Briefe beantworten	to reply to letters
etw **faxen**	to fax sth
Mitteilungen, Vermerke, Notizen schreiben	to write memos
Postausgang	outgoing mail; out-tray
Posteingang	incoming mail, inbox, in-tray
Post verteilen	to handle the mail
ein **Telefongespräch annehmen**	to answer the telephone
Textverarbeitung	word processing
Überstunden machen	to work overtime

169

Basic business vocabulary (German – English)

German	English
Unterlagen, Schriftstücke	paperwork
etw **weiterleiten**	to forward sth

Geschäftsbriefe – Commercial correspondence

Absatz	paragraph
Absender	sender
Adresse	address
Anhang	attachment
anhängen (E-Mail)	to attach sth
Anlage	enclosure (enc)
Anrede	salutation
Antwort	reply
beifügen (Brief)	to enclose
Betreff(zeile)	subject (line)
Briefkopf	letter head
Datum	date
Einschreiben	registered mail/post
Empfänger/in	addressee
Entschuldigungsschreiben	letter of apology
Freiumschlag	stamped addressed envelope
Mit den besten Wünschen	Best wishes
Mit freundlichen Grüßen (Hochachtungsvoll)	Yours faithfully
Mit freundlichen Grüßen	Yours sincerely
Mit freundlichen Grüßen, Viele Grüße	Best wishes, Regards
Mit herzlichen Grüßen	Best wishes, Cordially AE
Porto	postage
Postleitzahl	postcode
Schlussformel	complimentary close
Unterschrift	signature
vertraulich	confidential
Zeichen	reference (ref)
zu Händen	attention (attn)

Besprechungen/Präsentationen – Meetings/presentations

Abwesenheit	absence
Bericht	report
Einladung	invitation
Liniendiagramm	line chart
Protokoll	minutes pl
eine **Rede halten**	to make a speech
Säulendiagramm	bar chart
die **Sitzung leiten**	to take the chair / to be in the chair
stattfinden	take place
Tagesordnung	agenda
Tagesordnungspunkt	item on the agenda
teilnehmen	to participate
Teilnehmer/in	participant
Termin	date
Tortendiagramm	pie chart
Verschiedenes	any other business (AOB)
Vortrag	talk; lecture
vortragen	to report; to state

Dienstreisen – Business trips

absagen	to cancel
Anforderung	requirement
Anschlussflug	connecting flight
Ausstellung	exhibition
etw **besuchen**, an etw **teilnehmen**	to attend sth
Bitte, Anfrage	request
einfacher Flug	one-way flight
Hin- und Rückflug	return flight
Messe	(trade) fair
Passagier/in	passenger
Reservierung, Buchung	reservation
stornieren	to cancel
Termin	appointment
Unterkunft	accommodation
verschieben	to postpone

Geschäftspartner und Händler – Business partners and traders

Einzelhändler/in	retailer
Exporteur	exporter
Großhändler	wholesaler
Importeur	importer
Käufer/in	buyer
Klient/in	client
Konkurrent/in, Konkurrenz	competitor
Konkurrenz	competition
Kunde/Kundin	customer, client
Lieferant	supplier
Spediteur	carrier; forwarding agent; freight forwarder
Verkäufer/in	seller

Geschäftsvorgänge – Business transactions

Anfrage	enquiry
Angebot, Kostenvoranschlag	quotation
Auftrag, Bestellung	order
einen **Auftrag erledigen**	to fill an order
einen **Auftrag erteilen**	to place an order
Auftragsbestätigung	acknowledgement/confirmation (of an order)
einen **Auftrag bestätigen**	to acknowledge an order
Bestellformular	order form
Bestellnummer	order number

Basic business vocabulary (German – English)

German	English
Erhalt, (Waren-)Eingang	receipt (of goods)
Folgeauftrag	repeat order
Lieferbedingungen	terms of delivery *pl*
liefern	to deliver
Lieferung	delivery
Muster	sample
Probeauftrag	trial order
Reklamation, Beschwerde	complaint
eine **Reklamation** bearbeiten/regulieren	to adjust a complaint
Sendung	consignment
Umsatz	turnover
Verkäufe, Umsatz	sales *pl*
Versandanzeige, Versandmitteilung	advice of dispatch
Versandpapiere	shipping documents *pl*
versenden	to ship
versenden, absenden	to dispatch
Vertrag	contract
Ware(n), (Lager-)Bestand	stock
Zahlungsanzeige	advice of payment
Zahlungsbedingungen	terms of payment *pl*

Zahlung – *Payment*	
ausstehend	overdue
Dokumente gegen Akzept	documents against acceptance
Dokumente gegen Zahlung	documents against payment
Dokumentenakkreditiv	documentary letter of credit
fällig	due
Konto, Kreditkonto	account
letzte Mahnung	final demand
Mahnung	reminder
MwSt = Mehrwertsteuer	VAT = value added tax
Nicht(be)zahlung	non-payment
Rabatt, Nachlass	discount
Rate	instalment
Rechnung	bill, invoice
Skonto, Barzahlungsrabatt	cash discount
überweisen	to remit, to transfer
Überweisung, Zahlung	bank transfer, remittance
Vorauszahlung, Vorkasse	cash in advance
Wechsel	bill of exchange
zahlbar bei Lieferung, per Nachnahme	cash on delivery (COD)

171

Common irregular verbs

be – was/were – been	sein	leave – left – left	abfahren, verlassen, weggehen
become – became – become	werden	let – let – let	lassen
begin – began – begun	anfangen, beginnen	lose – lost – lost	verlieren
break – broke – broken	(zer)brechen	make – made – made	machen
bring – brought – brought	bringen	mean – meant – meant	meinen, bedeuten
		meet – met – met	treffen
build – built – built	bauen	pay – paid – paid	bezahlen
buy – bought – bought	kaufen	put – put – put	setzen, stellen, legen
catch – caught – caught	fangen	read – read – read	lesen
choose – chose – chosen	wählen	ride – rode – ridden	reiten, fahren
		ring – rang – rung	klingeln; anrufen
come – came – come	kommen	rise – rose – risen	(an)steigen
cost – cost – cost	kosten	run – ran – run	laufen, rennen
cut – cut – cut	schneiden	say – said – said	sagen
do – did – done	tun, machen	see – saw – seen	sehen
draw – drew – drawn	zeichnen	sell – sold – sold	verkaufen
dream – dreamt – dreamt	träumen	send – sent – sent	senden, schicken
		set – set – set	setzen, stellen
drink – drank – drunk	trinken	show – showed – shown	zeigen
drive – drove – driven	fahren		
eat – ate – eaten	essen	shut – shut – shut	schließen
fall – fell – fallen	fallen	sing – sang – sung	singen
feed – fed – fed	füttern, ernähren	sit – sat – sat	sitzen
feel – felt – felt	(sich) fühlen, empfinden	sleep – slept – slept	schlafen
fight – fought – fought	kämpfen	smell – smelt/smelled – smelt/smelled	riechen
find – found – found	finden		
fit – fit/fitted – fit/fitted	passen	speak – spoke – spoken	sprechen
fly – flew – flown	fliegen	spell – spelt/spelled – spelt/spelled	buchstabieren
forget – forgot – forgotten	vergessen		
		spend – spent – spent	ausgeben, verbringen
get – got – got (AE gotten)	bekommen	stand – stood – stood	stehen
		steal – stole – stolen	stehlen
give – gave – given	geben	swim – swam – swum	schwimmen
go – went – gone	gehen, fahren	take – took – taken	nehmen
grow – grew – grown	wachsen	teach – taught – taught	unterrichten, beibringen
hang – hung – hung	hängen	tell – told – told	sagen, erzählen
have – had – had	haben	think – thought – thought	denken
hear – heard – heard	hören		
hide – hid – hidden	(sich) verstecken	throw – threw – thrown	werfen
hit – hit – hit	schlagen	understand – understood – understood	verstehen
hold – held – held	halten, festhalten		
keep – kept – kept	behalten	wake – woke/waked – woken/waked	aufwecken
know – knew – known	kennen, wissen		
lay – laid – laid	legen	wear – wore – worn	tragen (Kleidung)
learn – learnt/learned – learnt/learned	lernen	win – won – won	gewinnen
		write – wrote – written	schreiben

Acknowledgements

Bildquellen

S. 6 Shutterstock Yuri Arcurs; S. 13 Alamy © Bon Appetit / Alamy; S.15/1 Alamy © Blend Images / Alamy, /2 Shutterstock Andrey Lipko, /3 Alamy © Hire Image Picture Library / Alamy, 4/ Shutterstock Konstantin Chagin; S. 17 Shutterstock iQoncept; S. 18(oben)/1 Shutterstock lithian, /2 Shutterstock Ariwasabi, 3/ Shutterstock Mathieu Viennet; (unten) A bis I Shutterstock, /K Shutterstock Fotovika; S. 24 Shutterstock Petinov Sergey Mihilovich; S. 24 Shutterstock Goodluz; S. 27/1 Shutterstock YanLev, /2 Shutterstock Helder Almeida; S. 29 Shutterstock Stuart Jenner; S. 33/1 Shutterstock HadK, /2 Shutterstock mzungu, /3 (Hintergrund) Shutterstock SVLuma; S. 34 Shutterstock Dmitriy Shironosov; S. 35 /1Shutterstock Smart-foto, /2 Shutterstock Karpova Alisa; S. 36 Shutterstock Amy Walters; S. 38 /1Shutterstock Glovatskiy, /2Shutterstock l i g h t p o e t; S. 41 Shutterstock RTimages; S. 42 /1 Shutterstock Phil Date, /2 Shutterstock Rido; S. 45 Alamy © Darroch Donald / Alamy; S. 49 /1 Shutterstock Viorel Sima, /2 Shutterstock TRINACRIA PHOTO, /3 Alamy © Jeff Greenberg / Alamy, /4 Shutterstock Venus Angel; S. 50 /1 Shutterstock Roman Sigaev, /2 Shutterstock Adriano Castelli, /3 Shutterstock, /4 Shutterstock Alex Ciopata, /5a Shutterstock Yuliyan Velchev, 5b Shutterstock Lasse Kristensen , 5c Shutterstock Patricia Hofmeester; S. 51 Shutterstock Dariusz Gudowicz; S. 52 /1Shutterstock, /2 Shutterstock, /3 Shutterstock Paul Matthew Photography, /4 Shutterstock; S. 54 /1 Shutterstock s_oleg, /2 Shutterstock Byron W.Moore, /3 Shutterstock Rafael Ramirez Lee; S. 57 (Hintergrund) Shutterstock Adriano Castelli / Shutterstock. com; S. 59 Shutterstock Monkey Business Images; S. 61 Shutterstock mangostock; S. 63 Shutterstock Monkey Business Images; S. 64 Alamy © Juice Images / Alamy; S. 71 /1 Shutterstock Lusoimages, /2 Shutterstock Oleksiy Mark, /3 Shutterstock, /4 Shutterstock Lipowski Milan, /5 Shutterstock, /6 Shutterstock, /7 Shutterstock, /8 Shutterstock, /9 Shutterstock Dmitry Lobanov; S. 80 /1 Shutterstock ifong, /2 Shutterstock RTimages, /3 Shutterstock mojito.mak[dog] gmail[dot]com, /5 Shutterstock Igor Shikov; /6 Shutterstock Mazzzur, /8 Shutterstock Christian Delbert; S. 91 Shutters ock Nataliya Hora; S. 93 /1/2/3 Shutterstock Bakelyt, /4 Shutterstock Radoman Durkovic, /5/6 Shutterstock valeriya_gold, /9 Dmitry Kalinovsky; S. 94: Oxford Designers & Illustrators; S. 97 Shutterstock Dmitry Kalinovsky; S. 101 Shutterstock Robert Kneschke; S. 104/1 Shutterstock James Flint, /2 Shutterstock Gabriela Insuratelu; S. 110 Shutterstock AVAVA

Textquellen

S. 36: Mark Sweney, guardian.co.uk, Wednesday 5 October 2011
S. 107: © Europäische Union; http://europass.cedefop.europa.eu
S. 116: © Europäische Union; http://europass.cedefop.europa.eu
S. 114: KMK mock exam, Track 36, Going global: This article has been re-printed with the permission of the British Council, and it is taken from http://learnenglish.britishcouncil.org/en/professionals-podcasts/going-global

AUSTRALIA & NEW ZEALAND

TUVALU

FIJI

Kermadec
Islands
(NZ)

NEW
ZEALAND

Pacific
Ocean

SALOMON ISLANDS

VANUATU

New
Caledonia
(F)

Norfolk
Island
(AUS)

North Island

Auckland
Hamilton
Bay of Plenty
Lake Taupo
Mt Ruapehu
2797
Hutt
Wellington
Christchurch

Chatham
Islands

South Island

Mt Cook
3764
Southern Alps
Cook Strait

Dunedin

PAPUA
NEW GUINEA

Coral
Sea

Brisbane
Gold Coast

Rockhampton

ACT = Australian
Capital
Territory

Tasman Sea

Invercargill
Stewart
Island

Townsville

Cairns

Great Barrier Reef

Great Dividing Range

Newcastle
Sydney
Wollongong

Torres Strait

Mitchell

Flinders

Queensland

New South
Wales

Charleville

Bourke

ACT
Canberra
Mt Kosciusko
2230

INDONESIA

EAST
TIMOR

Timor
Sea

Darwin

Katherine

Arnhemland

Gulf of
Carpen-
taria

Mount
Isa

Sturt
Desert

Copper Creek

Darling

Murray

Victoria
Geelong

Melbourne

Mt Ossa
1617

Hobart

Tasmania

Mt Bogong

Bass Strait

Arafura
Sea

Northern
Territory

Tennant
Creek

Alice
Springs

Macdonnell
Ranges

Simpson
Desert

Lake Eyre

Finke

South Australia

Lake Torrens

Port
Augusta

Adelaide

Flinders Range

AUSTRALIA

Musgrave
Ranges

Ayers Rock (Uluru)
867

Lake Argyle

Kimberley
Plateau

Fitzroy

Lake
Mackay

Great Victoria
Desert

Lake
Carnegie

Great Australian
Bight

Nullarbor Plain

Indian
Ocean

Broome

Port Hedland

Hamersley
1251 Mt Meharry
Range

Gibson
Desert

Great Sandy
Desert

Western Australia

Kalgoorlie

Albany

Southern
Ocean

Ashburton

Murchison

Carnarvon

Darling Range

Perth

0   250   500   750   1000   1250

km

002586: U3, Australia + New Zealand
° carlos borrell kartografie + infografik berlin

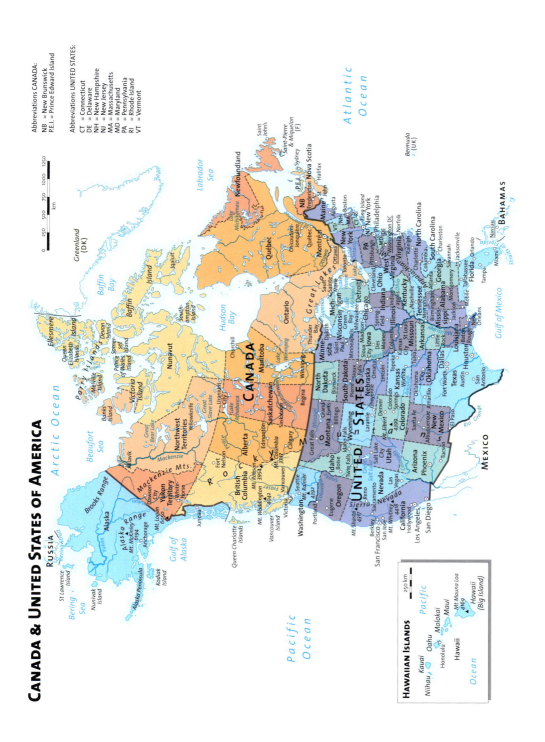

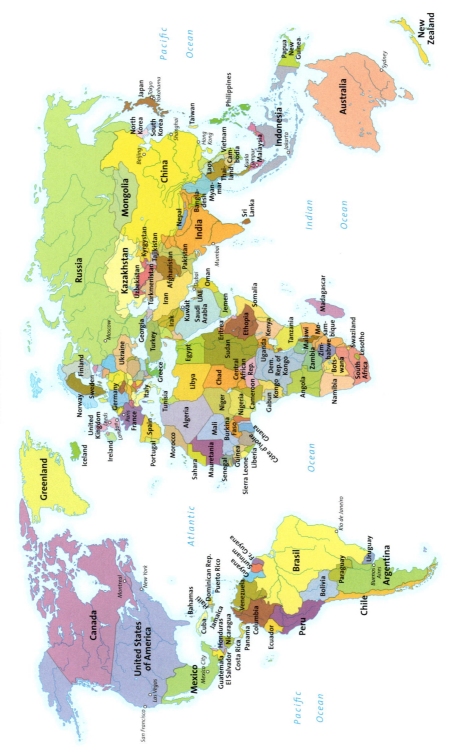